THE WORLD IN OUR HANDS

FOREWORD

To celebrate the turn of the century and the new millennium, **THE EVENTFUL CENTURY** series presents the vast panorama of the last hundred years – a century which has witnessed the transition from horse-drawn transport to space travel, and from the first telephones to the information superhighway.

THE EVENTFUL CENTURY chronicles epoch-making events like the outbreak of the two world wars, the Russian Revolution and the rise and fall of communism. But major events are only part of this glittering kaleidoscope. It also describes the everyday background – the way people lived, how they worked, what they ate and drank, how much they earned, the way they spent their leisure time, the books they read, and the crimes, scandals and unsolved mysteries that set them talking. Here are fads and crazes like the Hula-Hoop and Rubik's Cube . . . fashions like the New Look and the miniskirt . . . breakthroughs in entertainment, such as the birth of the movies . . . medical milestones such as the discovery of penicillin . . . and marvels of modern architecture and engineering.

Humans and nature have always lived in delicate balance, but never have the pressures been so intense as in the 20th century. **THE WORLD IN OUR HANDS** charts an extraordinary and paradoxical story. In the 20th century science and technology have given us unprecedented powers to exploit nature. Oil, for example, powers the motor car, which has given millions a freedom and mobility our forebears could only dream of. High-yield strains of wheat, rice, maize and other crops, along with newly available fertilisers, have enabled us to feed rapidly growing populations. Cracking the secrets of DNA holds out the prospect of banishing many hereditary illnesses. The benefits are real and we live with them every day, yet so, too, is the damage we have inflicted on our environment. Splitting the atom was one of the outstanding scientific achievements of the century, but it led to the bombing of Hiroshima in 1945 and disaster at Chernobyl in 1986. Our seas are polluted and some fish stocks almost exhausted. High in the atmosphere, the ozone layer is thinning dangerously. The rain forests are vanishing at a frightening rate; Antarctica may be melting. **THE WORLD IN OUR HANDS** tells an astonishing tale of power and responsibility, of dangers averted and new ones revealed.

THE WORLD
IN OUR HANDS

Reader's
Digest

PUBLISHED BY
THE READER'S DIGEST ASSOCIATION LIMITED
LONDON NEW YORK SYDNEY MONTREAL

THE WORLD IN OUR HANDS
Edited and designed by Toucan Books Limited
Written by Austen Atkinson
Edited by Andrew Kerr-Jarrett
Designed by Bradbury and Williams
Picture research by Christine Vincent

FOR READER'S DIGEST
Series Editor Christine Noble
Editorial Assistant Caroline Boucher
Production Controller Byron Johnson

READER'S DIGEST GENERAL BOOKS
Editorial Director Cortina Butler
Art Director Nick Clark

First English edition copyright © 1999
The Reader's Digest Association Limited,
11 Westferry Circus, Canary Wharf,
London E14 4HE

www.readersdigest.co.uk

Reprinted with amendments 2000

Printing and binding: Printer Industria Gráfica S.A.,
Barcelona
Separations: Litho Origination, London
Paper: Perigord-Condat, France

ISBN 0 276 42382 8

FRONT COVER
Background picture: Computerised image of the
seabed, created by Scripps Institution of
Oceanography, California, top; Tokyo by night,
bottom. From left to right: Environmentalist
protester, Merseyside, England; solar power used to
boil a kettle, Tibet; Nepalese girl taking part in a
tree-planting scheme; model of DNA.

BACK COVER
Clockwise from top left: Green sea turtle; burning
the Brazilian rain forest; seller of traditional
medicines, Brazil; bomb test, Nevada, USA, 1951.

Page 3 (from left to right): Charred clock from
Hiroshima, 1945; early motorised tractor; smog in
London, 1953; wildlife ranger collecting turtle eggs.

Background pictures:
Page 15: Optical fibres
Page 53: Computer graphic showing weather patterns
Page 87: Cloned cereal plants growing in test tubes
Page 117: Kayapo tribespeople, Brazil, with Sting
and Jean-Pierre Dutilleux

CONTENTS

THE QUEST FOR POWER

TECHNOLOGICAL CHANGE HAS GALLOPED AHEAD AT A TREMENDOUS PACE, BUT OFTEN THE ENVIRONMENT HAS SUFFERED AS A RESULT

Mankind has long sought to control and manipulate the environment, to find easier ways of living and of harnessing power. In the 20th century we have achieved these aims on a far greater scale than ever before. Science, technology and society itself have combined to produce a period of constant and rapid change in every field of human existence.

War played its part. The First World War (1914-18) involved millions of people and increasingly complex technologies. The Second World War (1939-45) forced technological advance at a still faster pace until a breakthrough was achieved with deadly potential – the nuclear bomb. A new era dawned in which mankind possessed an unprecedented capacity for destruction. Since 1945, the quest for power has led us to push

AGAINST THE ODDS Ill-equipped workers attempt to control oil pollution after a massive pipeline leak in Russia's autonomous Komi Republic on the north-western slopes of the Urals in 1994.

back ever farther the boundaries of what we can do with technology. We have benefited in all kinds of areas, from medicine to transport, home conveniences to the food we eat. But the costs – in, for example, pollution and the destruction of precious ecosystems – have also been brought home to us. By the end of the 20th century, mankind was increasingly aware of the responsibilities as well as the benefits of having 'the world in its hands'.

Energy and control

In 1900 technology and science were trumpeted as the joint saviours of humanity. They seemed to offer a steady increase in comfort, labour-saving devices, medical wonders and engineering marvels.

This was confirmed on July 2, 1900, when Graf von Zeppelin's company, Luftschiffbau Zeppelin, launched its first rigid-hulled airship. There was nothing particularly new about airships. The Frenchman Henri Giffard had made the first successful flight in one as far back as 1852, and many refinements had been made since then, notably by the Parisian-based Brazilian Alberto Santos-Dumont – he used to fly in to central Paris from his home at Saint-Cloud on the outskirts in special one-man airships. But Count Zeppelin was the pioneer manufacturer of the large rigid airships – ones with an internal metal framework – that would come to be known by his name.

This first 'zeppelin' was 425 ft (130 m) long, hydrogen-filled and powered by a 16 horsepower internal combustion engine – the kind of engine first used to 'motorise' vehicles in 1886 by Carl Benz, one of the inventors of the motor car. The zeppelin and other airships offered not only a

MAIDEN FLIGHT London showgirls help to haul a Blériot Golden Ray passenger plane onto the tarmac at Croydon airport on July 4, 1932, to inaugurate a new summer service from London to Le Touquet.

1900

1900 First zeppelin airship
1903 Wright brothers' powered flight
1913 Ford introduces assembly-line production
1914-18 First World War
1939-45 Second World War
1943 Colossus computer
1947 Transistor invented
1950

1950

1950-53 Korean War

2000

1997 Financial
crisis in East
Asia

means of escaping gravity but also of travelling in whatever direction their occupants wished. Until airships, the balloon had been the only means of travelling through the air, but it offered no opportunity to control the speed and direction of flight. The world at large was much more impressed by Zeppelin's craft than it would be on December 17, 1903, by Wilbur and Orville Wright's first flight in a powered heavier-than-air craft.

Mankind was conquering the air, and to many observers in 1900 it seemed that there would be no limit to the achievements of the next 100 years. It was also soon apparent that the internal combustion engine would become a driving force of change in the 20th century, much as the steam engine had been in the 19th. This became clear after 1901 when rich and steady supplies of oil were found, initially at Spindletop in Texas. With oil so abundant Benz's notion of harnessing an engine to a carriage offered an obvious replacement for horse-drawn transport. After 1913 Henry Ford's masterstroke of using assembly-line production techniques secured the future of motoring by putting it within the reach of 'the masses'.

Ready supplies of oil helped to stoke the growing 'motormania' which in its turn increased the demand for oil. Oil and the automobile were two factors contributing to a continuing expansion of industry on a more dramatic scale even than in the 19th century. Industrial expansion in turn brought a growing demand both for mechanical components and for skilled labour to make them. Wages rose and generated a cycle in which higher incomes stimulated consumer demand which in turn stimulated a greater demand for labour. From the 1920s onwards, particularly in the United States, higher levels of disposable income among the working classes opened up an entirely new market to manufacturers – for mass consumer goods.

OFF THE ASSEMBLY LINE Henry Ford's vision of mass-produced vehicles for the masses greatly increased output of his Model T, but reduced demand for specialist craftsmen.

The success of Ford's Model T made clear the benefits of standardised production. Products could be designed and manufactured to a standard pattern, reducing costs and facilitating the marketing of instantly recognisable brand names, from Ford for motor cars to Heinz for food products or Coca-Cola. Another development came in the form of great business empires or conglomerates. These were businesses composed of unrelated industries that sought to diversify into every area of commercial activity from extraction to production to distribution. The most famous example at the start of the century was John D. Rockefeller's Standard Oil. By 1911, this had gained a stranglehold on the

MARCONI RECEIVING APPARATUS ON AN ATLANTIC LINER'.

WIRELESS TELEGRAPH MOTOR CAR.

ITALIAN PORTABLE MARCONI STATION.

US oil industry, controlling 95 per cent of all petroleum-related companies. Another monopolistic behemoth was the American Tobacco Trust. In Europe and the USA governments introduced anti-monopoly legislation by which giants such as Standard Oil and the American Tobacco Trust were forcibly broken up to increase competition. Nevertheless, a new way of establishing a commercial power base had showed itself in action.

Communicating with the world

Increased mobility went hand in hand with one of the greatest revolutions in communications since the advent of writing 5000 years ago – a huge expansion in newspaper publishing, and then the arrival of radio, then television and later again the wonders of information technology. Various factors helped to stimulate the beginnings of this revolution at the start of the century, particularly the emergence of radio. They included the military and administrative needs of the great powers with their vast overseas empires, but the new conglomerates were important, too. Operating in disparate locations across the globe, the managers of these business empires needed to communicate with each

RADIO MIRACLE Marconi stands among the instruments on his yacht *Elettra*, which he used to carry out experiments into short-wave radio transmissions. Cigarette cards show some of the uses radio had been put to by 1910, allowing communication in remote areas.

other and their workers. Guglielmo Marconi's radio transmitter and receiver apparatus, invented in 1896, fitted their needs. The first truly global radio transmission took place on December 12, 1901, when Marconi tapped out a message in Morse code from a transmitter in Cornwall, England, to a receiver on

PACIFIC OUTCRY Anti-nuclear campaigners were outraged in 1995-6 by French nuclear tests in the Pacific. European groups spread posters and leaflets (right), and there were widespread protests, such as this one in London.

the other side of the Atlantic in Newfoundland. At this point in its history, the radio was seen as a means of sending messages from one place to another, a supplement to the network of undersea cables that had been linking the continents since the first transatlantic cable was laid in 1858; this had been expanding steadily, allowing people to exchange telegraph messages over thousands of miles of land and sea. Only later did people come to see radio as a means of bringing entertainment into the home – in Britain, the use of radio for entertainment was banned until the start of the 1920s.

COLD WAR FEVER A US anti-communist makes his feeling clear during the 1951 trial of Julius and Ethel Rosenberg, a husband and wife accused of passing on nuclear secrets to the Soviets. They were found guilty of espionage and executed in June 1953.

Technological innovation played its part in the international rivalry that eventually erupted in the First World War. This was seen, for example, in a naval armaments race between Britain and Germany, with both countries building more and more of the new dreadnought-class superbattleships. Later in the century, during the Cold War, the arms race developed between the Soviet Union and the USA as both superpowers built ever-larger stockpiles of nuclear weapons. They eventually created enough of them to produce an explosion equivalent to 10 billion tons of TNT. More peacably, the use of aircraft in both world wars helped to foster the development of passenger aircraft in the 1950s and a greater reliance on air transport to move food, goods and raw materials around the world.

Computer power

The Second World War also saw the beginnings of the computer age, when in 1943 British scientists built the first Colossus, a 2000 valve monster, constructed for the top-secret code-breaking establishment at Bletchley Park near London. US scientists later built their own computer, ENIAC (Electronic Numerical Integrator and Computer), in 1945. After the war's end came the transistor, invented in 1947 by the Americans John Bardeen, Walter H. Brattain and William B. Shockley, working at the Bell Telephone Laboratories. It was the advent, however, of the integrated

WORLDWIDE OFFICE The advent of portable computers brought the possibility of a new high-tech flexibility. Theoretically at least, you could even work on the beach.

circuit or microchip that transformed communications and computing. By the late 1980s the computer had become an essential part of the office environment. By the late 1990s it had become a workplace in itself (thanks to 'teleworking', using telephone lines to send information between one machine and another) as well as an entertainment centre and a research and marketing tool. Today, the Internet, a global network of computers

MIGHTY MINIS – ROBOTS FOR ALL OCCASIONS

A Czech playwright, Karel Capek, coined the term 'robot' for his play *R.U.R.*, first performed in 1920. What started as science fiction has, since the 1960s, become reality on robot-operated factory assembly lines. And new generations of robots are still emerging. In the 1990s Mark Tilden of Los Alamos National Laboratory in New Mexico has pushed robot design into new dimensions. Wherever you look in his home tiny robots are cleaning floors, gliding up and down windows. Unlike ordinary robots, these ones, built from discarded electronics, operate by means of what Tilden calls a 'nervous net', a ring of artificial nerve cells which transmit electric pulses to one another. Each robot is designed for a particular function, such as a 'satbot' to be sent into orbit around the Earth to measure the magnetosphere. Tilden's stable also includes a robot that crawls suicidally through minefields, disposing of landmines.

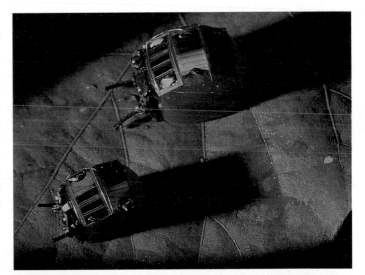

ROBOTS INTO ACTION Solar-powered 'ladybird' robots crawling across a leaf. Below: The 'spider' is used in Tokyo to check natural gas tanks for flaws.

SILICON TIGERS Kuala Lumpur's Petronas Twin Towers symbolise the achievements of the Malaysian economy before the crisis of 1997. Employees of Celcom parade in futuristic costumes during Malaysia's National Day celebrations in 1996.

along with the information stored on them, is accessed daily by millions of people. It is also used to send electronic mail (e-mail).

Electronics have revolutionised industry, carrying the production-line process, pioneered in Henry Ford's car plants, several stages further. Nowadays, much of the dangerous welding and heavy lifting in factories is performed by specialised robots, while design is often carried out on a computer, replacing the cumbersome drawing board. Using computers experts can carry out simulated tests of any new design, such as that of a car, thus reducing the need to build numerous prototypes.

Among the beneficiaries of the electronics revolution have been the 'tiger economies', such as South Korea, of East and South-east Asia. Since the Korean War (1950-3), the

South Korean economy has leapt forward, thanks in part to initial investment from Japan, the USA and Europe. Through the 1960s and 70s it grew at a staggering rate of 8.5 per cent on average per year. The country's gross national product grew by 10 per cent per year during the 1980s, though growth had slowed to an average of 1 per cent by 1992. By the early 1990s South Korea had gained a significant share of the world's electronics market, competing on almost equal terms with Japan. It was exporting goods and services worth US$80 billion per year.

World trade was changed by these events as Japan, South Korea and Malaysia, in particular, became net exporters. They relied heavily, however, on the stability of international markets, and in 1997 many economists' worst fears were fulfilled when a downturn in demand for electronics and other exports resulted in a near-catastrophic crash in the tiger economies. In December 1997 the Malaysian government called on its people to help to support the economy by handing over their gold and silver jewellery to the state. The World Bank had to step in with an $11 billion loan.

Between them, the two world wars and the Depression of the 1930s fragmented previous patterns of world trade. By 1900 the European powers, Britain, France and Germany, had already been outstripped by the US economy. Later, during the Second World War, Western Europe's position as a leading world exporter was further dented, when colonial markets so long dependent on

EAST MEETS WEST McDonald's has reached Nanjing Road in Shanghai, a city that saw an explosion of both local entrepreneurial activity and foreign investment in the 1990s.

European exports substituted their own products. Even so, the Western economies along with Japan and the Russian Federation still controlled three-quarters of all world trade in the 1990s. For all its ups and downs, the 20th century had seen a remarkable degree of stability in a handful of economies, while doing comparatively little to further economic development around the rest of the globe except in Asia.

ECONOMIC POWERHOUSES In a century of social and technological change, economic power has shifted remarkably little. The same countries that dominated the world's total gross domestic product (GDP) in 1900 mostly did so in 1990, though some, such as the UK, have taken a tumble and others, such as Japan, have seen a rise.

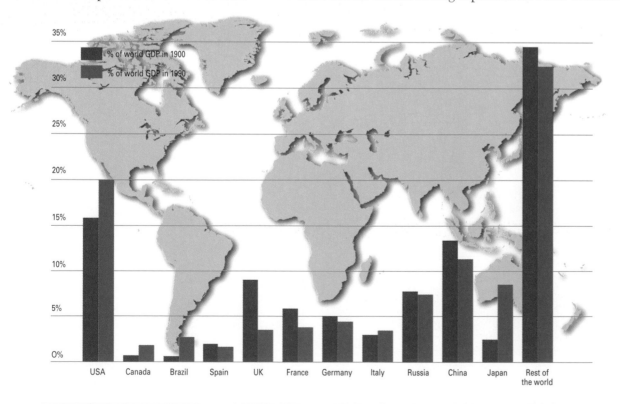

35%

30%

25%

20%

15%

10%

5%

0%

■ % of world GDP in 1900
■ % of world GDP in 1990

USA Canada Brazil Spain UK France Germany Italy Russia China Japan Rest of the world

EXPLORATION AND DISCOVERY

NEW TECHNOLOGY HAS ENABLED HUMANKIND TO EXPLOIT THE EARTH'S RESOURCES ON AN UNPRECEDENTED SCALE. IT HAS ALSO BEEN A DEVOURER OF RESOURCES IN ITS OWN RIGHT, FROM COAL AND OIL TO DIAMONDS AND SILICON. OIL HAS POWERED INDUSTRIAL EXPANSION – AND THE HUNT FOR IT HAS BEEN A BILLION-DOLLAR BUSINESS – WHILE THE ENERGY RELEASED BY SPLITTING THE ATOM HAS LEFT ITS MARK, FOR GOOD OR ILL, ON THE CENTURY'S SECOND HALF.

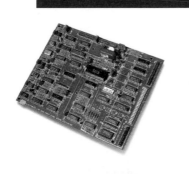

THE OIL AGE

THE INTERNAL COMBUSTION ENGINE BROUGHT THE AGE OF OIL, A SUBSTANCE SOUGHT OUT FROM DESERTS TO FROZEN WASTES

Future historians are likely to remember the 20th century for its obsession with one particular substance: oil. The drive to find, extract and use oil has been the cause of wars and created vast industrial empires. In many ways modern society is founded upon the myriad properties of this mineral slime.

Oil has been used by most societies in history. The Babylonians, Assyrians and Sumerians of the ancient Middle East used petroleum as pitch; the ancient Egyptians used it as a medicine and to dress wounds. The Chinese used small quantities of it to heat their homes. Little more than a century ago the chief use for petroleum was as a fuel for oil lamps, an alternative to the more frequently used sperm whale oil, a wax-like substance extracted from the huge spermaceti 'case' inside the head of a sperm whale. Until the mid 19th century petroleum was extracted only from surface deposits which emerged, often in the form of tar, from fissures beside creeks and inland water. It was invariably collected by small companies and distilled to produce paraffin (kerosene).

This changed on August 29, 1859, when Edwin Drake, a 38-year-old railway conductor, struck an oil field in Pennsylvania – well known for its abundance of surface oil. Drilling to a depth of 72 ft (22 m), he struck a fissure that yielded 330 gallons (1500 litres) of crude oil in a single day. Pennsylvania was soon in the grip of oil fever as prospectors, including many whalers who had given up the sea, joined in the rush for 'black gold'.

The next major development came in Texas on January 10, 1901, when a column of oil blew a drilling rig apart: oil had been struck at Spindletop. The find was massive – a 'gusher' – the biggest source that had so far been discovered. The oil age had begun. The man who struck lucky at Spindletop was Captain Anthony F. Lucas, an expert driller – he and another prospector at the same site, Patillo Higgins, made millions from the discovery. Spindletop not only created the first bulk supply of crude oil in history, but also ensured the successful launch of three petrochemical giants: Guffey (later renamed Gulf), Humble and Sun Oil. By the start of 1902 more than 400 wells had been sunk in the vicinity of Spindletop, and

by 1905 the Texas fields were producing 28 million barrels of crude oil a year (1 barrel is equivalent to 35 imperial gallons – roughly 160 litres).

HEIGHTS OF FORTUNE The Spindletop 'gusher' (right) produced its first fountain of oil in 1901. Marcus Samuel (left) was fascinated by seashells, hence the name for his company, formed in 1897.

1901 Spindletop 'gusher' – oil found in Texas
1903 Ford Motor Company founded

1908 Oil discovered at Masjed Soleyman, Persia

1913 Burton patents 'cracking' process

1918 First US petroleum pipeline – from Salt Creek to Casper, Wyoming

1938 First commercial oil finds in Saudi Arabia

1947 Oil struck in Gulf of Mexico

In Europe, meanwhile, demand was quick to respond to the new supply. Guffey Oil commissioned five tanker ships to transport the oil across the Atlantic. The Englishman Marcus Samuel, of the Shell Transport and Trading Company, telegraphed Guffey and negotiated for Shell to become the first European company to import the Texas oil. Samuel had a plan to persuade the Admiralty of the British navy to convert their vessels to become oil rather than coal burners.

The Samuel family were well-known spice traders, but Marcus Samuel had long appreciated the potential of oil. By 1902 John D. Rockefeller's Standard Oil had gained an effective monopoly of the US industry. Samuel was determined to prevent it from getting the same kind of stranglehold in the markets of Britain and its empire. Backed by the merchant bank Rothschild's, he persuaded the governors of the Suez Canal to let his oil-carrying ships use the waterway on their way to the East; they denied this privilege to Standard's vessels which had to sail around the Cape of Good Hope. The shorter route gave the Shell fleet an edge over its rivals, but to achieve Samuel's ambition in full, his company needed its own supply. The Dutch colony of Borneo provided

HUNTING FOR OIL

When searching for seabed gas and oil deposits, seismologists drop an explosive charge from a ship and detonate it on the sea floor. A shock wave travels across the seabed and then bounces back. A seismograph records the amount of returning energy as peaks and troughs on a graphic display. Shock waves travel through different materials in different ways. From the differences, seismologists can determine the location of certain rock types and suggest where and at what depth oil may be found. Exploratory drilling is always needed to verify this data.

that. In 1905 Shell formed an alliance with Royal Dutch, an oil company already operating in Borneo. Royal Dutch Shell was set to become one of the century's dominant petrochemical companies.

Around the same time, another entrepreneurial Englishman, William Knox D'Arcy, had conducted successful negotiations with

GOLD TO OIL William Knox D'Arcy (right) made a fortune in the Australian gold fields before founding Anglo-Persian. His prospectors struck oil at Masjed Soleyman (above) in 1908.

Muzaffar al-Din Shah, the ruler of Persia. These gave him the rights to search for and exploit oil reserves in Persia for 60 years. D'Arcy's finances had been severely stretched by seven years of fruitless exploration, but on May 24, 1908, a fountain of oil burst past the drill bit at Masjed Soleyman in western Persia. Surging up from a depth of 1180 ft (360 m) below the Earth's surface, the oil spurted 80 ft (25 m) into the sky.

D'Arcy's company, Anglo-Persian – later renamed BP (British Petroleum) – managed to outmanoeuvre Samuel's Shell by finally winning over the British prime minister, H.H. Asquith, and the First Sea Lord, 'Jackie' Fisher. In 1912 the Royal Navy converted its fleet of dreadnoughts to oil. Shell was now affiliated with a foreign power – the Netherlands. D'Arcy played on this fact. In May 1914 the British government injected £2 million into Anglo-Persian in return for a majority shareholding, and contracted the company to provide 40 million barrels of oil for the Royal Navy over a 20 year period.

Moving the masses

While oil magnates fought to achieve market dominance, another entrepreneur, Henry Ford, came to a decision that would make oil the single most important commodity in the

Western world. In 1903 he founded the Ford Motor Company. 'Horseless carriages' were increasingly popular among the rich, but Ford's vision was to bring car ownership within reach of the working man. As the train had symbolised all that was dynamic about the 19th century, so the motor car, Ford believed, would symbolise the 20th century.

How would Ford's vehicles be powered? The German engineer Karl Benz is usually credited with pioneering the automobile. His first car, patented in 1886, was a three-wheeler powered with a single-cylinder internal combustion engine – one in which fuel is burned within the engine rather than in a separate furnace. But the motive power for any future car remained undecided. At the turn of the century, many manufacturers were making cars that depended on batteries to power an electric motor, whilst others depended on steam. In the United States at that time, only 22 per cent of cars had internal combustion engines – 40 per cent were steam powered, 38 per cent electric powered. Yet the internal combustion engine did have notable advantages. It was cheap to manufacture and to power, thanks to the ever-growing supply of refined oil.

The Great Road Race of 1908 helped the internal combustion engine to establish its

PARIS OR BUST The Thomas Flyer showed itself worthy of its name when it won the Great Road Race of 1908.

supremacy. Sponsored by two of the world's leading newspapers, France's *Le Matin* and the *New York Times*, the race began in New York's Times Square on February 12, 1908. Waved off by a crowd of 250 000 people, six motor cars embarked on a journey across North America to San Francisco. From there they were transported by ship across the Pacific to Japan, and thence to Siberia. They traversed Russia to Moscow, and then cut down via Berlin to the finishing line in Paris.

The German team arrived first in Paris on July 26, 1908 – 165 days after leaving Times Square. Driving a Protos, the team's members all came from the German army and were sponsored by Kaiser Wilhelm II. Four days after the Germans, on July 30, George Schuster, the sole US contender, arrived in Paris. Despite arriving first, the Germans had incurred a number of penalties. They had crossed sections of the United States by train because of severe weather conditions and later sailed around Japan, rather than driving through it, before crossing to Siberia. Schuster, by contrast, had travelled overland across Asia, including Japan. Having driven 13 360 miles (21 500 km) without the penalties incurred by his German rivals, he was declared the winner. Schuster's car, a US Thomas Flyer, became an instant sensation – sales of it increased by 27 per cent.

Meanwhile, it was also in 1908 that Henry Ford unveiled the Model T, the first car designed to meet the demands of the masses. Known as the Tin Lizzie, the Model T was a simple vehicle, but boasted a four-cylinder internal combustion engine capable of generating 20 horsepower. Initially available for

US$850, the Model T rapidly dropped in price, largely due to innovative assembly-line techniques devised by Ransom Olds and first introduced in Ford's Highland Park assembly plant in Michigan in 1913.

By 1919, 50 per cent of all motorised vehicles in the world were Model T Fords. By 1923, Ford's workers, paid $5 a day, could buy a Model T for $290 – the equivalent of 58 days' wages. More than 15 million had been sold by May 1927 when production ceased. The Model T had helped to ensure the success of the motor car and of motorised vehicles in general. At the same time, it ensured that oil became a key commodity.

How to crack oil

But the escalating demand for petrol (gasoline) had created a supply problem. The distillation technology used to extract petrol from crude oil at the start of the century was highly inefficient. Based on a system devised

in the 1870s, it produced a yield of 20 per cent at best, until William Burton, at Standard Oil, devised a new method in 1913. In the process called 'thermal cracking', oil molecules are heated in stills (known as Burton stills after the technique's inventor) until they split into smaller more energised molecules. This technique doubled the yield and raised the general quality of fuel available to the consumer.

Demand grew and grew. The two world wars saw a rapid increase in the use of motorised vehicles, from oil-powered ships to tanks to planes. During the First World War air aces won renown as they fought it out in aircraft such as the German Fokker *Eindecker* (monoplane) and the British Sopwith Camel biplane. Between the wars some of the same pilots went into the new and expanding air transport industry. During the 1930s, passenger aircraft such as the Boeing 247 came into their own. By the time of the Second World War, the automotive industry amounted to 20 per cent of the United States' total manufacturing output: $29 billion-worth of equipment, including aircraft, tanks and engines.

At the same time, breakthroughs in oil-refining had continued through the 1920s and 30s. These had allowed petrochemical companies to exploit by-products of the refining process to manufacture solvents,

AFFORDABLE FORD Ford produced the first Model T in 1908. The next year a Model T won a transcontinental race from New York to Seattle.

plastics and even animal feed. They began to realise that oil, largely composed of carbon atoms (the fundamental building blocks of life and organic material), could be refined to produce virtually any commodity: it was simply a matter of developing the appropriate techniques.

During the Second World War, the escalation in aviation, thanks to bomber and fighter sorties, encouraged this process. It pushed the refining industries to develop

After the five-year hiatus of the Second World War, passenger air travel resumed in the late 1940s, and the increased demand for specialised fuels forced the petrochemical industry to find new sources of oil.

Rise of the Middle East

Between 1951 and 1970 world production of oil grew from 12 million barrels a day to 46 million barrels, with demand growing by 7 per cent every year. This growth in production

and it was not given back its monopoly; it had to compete against other companies.

The Suez Canal, which had been so vital to the success of Sir Marcus Samuel's Shell Oil, was nationalised by the Egyptian government in 1956. The former colonial powers which had dominated the area for so long were obliged to find additional supplies and alternative routes. In the event of war the Suez Canal could no longer be relied upon as a safe route from the Middle East to Europe. One result was an increase in the average size of oil tankers from a capacity of 50 000 tons to more than 200 000 tons. This helped to ensure a steady supply when tankers were forced to take the longer route to the West around the Cape of Good Hope.

Soviet oil flooded Western markets in 1959, prompting another fall in world prices. The time was ripe for Venezuela and the states of The Gulf to take further control into their hands. After the success of the Iranian nationalisation in 1951 and the Suez revolt, they formed the Organisation of Petroleum Exporting Countries (OPEC) in 1960 and established a price-fixing cartel.

TRANSATLANTIC TRAVELLER This German-built Fokker monoplane, 'Old Glory', belonged to the Hearst Corporation in the mid 1920s. Here, it is being prepared at an airfield on Long Island, New York, for a flight to Rome.

techniques for extracting higher octane fuel – a more powerful fuel that combusts more smoothly within an engine. Similarly, the large number of military aircraft and motor vehicles that needed rubber for tyres and engine hoses forced European and US refining industries to develop methods of producing benzene and other petroleum-derived chemicals in order to make synthetic rubber. By 1945 parachutes, too, were made of nylon, replacing the traditional silk cloth.

was mostly concentrated in the Middle East. Oil became ever more affordable and the West, in particular, soaked it up.

During the 1950s, Western companies found themselves outmanoeuvred as countries in the developing world took control of their reserves, particularly Iran (Persia), Iraq and Kuwait. In 1951 Iran nationalised its oil fields, revoking its agreements with BP. It took three years of negotiations before BP was allowed to start operations there again,

PETROL ON TAP During the 1930s roadside petrol pumps became a common piece of street furniture. They were often installed at street corners without the various station buildings that became familiar from the 1950s.

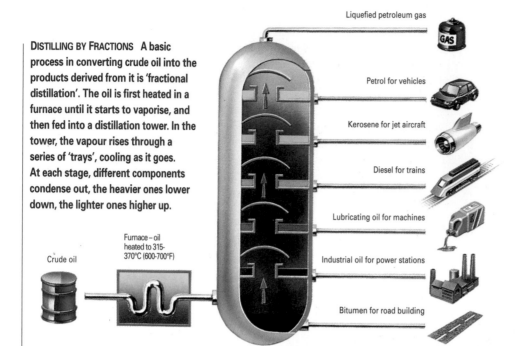

Liquefied petroleum gas

Petrol for vehicles

Kerosene for jet aircraft

Diesel for trains

Lubricating oil for machines

Industrial oil for power stations

Bitumen for road building

DISTILLING BY FRACTIONS A basic process in converting crude oil into the products derived from it is 'fractional distillation'. The oil is first heated in a furnace until it starts to vaporise, and then fed into a distillation tower. In the tower, the vapour rises through a series of 'trays', cooling as it goes. At each stage, different components condense out, the heavier ones lower down, the lighter ones higher up.

Crude oil

Furnace – oil heated to 315-370°C (600-700°F)

GOODS GALORE The range of petroleum-derived goods is huge. One barrel of crude oil yields the chemicals from which manufacturers can produce any of the items below.

21 shirts OR 6 dustbins OR 479 ft (146 m) of gas pipe

4 milk crates OR 21 sweaters

1 car tyre OR 3 car inner tubes

500 pairs of tights

Saudi Arabia, Iran, Kuwait, Iraq and Venezuela were united against the Western oil companies, determined to control world oil prices in their own favour. OPEC managed to stabilise prices at an average of US$1.65 per barrel during the 1960s. Although the Western oil companies tried to ignore OPEC's growing power, the potential for an artificially created supply crisis now existed.

Oil crises

The Arab-Israeli War of October 1973 gave the OPEC cartel a huge boost. The Arabs enforced an oil embargo against the West, causing prices to triple and precipitating an oil crisis. Suddenly, petrol stations were short of fuel.

Less than six years later, in early 1979, a similar situation arose when the Shah of Iran was overthrown and Ayatollah Khomeini came to power. The Shah had fostered close links with the USA. Khomeini, by contrast, was vehemently anti-American. In November 1979 a mob of his supporters stormed the US Embassy in Tehran, seizing 66 hostages. In response, President Jimmy Carter ordered the sequestration of all Iranian assets in US territories. Western trade with Iran was effectively suspended, sparking another oil shortage and price hike. The crisis in the Middle East deepened still further when Iraq invaded Iran on September 22, 1980. All this time, 52 of the original 66 US hostages had

remained in captivity. They were not finally released until January 1981.

OPEC's price-fixing policy was, to a certain extent, superseded by events. The political and religious crises of the Middle East pushed prices up – with the result that world oil consumption went into serious and prolonged decline for the first time in the 20th century. Oil dropped in importance as a fuel for energy production. In 1979 it accounted for 50 per cent of world energy production; this fell to 39 per cent by 1985.

In 1947 a new technology of offshore drilling had produced its first results when oil was struck in the Gulf of Mexico. Offshore oil from the Gulf came to provide 25 per cent of the United States' output – over 10 billion barrels since 1947. But the new technique would have an even greater impact in

PIPING THE RESOURCE Pipelines – such as this one in Kuwait being laid in 1967 – transport crude oil to the coast for shipping and distribution around the world.

Europe, where in the 1960s it offered a way out of OPEC's threatened stranglehold.

Offshore drilling is impossible without a semipermanent base on the surface of the sea. This is built around a large hollow drill, or 'rig', which is lowered onto the ocean bed.

CANAL CRISIS

SUEZ STRANGLEHOLD   During the Suez crisis, Nasser blocked the Suez Canal by sinking old ships.

In July 1956, the US government withdrew from plans to co-fund a new dam on the Nile; isolationism was running high in Congress which was keen to limit foreign aid to Egypt's President Nasser, perceived as a socialist. Britain also withdrew from the scheme, and Nasser responded on July 26 by nationalising the Suez Canal, the profits of which would be used to fund the dam. The British and French governments, who had previously controlled the canal, were enraged. The movement of oil from the Middle East would now be at the behest of Nasser. London and Paris appealed to the International Court of Justice at The Hague to overturn Nasser's actions. Instead, it ratified them. Britain, France and Israel then agreed on an operation to recover control of the canal by force. Israel was to attack Egypt to give British and French troops a pretext to occupy the canal zone and 'restore order'. The Israelis duly attacked on October 29, followed a few days later by Anglo-French forces. The USA, however, would have no part of the action, calling instead for a ceasefire, while Moscow threatened a nuclear attack. This brought the operation to an end on November 6 in an embarrassing defeat for Britain and France.

The drill bit bores through the bed, sometimes reaching depths of 6000 ft (1800 m) during exploratory drilling. Oil is usually struck between 980 and 2900 ft (300 and 900 m) below the seabed. Oil fields contain flammable gases which pressurise the pockets in the rock that hold the oil. When a drill bit ruptures the surrounding rock and enters the

A MATTER OF SCALE   The supertanker is a colossus of the seas. Able to carry 200 000 tons of oil, it is 34 times longer than a double-decker bus.

pocket the pressure forces oil out of the reservoir and up the hollow drill pipe to the surface. This pressurisation allows platforms to recover approximately 20 per cent of the oil in a reservoir. By pumping sea water into the pocket another 30 per cent can be recovered. The extracted crude oil is

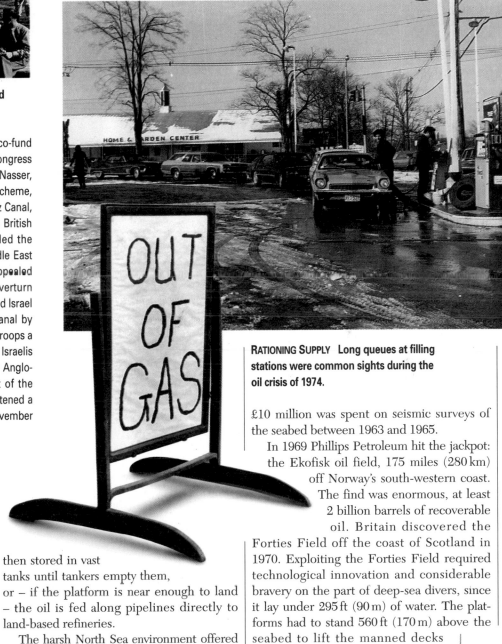

RATIONING SUPPLY   Long queues at filling stations were common sights during the oil crisis of 1974.

then stored in vast tanks until tankers empty them, or – if the platform is near enough to land – the oil is fed along pipelines directly to land-based refineries.

The harsh North Sea environment offered Europe's petrochemical industries a

chance to prove their mettle. The turning point came in August 1959, when seismologists discovered a gas field off the coast of Groningen in The Netherlands. This field, the second-largest known gas field in the world, opened the floodgates for investors. Petrochemical companies hired seismologists to hunt in earnest for reserves of gas and liquid oil beneath the North Sea. More than £10 million was spent on seismic surveys of the seabed between 1963 and 1965.

In 1969 Phillips Petroleum hit the jackpot: the Ekofisk oil field, 175 miles (280 km) off Norway's south-western coast. The find was enormous, at least 2 billion barrels of recoverable oil. Britain discovered the Forties Field off the coast of Scotland in 1970. Exploiting the Forties Field required technological innovation and considerable bravery on the part of deep-sea divers, since it lay under 295 ft (90 m) of water. The platforms had to stand 560 ft (170 m) above the seabed to lift the manned decks above the reach of 100 ft (30 m)

ALL HANDS ON DECK Shifts of men work round the clock to maintain a steady supply of oil from deep-sea oil rigs. Right: The Forties Bravo rig in the North Sea.

waves, though this height increased the dangers of structural stress. Despite these problems, North Sea oil reached Britain's shores on June 18, 1975, and flowed through the first pipeline – from the Forties Field to a refinery in Grangemouth – on November 3, 1975.

Companies such as BP had been drilling for oil in Europe since the end of the First World War, but results had mostly been disappointing. Before the 1970s, oil production in Britain, for example, yielded only 0.5 million barrels a year. North Sea oil changed all that. By 1975 the pipeline from the Forties Field was producing that amount a day.

Crossing Alaska

After the Suez crisis of 1956, the US government was as keen as the Europeans to locate additional sources of oil. In March 1968, the last great petrochemical frontier was crossed: the largest oil field in North America was discovered at Prudhoe Bay on Alaska's northern coastline. Here, 10 billion barrels of oil are locked beneath a permanently frozen landscape, equal to the reserves of the Middle East and North Africa combined. Battered by Arctic winds, in temperatures of –30°C (–22°F), capable of causing frostbite within seconds, oil workers penetrated the Alaskan wilds to exploit the find. Petrochemical companies now had the oil reserves they sought . . . but could not move them, by truck or by sea, from the frozen coast of Prudhoe Bay.

The solution was a grand feat of civil engineering: a pipeline, crossing 800 miles (1300 km) of Alaskan valleys, rivers and mountain ranges to reach the ice-free port of Valdez at the southern end of the Alaskan Gulf. It cut through the Atigun Pass between mountain peaks rising to heights of 4900 ft (1500 m) above sea level, and ran along the bed of the Tosina river. After four years of construction and 71 000 welds, the pipeline was finally completed at a cost US$8 billion.

BREAKING THE WAVES

David Warwick, a well-site geologist, was one of the pioneers who first explored the North Sea oil frontier. Working at sea, Warwick weathered a storm on November 19, 1973, which nearly destroyed the *Bluewater III* oil platform in the Argyle Field:

'The wind built up to a steady 90 miles per hour [145 km/h], gusting up to 120 miles per hour [190 km/h], and one of the rig's anchors popped apart until we ended up with just two anchors on one corner holding the rig in position. Each time the anchors broke, the rig swung round to a different heading and the balance shifted dramatically. At one point the deck was tilting at 15 degrees which we later found out was just a few degrees off the critical angle at which the rig would have turned over . . . The last two anchors began to drag and we started to drift to the south-east, on a heading towards Rotterdam . . . Mayday messages were duly transmitted and two ocean-going tugs were dispatched, one from Aberdeen and one from Hull. The skipper of the Aberdeen tug fell on the bridge on his way out and broke his leg, so the tug had to return to port. The other tug *Euroman* from Hull . . . caught up with the *Bluewater III* and got a line attached. I was . . . one of the non-essential personnel to be evacuated by chopper several hours later.'

DISASTER SLICK

On March 24, 1989, more than 9 million gallons (41 million litres) of crude oil poured out of the grounded *Exxon Valdez* tanker into the waters of Prince William Sound in Alaska. A huge slick formed and during the spring drifted south-west. National parks, wildlife refuges and shoreline communities were all badly affected, and wildlife was massacred. Around 1000 sea otters were killed, only 200 saved. Clean-up efforts were, many environmentalists claim, ineffectual. On Naked Island in the sound, workers blasted the oil slick from beaches, pushing the oil out to sea, where skimmers sitting on top of the water could collect the oil and siphon it off. Unfortunately, the vast amount of oil meant that as soon as the beach was clean, the tide and wind would cover it in a new layer.

Despite the size of the spill, nearly four times the amount of oil lost remained in the tanks of the *Exxon Valdez*. This was pumped off onto other ships and to shore. Had the tanker broken up, the spill would have caused unimaginable devastation. As it was the effects of the catastrophe were far-reaching. Fishermen in the North Pacific have reported large hauls of polluted fish, probably poisoned by the *Exxon Valdez* spill.

In 1994 Exxon and the ship's captain, Joseph Hazelwood, were found guilty of recklessness and ordered to pay more than $5 billion in punitive damages. Already in 1990, the US government had passed the Oil Pollution Act in an attempt to calm fears about future disasters. By the year 2015, all tankers operating in US waters will have to have double hulls to protect against holing and spills – though for the time being older designs continue to predominate.

DAUNTING TASK Hand-scrubbing may be the only way to clean a polluted beach.

On June 20, 1977, oil began to flow across the Arctic Circle to Valdez. By 1978 the Trans-Alaskan Pipeline was carrying a million barrels of oil a day: the USA had its new oil reserve.

How long will Earth's oil last? One oil company estimated that 'proven' reserves – from which oil can be extracted economically using current technology – amounted to more than 1 million million barrels at the end of 1996. There are at least as many reserves that can be viably tapped as technology improves. In 1996 world consumption of oil stood at just under 70 million barrels a day. At that rate, the proven reserves will last 40 years, but that takes no account of any other reserves; nor does it allow for a world-wide shift away from fossil fuels towards alternative energy sources. One thing, however, is sure. The oil that has powered so much of the 20th century is a finite resource; inevitably, future generations will have to find other ways of generating power.

RAISED ON HIGH The Trans-Alaskan Pipeline has to be raised on stilts for much of its length to prevent the warm oil from melting the permafrost beneath.

HARVESTING THE ELEMENTS

COAL HAS DIPPED IN GLOBAL IMPORTANCE; SILICON HAS COME UP; DIAMONDS HAVE STAYED STEADY AND EVEN FOUND NEW USES

As the British politician Anthony Crossland once observed: 'What one generation sees as a luxury, the next sees as a necessity.' Certainly, the role of diamonds, gold and other precious commodities has changed over the 20th century. What were once viewed almost entirely as luxury items are now seen also as economic necessities – diamonds, for example, are widely used in industry. By contrast, minerals such as coal, once seen as supremely vital commodities, are now much less important than they were.

Coal was the main power source of the 19th century. It fuelled the dominant form of transport – steam trains – and powered industry. In less than a generation between 1875 and 1900, annual world production of coal nearly tripled from 285 million tons to 766 million tons. By the 1920s, however, although world production was still expanding, it was doing so much more slowly – it rose from 1212 million tons in 1920 to just 1275 million in 1930. Between 1930 and 1938, it fell to 1271 million tons. Coal had peaked as the world's most important fuel, to be replaced by new and cheaper supplies of oil and gas.

The lot of coal miners at the turn of the century was also changing. Working in cramped conditions at a coalface which was sometimes only 3 ft (900 cm) high, miners were still cutting coal by

LIKE THEIR FATHERS BEFORE THEM German coal workers in 1900 (right). Men like these worked in much the same way as their forefathers. By 1920 mechanisation was becoming common, enabling miners to exploit more remote seams.

hand. Black lung – a bronchial disease caused by inhaling fine particles of coal dust – was common. But casualty figures were improving. In 1865, nearly four underground miners in every thousand in the UK died from mining-related diseases or accidents; by 1905, that figure had fallen to 1.4 per thousand. The improvement was due to better ventilation provided by more efficient steam-powered pumps. Conditions would continue to get better, thanks chiefly to the increased use of mechanisation at the coalface. In the UK alone, the amount of coal cut by machine increased from under 8 per cent in 1913 to approximately 60 per cent in 1938.

Despite the increased deployment of technology, extracting coal was more difficult than drilling and exploiting new-found oil wells. The greatest challenge for coal producers in the first half of the 20th century was the development of the internal combustion engine. Once General Motors had produced its first compact diesel engine in 1919-20, diesel trucks and locomotives started to replace the steam engine. The petroleum industry was marching into coal's market share. By the 1950s in most Western countries the diesel locomotive was sidelining the steam engine to menial shunting duties. Consequently, the transport network's demand for coal, which had been growing ever since 1828, had all but died by 1950.

But coal was not finished as a fuel. By 1950 the petrochemical industry still accounted for only 10 per cent of Europe's electricity production, for example, leaving coal to provide the bulk of the remaining 90 per cent. Nonetheless, by the mid 1950s the role of smog in causing illness and even death was a well-established fact. In 1953 the *British*

1902 Death of
Cecil Rhodes

1930 World coal
production peaks at
1275 million tons

1945 ENIAC computer
1947 Brattain, Shockley and
Bardeen invent transistor

DIGGING FOR THEIR COUNTRY In 1947, postwar Britain faced an energy crisis, and the country's miners, such as these men of Betteshanger Colliery in Kent, were seen as an essential human resource.

Medical Journal published a report which stated that more than 4000 people had died in London as a result of five days' smog in December the previous year. 'Clean air' acts followed in most Western countries. Homes in urban areas would no longer be allowed to burn smoke-creating fuels. Fuels such as gas and electricity were embraced by consumers keen to break away from the dirt and drudgery of solid-fuel heating.

By the 1980s there were further environmental concerns, this time about sulphur and nitrogen emissions from coal-fired power stations. When sulphur dioxide and nitrogen oxides enter the atmosphere, they create sulphuric and nitric acids which fall back to Earth in 'acid rain'. This is believed to be responsible for widespread damage to lakes and forests, particularly in Scandinavia.

Another set of worries came to prominence in the 1990s – about emissions of carbon dioxide and nitrous oxides. These are released into the atmosphere when coal, oil and natural gas are burned in power stations or motor vehicles. Many experts believe that they act as a heat barrier within the atmosphere, triggering global warming. This was another knock for the coal industry. Agreements to use coal reserves to fuel power stations expired in the 1990s, leaving the mining industry without a guaranteed market.

In the USA, 90 per cent of all coal mines closed between 1985 and 1994, leaving fewer than 20 profitable coal mines in operation. In Europe miners fared little better. In the UK more than 130 coal mines closed in a little over seven years between 1985 and 1992 at the cost of 180 000 jobs.

Diamonds are forever

In 1902, the British entrepreneur, magnate and empire builder Cecil Rhodes died in Cape Town at the age of 48. His relatively short life had been distinguished by a vision to unite Africa under European domination, and to create there an economy greater than that of the United States. In the end, he never created his giant economy, but his financial legacy survives in De Beers Consolidated Diamond Mines, founded on March 12, 1888.

During the 20th century the diamond's importance has grown with its increased use in manufacturing and science. By 1927 South Africa's annual production of diamonds was valued at US$18 million and by the 1950s De Beers diamond mines alone were mining and selling 50 million carats (roughly 10 tons) of diamonds every year.

Diamonds have always been treasured for their beauty and the status that comes with owning and wearing them. So it was almost inevitable that new technologies in exploiting the Earth's reserves would be applied to diamond mining. But the growth of mechanisation in the 20th century did more than simply improve the supplies of diamonds; it also found new ways of exploiting them.

SIFTING THE SANDS OF WEALTH De Beers workers at South Africa's diamond capital Kimberley near the start of the century. They were experts at detecting diamonds and diamond fragments in the gravel produced by open-cast mining.

Diamonds are carbon, the purest kind of carbon deposit. They are one of the hardest substances known to science and one of the most heat-conductive materials on Earth, making them a vital component in many precision electronics machines. They are often used as a 'heat sink', a component within an electronic product that harmlessly radiates any heat generated. Virtually indestructible diamond drill bits are used to extract other resources from the Earth, such as oil and gas, and in precision engineering.

Another use for diamonds was the result of research by the German physicist Karl

1955 General Electric create synthetic diamond
1958 First microchip

1969 Arpanet, forerunner of Internet

1990 World Wide Web established

RAW BEAUTY Uncut diamonds look more like coloured glass than precious gems. The quality of the cutting can enhance or reduce their value.

Braun. As early as 1897 he had invented the cathode-ray tube which would later make television possible. He then turned his attention to wireless telegraphy, especially the problem of how to send radio messages in a particular direction. For his work in this field he was awarded the 1909 Nobel prize for physics with Marconi. He also made the discovery that radio reception is improved by passing the signal through a crystal. To be registered as sound, certain kinds of radio waves have to be converted, or 'rectified', from high frequency oscillating signals into currents flowing in one direction. The uniform nature of crystalline structure prevents radio waves from travelling in more than one direction. Braun's crystal rectifier was one key factor that made possible the dramatic development of radio broadcasting after the First World War. Diamond, by far the best form of rectifier, was in great demand for use in the early radios known as 'crystal sets'.

In 1926 Carol Chatham, a teenage amateur scientist from San Francisco, was the first person to attempt to 'grow' artificial diamonds, and he came very close to doing so. Unfortunately, his method required the use of molten iron to dissolve his raw material, graphite. Once the graphite had dissolved, he threw it in a container of liquid nitrogen – used as a supercoolant – which wrecked his family home in a large explosion. Despite this alarming experience, he persisted with his experiments throughout his late teens and early twenties. Although he never succeeded in producing pure synthetic diamonds, he did create the world's first synthetic gem – a synthetic emerald – in 1938.

Research scientists at the US firm General Electric finally created a synthetic diamond for use in industrial production in 1955. They did it by subjecting carbon to pressures of 3000 lb per sq in (210 kg per cm^2) and temperatures in excess of 350°C (662°F). By the 1980s the technology was so well developed that the production of synthetic

CRYSTAL CLARITY Karl Braun's crystal rectifier helped to make practical radio a reality. The Cosmos crystal radio set (below) was widely marketed in the 1920s.

A GIRL'S BEST FRIEND?

**DIAMONDS HAVE RETAINED THEIR TRADITIONAL ROLE AS PRIZED POSSESSIONS
AND ADORNMENTS OF THE RICH, FAMOUS AND POWERFUL**

Glamour and diamonds still go hand in hand. In 1990, according to one estimate, the jewellery collection of Hollywood star Elizabeth Taylor was worth £5 million. Her most famous gems were gifts from her twice-married husband, Richard Burton. In 1968 he gave her the 33 carat Krupp diamond. The following year he paid over $1 million for a large pear-shaped stone that became known as the 'Taylor-Burton'. Elizabeth Taylor wore it for the first time that year at the 40th birthday party of Princess Grace of Monaco. In 1978, however, she announced that she was selling it and planned to use the proceeds to build a hospital in Botswana. It went in June 1979 for nearly $3 million and was last heard of in Saudi Arabia. Another great jewellery owner was the Duchess of Windsor, whose collection was sold in Geneva after her death in 1986. It raised $45 million for the Pasteur Institute in Paris.

One diamond, the Hope Diamond, has left a trail of unlucky owners. Originally mined in India, it was brought to France in 1668 and sold to Louis XIV. By the start of the 20th century, it had come

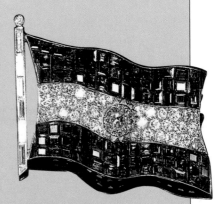

TEAR OF JOY Jewellers in the 1930s were inspired by the current art deco style. This French diamond clip brooch is shaped like a teardrop.

HOLLYWOOD QUEEN Elizabeth Taylor in Paris in 1967. Her tiara was created by the jeweller Alexandre at a reported price of US$1.2 million.

into the hands of an East European prince who gave it to his mistress, a dancer at the Folies-Bergère; the first time she wore it he shot her across the footlights. A subsequent owner, the Turkish Sultan Abdul-Hamid II, had the diamond for only a few months before losing his throne in a coup. In 1911 the American socialite Evalyn Walsh McLean bought it. A catalogue of disasters followed, from her son being killed in a car crash to her husband dying in a mental hospital. It is now safely in the Smithsonian Institution in Washington.

By the 1990s, diamonds worn in unusual places were the trend. Supermodel Naomi Campbell wore a chain of diamonds looped around her waist and through a navel ring. Pop icon Madonna had a diamond horseshoe charm in her navel and a diamond stud in her nose.

FOR THE PRESIDENT'S LADY Sapphires and diamonds pick out the Argentine flag in a brooch made for Eva Perón.

BEJEWELLED INSTRUMENT
Modern dental drills, like this one photographed through an electron microscope, are encrusted with diamond particles.

60 per cent of the Earth's landmass is composed of it, this grey fragile crystalline substance – neither a metal nor mineral but a 'metalloid' – became significant with the rise of computing.

The construction and use of computing devices had existed only in the imaginations of science fiction writers until the 1940s. Then, in 1943, in the thick of the Second World War, a British team, led by Cambridge mathematician Max Newman and Post Office engineer Thomas Flowers, built the world's first electronic digital computer, the Colossus; it was to be used at the code-breaking centre at Bletchley Park in Buckinghamshire. In the end, ten Colossus computers were built and used during the last years of the war.

Across the Atlantic, meanwhile, a team at the University of Pennsylvania in Philadelphia was working on a similar machine for the US army. The ENIAC (Electronic Numerical Integrator and Calculator) was revealed to the public at the start of 1946. This vast machine, which weighed more than 30 tons,

diamonds exceeded the quantity extracted from diamond mines.

Another recent development in the use of diamonds relates to their durability. Researchers have conducted experiments to try to produce microscopically thin, cost-effective diamond coatings on machinery. The aim is to extend greatly the life of moving parts.

Elements of the century

While coal has declined in importance in the advanced economies, silicon has risen. Long overlooked, it began to fulfil its potential in the 1950s, as scientific advances made it possible for the first time to exploit its various properties. Plentiful in supply since more than

FIRST GENERATION The earliest computers contained thousands of vacuum tubes: ENIAC (above) had 18 000. The work of Shockley, Brattain and Bardeen (left to right) led to the invention of the far more practical transistor.

ELEMENTAL POLITICS

If it had not been for the US Helium Act of 1927, we might nowadays crisscross the world in helium-filled airships rather than fixed-wing jet liners. At the start of the century, it seemed obvious to most observers that mankind would conquer the skies in airships. Although the Wright brothers succeeded in piloting an aircraft that was heavier than air in 1903, the airship was widely seen as more practicable. In the end, however, international politics got in the way, for the clear leader in airship design was the German Zeppelin company. By the 1920s, Germany's European neighbours, with memories of the First World War fresh in their minds, were concerned, as was the US government. Airships were quiet and could operate at great altitudes, allowing them to make a stealthy approach to any site.

By then the Zeppelin company had designed airships to be fuelled by nonflammable helium rather than hydrogen. There was one snag: the USA was the only mass producer of the helium, and in 1927 Washington restricted its export. Zeppelin had to go back to using hydrogen. By the 1930s, airships were vast; the most famous, the *Hindenburg*, held 7 million cu ft (200 000 m³) of hydrogen in its gas envelope. Originally designed to use helium, this first transatlantic airliner was a bomb waiting to explode. All the same, it flew 18 successful trips until May 6, 1937, when it ignited during landing manoeuvres at Lakehurst, New Jersey, with the loss of 36 lives. Had it been using helium, as it was designed to, the catastrophe would not have occurred. After that, few people wanted to travel by airship any longer.

SKY LINER Although the *Hindenburg* was designed to use helium, it went into operation using hydrogen, with disastrous consequences.

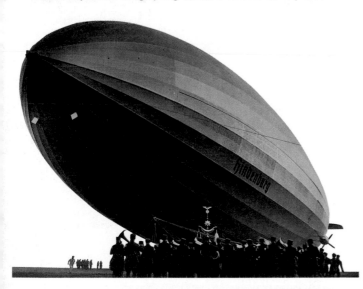

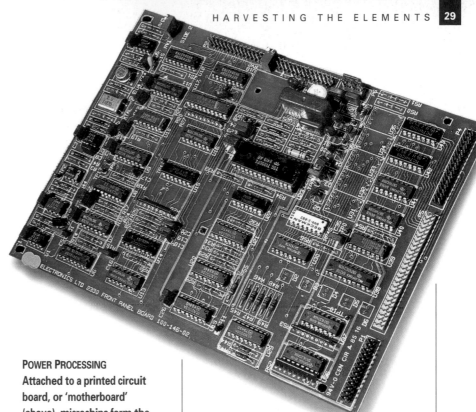

POWER PROCESSING Attached to a printed circuit board, or 'motherboard' (above), microchips form the central processing unit in modern personal computers.

As science progressed and dealt with ever-more complicated calculations, a more practical system was needed. Solid-state physics offered the solution. In 1931 Walter Brattain at the Bell Laboratories in the USA had noticed that silicon conducted electricity when it was chemically treated. Silicon had long been regarded as an insulator, but the discovery that it could conduct as well as insulate – that it is a 'semiconductor' – led to a breakthrough. In 1939 one of Brattain's colleagues at Bell Laboratories, William Shockley, realised that if minute areas of a sliver of silicon were chemically treated, they might be used to replace the vacuum tube to

In 1958 some physicists who had worked with Shockley established the next and most pivotal breakthrough in semiconductor technology: the microchip. Led by Robert Noyce, the team wanted to combine transistors and circuits into one integrated circuit, avoiding the need for hand-soldered connections. In the end, Noyce devised a method of sandwiching silicon semiconductor membranes between insulating layers. At about the same time, an employee of the Texas Instruments company, Jack Kilby, was achieving similar results. He formed a microscopic capacitor, transistor and resistor out of one sliver of silicon. He then linked them with microscopic wires, producing another integrated circuit.

During the 1970s microcomputers were designed and marketed in kit form to be sold to amateur electronics engineers. This

VIRTUAL COMMODITY The Internet and World Wide Web are revolutionising the way we disseminate information. Web browsers enable users to tap into millions of 'sites' carrying information and entertainment.

depended on vacuum tubes to allow it to function. Indeed, the entire field of electronics, then in its infancy, depended on these glass tubes which contained electrodes in a vacuum and could generate or alter an electronic signal. They were large – somewhat similar to light bulbs – and prone to failure. They also generated a terrific heat and needed dedicated air-conditioning units to prevent systems from combusting.

generate or alter electronic signals. The Second World War interrupted their work, but in 1947 Brattain, Shockley and a team mate, John Bardeen, produced the transistor, an effective replacement for the vacuum tube. In 1956 the three men shared the Nobel prize for physics.

FIBRES OF LIGHT

Since its development in the 1950s, fibre optics has revolutionised communications. Silica (silicon dioxide) is fused at high temperatures and stretched to create glass strands. These glass fibres absorb very low quantities of light. When attached to lasers, they can carry pulses of information around the globe. Transmissions consist of signals in the form of short flashes of light, akin to a switch being turned on and off. Boosters amplify the signal so that it gets to the receiving end. Because one optical cable can carry millions of pieces of information at the same time, fibre optics have replaced metal cables in telecommunications.

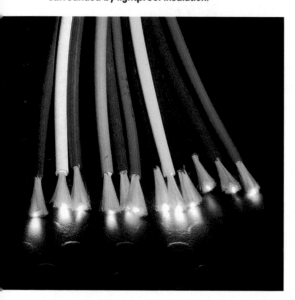

GLASSFULS OF LIGHT Optical fibres are surrounded by lightproof insulation.

presaged the development in the 1980s of the market for personal computers (PCs). The computer rapidly replaced older systems in almost every industry. Printing and design industries embraced the design and word-processing abilities of the computer, while the development of a system that could allow computers to transmit and receive data using the telephone network via modems began yet another revolution. As early as 1969 a group of military computers in different parts of the USA had been linked together in a network called Arpanet. Similar networks, for civilian as well as military use, were established in increasing numbers during the 1970s and 80s. In due course, the telephone system was used to link these networks into an 'interlinked network' or Internet. With the advent of cheap and easily accessible satellite telephone communications, the Internet became an international network, carrying billions of pieces of information. Technology is now so developed in this area that radio and television broadcasts are being tested on the 'net', and video cameras are able to operate alongside standard voice signals to carry sound and 'videophone' images over it.

Computers have become a common part of life, whether as a desktop tool or to regulate the internal combustion in cars. The silicon microprocessor has changed patterns of work

URANIUM'S HIDDEN POWER

Uranium has become a precious commodity. It was discovered in 1789 by a German apothecary, Martin Klaproth, who named it after the recently discovered planet Uranus. It was used as a dye for glassware, but for the most part remained an oddity. Then, in 1896, the French physicist Henri Becquerel discovered that it gave off radiation. Uranium held a power that might be tapped: Klaproth's oddity was used to create the atomic bomb and exploit nuclear power in general.

and those of economic dominance. In the West, it is estimated that 20 per cent of all households now own a computer, and by the year 2000 as many as 4 billion PCs will be in everyday use around the world.

ROBOT WORKERS The computer age sees 'Motoman' robots used in motor manufacturing (below). Experiments are well advanced to develop a robot-controlled car that will allow the human occupants to work or relax (right).

PROBING THE OCEANS

FISH STOCKS ARE IN PERIL THROUGH OVERFISHING, BUT EXPERTS ARE FINDING NEW FORMS OF OCEAN WEALTH – FROM MINERALS TO DRUGS

People have sailed the seas since the beginnings of history. There is evidence of trade between the Greek mainland and the island of Melos from the 11th century BC. The inhabitants of the Near East had reed boats for river transport by 7000 BC. By 1200 BC the ancient Phoenicians were sailing from their home ports in the eastern Mediterranean out into the Atlantic and as far north as England. Yet despite this long history of seafaring we still know relatively little about the oceans, the alien environment that covers 71 per cent of our planet. After centuries of speculation but limited technology, it is only in the 20th century that we have finally started to explore the deeps and exploit their untapped resources.

The most obvious wealth of the oceans is their fish. As early as the Middle Ages, fishermen from Europe were catching herring in large quantities in the North Sea, and by the 15th century they were making their way across the Atlantic to the Grand Banks of Newfoundland to harvest the cod there. Large-scale whaling began in the 17th century. By the end of the 19th century technology was transforming the industry as steamers and motor vessels started to replace the old sailing boats. By the start of the 20th century, even smaller fishing vessels in developed countries were being motorised.

Yet fishing remained an intuitive business. In 1900, without modern scanning techniques, a fisherman was dependent on his instincts and experience; he prospered or failed by following his gut feeling. Lack of refrigeration equipment – large blocks of ice preserved catches while at sea – dictated schedules, preventing vessels from staying at sea for more than ten to twelve days at the outside.

Changes in a new century

As early as the 1890s the British House of Commons raised grave concerns over the levels of fish stocks in the North Sea and North Atlantic fishing grounds. In 1899 a conference was arranged for the North American and European fishing communities to discuss the issue. In 1902, the International Council for the Exploration of the Sea (ICES) was established, with the aim of regulating fishing in the North Sea and North Atlantic.

The Grand Banks, off the south-eastern coast of Newfoundland, stretch for 420 miles (680 km) from east to west where the warm Gulf Stream meets the cold Labrador Current. For thousands of years, crabs, worms and shrimps carried by the Labrador Current fed a great population of fish including cod, mackerel, herring and haddock. But by 1902 the state of stocks on the Grand Banks was causing concern. Catches of haddock in particular were plummeting. The countries of the ICES realised that the 'ever bountiful seas' were in fact exhaustible.

Excessive fishing had probably already pushed the levels of haddock below the point of survival. Although the species continued to populate the area, catches dwindled more and more, while fishing activity in the Grand Banks increased – despite the international concern. The fishing grounds there were finally exhausted in 1993. Haddock and other key species were so rare that they were declared commercially unviable. Yet it was

FISHING TRADITION
Hudson River fishermen
sort through their catch
of shad around 1900.

1902 International Council
for the Exploration of the
Sea established

1925 SS *Meteor* uses
echo sounders to
chart South Atlantic

HERRING APLENTY Women prepare fish for market in Great Yarmouth on England's east coast around 1930. The women often came from eastern Scotland, following the herring catch south during the summer months.

not just the persistence of the fishing that had caused the virtual extinction on the Grand Banks fisheries; this was also the result of changes in technology. In the nine decades between the establishment of ICES and the closure of the Canadian cod fishery in 1993, the fishing community had undergone an industrial revolution.

Dawn of the trawler

An ever-increasing demand for food to feed a fast-expanding world population encouraged the growth of the fishing industry during the 20th century. This is reflected in the size of the catch. In 1900 the world total was only 3 million tons. Fifty years later the catch had grown sevenfold to 20 million tons of fish per year, and by 1989 to 85 million tons. Between 1970 and 1990 alone, the world's fishing fleet doubled in size, from 600 000 ships to nearly 1.2 million, including support and feeder vessels. And the ships were not of the traditional kind, familiar in the ports of Europe and North America at the turn of the century. This was the period of the factory ship.

The former Soviet Union was the first to industrialise fishing. The factory trawler is a large ship, often 330 ft (100 m) long, and it carries a crew of 100 people. They are specialists: sonar operators who detect shoals of fish, navigators trained in the use of satellite data and production-line workers who gut, fillet and freeze the fish. The factory ship is a self-supporting community, capable of staying at sea for months at a time and catching hundreds of thousands of fish. No longer an occupation handed down from father to son, fishing is literally an industrial process. Environmentalist groups, particularly Greenpeace, have accused these industrial giants of raping the oceans. By the late 1970s the Soviet fleet alone comprised 100 factory ships fed by an armada of 700 large trawlers and 3000 smaller fishing boats.

The problem of overfishing is, to a large extent, a result of this process. The World Wide Fund for Nature estimates that the European Union has 40 per cent more fishing vessels than it actually needs to provide food for its

A DWINDLING HAUL North Sea trawlers (right) are pursuing a diminishing stock, threatened by both overfishing and pollution.

population and export sales. Yet its fishing industry continues to overfish simply to support its workers. Unfortunately, fish stocks will not allow this to continue and could, some environmentalists believe, crash. They are so depleted in European areas that 25 per cent of the EU total catch is now taken in African, Pacific and Caribbean waters.

Setting limits

Quotas are the main tool for limiting fishing. Levels are set by governments and international bodies such as the North Atlantic Fisheries Organisation, established in 1979. The trouble with quotas is that they have proved to be largely unenforceable. Spanish trawlers, for example, are regularly accused of violating quotas, particularly in Canadian waters, by using nets with too small a weave – these trap even the youngest fish. Yet there is no easy way of monitoring trawlers when they are working in the vast Atlantic fishing grounds.

Another problem is wasteful fishing: a product, in many respects, of the quota system. Inevitably, fishermen catch a variety of

1960 *Trieste* explores Marianas Trench

1968 Deep Sea Drilling Project begins

1979 North Atlantic Fisheries Organisation founded

fish in their nets. Under quota regulations, however, ships are licensed to catch a particular species; so any fish caught that do not belong to that species must be thrown back into the sea. This wasteful fishing is the main cause of a nose-dive in the North Sea herring population. Environmental groups believe that more than a quarter of all fish caught are thrown back, dead or dying, into the sea as waste or 'bycatch'.

Fish stocks have proved their ability to regenerate in the past. During the two world wars, fishing areas in the Atlantic and North Sea became a different sort of killing ground – Allied ships were in constant danger from German submarine and surface attack. Fishing was scarcely possible, and stocks soon started to bounce back. Some scientists predict that the total world catch could exceed 100 million tons per year if stocks were once again allowed to regenerate. It is unlikely, however, that such a pause will happen in the foreseeable future. The fishing industry is a powerful force. Millions of people depend

POLICING THE CATCH At a press conference in 1995 a Canadian Fisheries officer shows that the nets used by a Spanish trawler are finer than is permitted by international law.

SEA WARRIORS Greenpeace protesters prepare to board a factory ship in the North Sea in 1996. It was part of a campaign to halt the overfishing of herring and herring roe.

upon it for their income and are unlikely to participate willingly in a moratorium. Only an internationally agreed policy, rigorously enforced, would establish an environment in which fish populations could start to grow again. There is little agreement among nations on this issue – even within the European Union. As a result, some species of once-abundant fish, such as the herring, could face extinction.

While the international community tries to deal with the fishing crisis, other industries are beginning to tap the potential of

the wider marine environment. By the mid 1960s big business had come to see the oceans as a resource. All minerals extracted from the Earth until the beginning of the 20th century came from land. If the distribution of minerals is as generous on the ocean floor as it is on dry land, new oceanographic technology seems to offer industrialists the chance of capitalising on a treasure trove of mineral wealth.

To date true commercialisation of the oceans has been limited to extracting oil, coal and gas. But other possibilities have begun to open up, though there are often difficulties in the way of taking advantage of them. For example, in the 1970s manganese nodules, golf-ball-sized nuggets of manganese, were discovered on the seabed in parts of the Pacific and Indian Ocean. They also contained copper, nickel and cobalt. There were plans to collect these, using unmanned submersibles dredging the ocean floor with large trawls, rather like metal fishing nets. Although the scheme was feasible, it was found to be more economic to mine manganese in the traditional way on land.

Mapping an invisible world

Exploration continues, however, helped by an army of cartographers. Mankind has tried to map the sea floor for hundreds of years, using essentially the same technique from ancient times until as late as the 1920s. A line of rope with a weight (sinker) attached is lowered until it reaches the seabed. By marking the rope, cartographers are able to chart the contours of the ocean floor and create maps. The process is laborious and time-consuming, however, and little progress was made until 1925 when a German research vessel, the SS *Meteor*, set out on a two-year mission. The *Meteor* was the first such ship to be equipped with a crude form of an electronic device known as sonar.

Sonar – an acronym from 'sound navigation and ranging' – is a system which uses sound echoes to measure

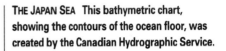

YAMATO
BASIN

YAMATO

2000

1000

200

DEATH OF A SEA

The Aral Sea in Central Asia was once the world's fourth-largest lake, but now it is dying. Since the 1960s, 70 per cent of its water has been drained away to irrigate cotton fields and rice paddies. Now only just over 11 600 sq miles (30 000 km²) in area – half its former size – the sea is a disaster area. The region surrounding it has become a desert, with dust carried on the winds filling every crevice. A million people live in the former Soviet republic of Kara-Kalpak (now an autonomous republic within Uzbekistan) near the Aral. They are suffering without their sea, poisoned by salt, heavy metals and pesticides in their drinking water. The area has the highest infant mortality rate in the former USSR. United Nations experts estimate that unless an orchestrated attempt is made to save the Aral Sea, it has only a decade of viability before the whole area becomes desert.

SEA OF SAND Rusting hulks bear witness to the shrinking of the Aral Sea. What once was sea is now dry desert.

distance in much the same way that radar does. Developed by a consortium of French, US and British scientists during the First World War to detect submarines, sonar sends

UNTAPPED RESOURCES Manganese nodules scatter parts of the ocean floor, such as off the Galápagos Islands. They are rich in copper, cobalt and nickel as well as manganese.

pulses of sound through the water and records the time taken for the sound to bounce off objects and return. On the basis of that information, an accurate measurement can be made of the distance between the object and the ship generating the sound. In cartography it is the distance between the ship and the seabed that is measured. As the ship moves through the sea, it collects from the sonar strips of data which build up into maps of the area traversed. While highly effective, the sonar data is limited to the area covered by the ship. Mapping the ocean floor in this way is still a laborious process. The *Meteor* had to cross the Atlantic 13 times, making more than 70 000 echo soundings.

After more than 70 years of expeditions, sonar measurements had charted only about 5 per cent of the seabed. By the 1990s, these highly accurate sonar maps were being combined with more efficient satellite measurements to form the first truly global map of the submerged landmass. This was produced in 1995. Developed by two Americans, Walter Smith of the US National Oceanic and Atmospheric Administration and David Sandwell of Scripps Institution of Oceanography, the computerised image heralds a new era in the exploitation of the underwater environment.

Satellites are unable to produce direct photographic images of the seabed – sea water is too dense to allow light to penetrate its depths. However, radar that is mounted on

THE JAPAN SEA This bathymetric chart, showing the contours of the ocean floor, was created by the Canadian Hydrographic Service.

a satellite can bounce a beam of microwaves off the sea and measure minute height differences in the ocean surface. These reflect the structures beneath. Peaks and troughs of the ocean bed create different fields of gravity. These exert differing pulls on the water, causing varying heights on the ocean surface. Removing the distorting effects of currents, eddies and tides, Smith and Sandwell were finally able to deduce the hidden geography of the ocean bottom.

In commercial terms their map is of incalculable value. In the 1980s a number of governments declared their interest in the

SCANNING THE SEA FLOOR Sonar signals bounced from the sea floor by a survey ship provide detailed information about the contours of the submerged landmass.

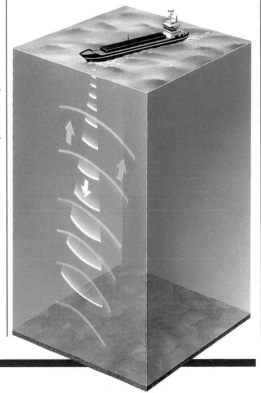

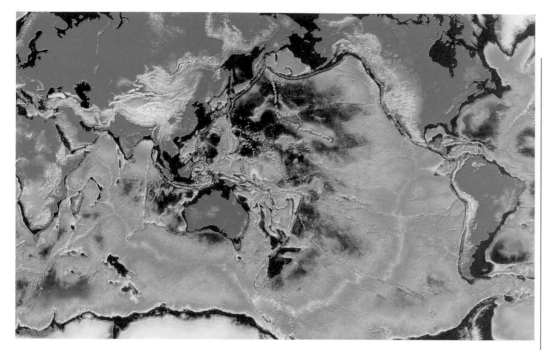

SEABED CONTOURS Combining sonar and satellite findings, scientists at the Scripps Institution of Oceanography in California are creating the most accurate maps of the ocean floor ever made. Continental shelves are shown in pink, trenches in blue and ridges in green.

recreational areas, becoming sea-based communities. The world's largest concrete barge, 720 ft (220 m) long and weighing more than 70 000 tons, was built in Marseilles by the Paris-based construction company, Boygues. Owned by the oil giant Elf Congo, the island is equipped with accommodation and oil-processing equipment and has become a production centre in its own right. It was towed to its final destination off the West African coast in 1995.

An even more ambitious and highly successful example of an artificial island is Japan's Kansai International Airport in Osaka

ARTIFICIAL ISLAND Huge floating 'barges', like this one belonging to the French oil company Elf, provide a mobile base from which to exploit the riches of the ocean floor.

potential of the oceans. In 1981 the US government announced that the waters and sea floor within 190 miles (300 km) of its coastline were an exclusive economic zone. Without a licence, no other nation would be allowed access to exploit any resources within that area. Most nations have followed the US lead.

An exhaustive process has begun in which the formations of the sea

COLUMNS OF WEALTH Deposits of zinc and copper in the Bismarck Sea are constantly being renewed as mineral-rich water from the Earth's crust seeps into the ocean depths.

floor are analysed in order to determine the location of mineral deposits. One exciting find was made in 1991 in the Bismarck Sea in the territorial waters of Papua New Guinea. Scientists from Australia's Commonwealth Scientific and Industrial Research Organisation (CSIRO) discovered strange chimney-like formations on the seabed, rich in zinc and copper and with small amounts of silver and gold as well. In this region there are a number of vents in the ocean floor where hot water from the Earth's crust bubbles through into the sea. It contains large amounts of melted minerals, and these precipitate out as the hot water makes contact with the cold ocean water, forming the 'chimneys' found by the CSIRO researchers.

Experts are exploring the possibility of exploiting these deposits commercially. They believe that there could be a number of advantages. These deposits, unlike those found on land, are constantly being renewed, and because of their purity, there would be much less waste. They are also in more accessible waters than, for example, the manganese nodules which caused so much excitement in the 1970s. Moreover, there would be no human populations whose way of life would be threatened by exploitation.

In other parts of the world, meanwhile, companies are considering the use of floating concrete islands for exploiting seabed riches. These man-made structures could provide large stable bases for the extraction of minerals – as well as for other purposes, such as commercial rocket launches. They would be fitted with living, working and

Bay. Opened in September 1994, the island covers 1263 acres (511 ha). It has one 11 480 ft (3500 m) runway and, as well as all the usual airport facilities, a 576-room hotel, a post office, a power plant and plants for treating waste and water. A 2⅓ mile (3.8 km) double-decker bridge, with a motorway on top and a railway beneath, links it to the mainland. In mountainous Japan, where flat land is at a premium, building an airport on an artificial island has obvious advantages; moreover, because there are no residents nearby, it can operate 24 hours a day. There are plans to extend the island, allowing for two more runways.

Reaching the limit

The deepest chasms in the Earth's crust, hidden under more than 20 000 ft (6100 m) of water, form the 'hadal zone' – from Hades, the

DEPTHS OF BEAUTY A huge sausage-shaped buoyancy tank dwarfs the bathyscaph *Trieste* beneath it. *Trieste's* success opened up a new era in the exploration of the ocean depths. Left: This photograph of the Marianas Trench was taken in 1976.

underworld in ancient Greek mythology. Most famous of them is the Marianas Trench, a curved valley, 200 miles (320 km) east of the Mariana Islands in the Pacific Ocean. In January 1960 humans visited the trench for the first time. A small spherical vessel, known as a bathyscaph (from the Greek *bathus*, 'deep', and *skaphe*, 'light boat'), was designed and built for the task by a Swiss explorer, Auguste Piccard. It was attached to a large buoyancy tank above it. The crude submersible – named the *Trieste* – carried Piccard's son, Jacques, and a US naval officer, Lieutenant Don Walsh, to a depth of some 38 000 ft (12 000 m). This was a journey into the unknown, as risky to the bathyscaph's occupants as the first rocket launches were to the pioneering astronauts. Jacques Piccard and Don Walsh faced the possibility that their craft might be crushed by the high pressures at such depth.

Scientists already knew from previous experiments that pressure increases at the rate of roughly 1 atmosphere – the normal pressure encountered at sea level – per 30 ft (9 m) of depth. So Auguste Piccard had to design a vessel that could function at an almost inconceivable level of pressure. A diver would be crushed by the pressure of the sea above him long before he reached 38 000 ft (12 000 m). If Piccard's design failed, there would be no chance of survival. As a result he chose one of the strongest and sim-

TO THE CORE

The Deep-Sea Drilling Project was an international programme established in 1968 to drill core samples of the Earth's crust at different levels beneath the seabed. It proved that the plates of the Earth's upper crust move and slide over the inner core. The continents sit on the surface of the plates and are slowly moving apart in some cases, together in others, as the plates move.

plest shapes known to man: the sphere. He hoped that, as the craft descended, the escalating pressure would force the metal plates of the bathyscaph's hull closer together – improving the strength of the overall structure. Jacques Piccard and Don Walsh heard the small bathyscaph's hull creak and moan as they descended into the dark waters of

A LIFE IN PURGATORY

For three years from 1991 two US marine scientists, Rachel M. Haymon and Richard A. Lutz, carried out a study of one of the oceans' most hostile environments, a volcanic vent. On the bed of the Pacific, 1¹/₂ miles (2.4 km) from the surface, Haymon and Lutz witnessed a stunning display of catastrophe and rebirth. They found an environment devastated by a deep-sea eruption. Persisting with their visits, they also saw the recovery of the vent's flora and fauna:

'It was obvious that an eruption had just occurred. Dusted by fine grey ash, fresh lava lay in shards, which we later learned were less than two weeks old. It seemed that we had barely missed an explosion. Dead tube worms looked like spent fire crackers. Since the specimens we carried to the surface had freshly charred flesh, we dubbed the spot Tube Worm Barbecue. At a gaping new fissure we called Hole to Hell, lava was blanketed by acres of thick white mats of bacteria. A year later at Hole to Hell brachyuran crabs had arrived and were scrambling around like Pac-Men of video-game fame, stuffing their mouths with bacteria. Foot-long [30 cm] Jericho worms (*Tevnia jerichonana*) with accordion-like tubes were reaching toward the shimmering new vent. We dropped marker nine in a mile-long [1.6 km] trail of foot wide signposts – like a yellow brick road – for future voyages. At this same spot only 21 months later giant tube worms (*Riftia pachyptila*) had grown to four feet [1.2 m], engulfing the Jericho worms and marker nine.'

the abyss. Yet despite springing several leaks during its two and a half hour descent the *Trieste* not only succeeded in penetrating the remotest part of the planet, but also returned its occupants safely to the surface and took measurements of pressure, temperature and salinity levels throughout the mission.

With only the *Trieste*'s lights to illuminate their path, Piccard and Walsh were delighted to find diverse life forms at the bottom of the trench. Crustaceans, molluscs and coelenterates (the biological group that includes jellyfish, sea anemones and corals), all thrived in this environment which, with its red sedimentary clays, resembled an alien world.

While most oceanic exploration has concentrated on areas closer to the surface, the *Trieste*

LIFE WILL FIND A WAY Outsize bacteria and other strange creatures cluster round a sea-floor volcanic vent. Scientists see marine microorganisms as a potential source of new antibiotics and disease-fighting drugs.

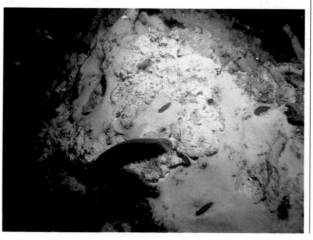

mission set a benchmark for oceanic exploration. Piccard's submersible had sat on the bottom of the ocean. Henceforth, science and commerce alike knew that it was possible to construct vessels that could navigate in the deeps beyond the continental shelf. Modern oceanic craft, often robotic or remote-controlled – such as the *Argo* which was used to find the wreck of the *Titanic* in 1985 – can take samples of flora and fauna and film their activities as directed from a controlling ship above.

Ocean industry

During the last two decades of the 20th century a new science has come into its own. Biotechnology depends upon the Earth's living resources, and in the 1990s, in particular, minerals, fish, coral and newly discovered forms of life, prospering in colonies around poisonous sulphurous vents, have provided industry with a fresh cache of raw materials.

Coral and coral reefs are proving to be among the most useful. Reefs are crowded places and competition is intense as different organisms struggle to survive. Among the most vulnerable are soft-bodied invertebrates, many of which have developed sophisticated chemical defences as a result. These are a rich source of chemical compounds which several research institutes in North America, Europe, Australia and Japan are isolating and testing for possible future use as drugs. One example, among many others, is the group of compounds known as pseudopterosins, found in the Caribbean sea whip (*Pseudopterogorgia elisabethae*). Studies have shown that they

LIFESAVING SEA LIFE The Indian Ocean coral *Eleutherobia aurea* manufactures a compound that may be effective in preventing cancer cells from reproducing themselves.

may be effective as anti-inflammatories for use in treating arthritis.

Similarly exploitable, though not living in coral reefs, are the so-called moss animals (Bryozoa). These are the communities of invertebrates found all over the world fouling the pilings of piers or the hulls of ships. A compound discovered in the common bryozoan *Bugula neritina* has been found to be effective against leukaemia. Bryostatin 1, as the compound is known, is at a relatively advanced stage of testing and promises to be an important anti-cancer drug.

Coral itself has been a source of interesting compounds. An invertebrate, it secretes a calcium skeleton which creates the familiar protective structures that are found on coral reefs. In 1993, the US scientist William H. Fenical, from the Scripps Institution of Oceanography in La Jolla, California, started investigating a compound produced by a rare yellow coral, *Eleutherobia aurea*, living in reefs off Western Australia. Fenical and his colleagues tested the compound to see if it had any effect against cancer cells. The results were encouraging. The chemical, later patented in 1995 as Eleutherobin, seemed to have potential as a cancer cell killer, particularly effective against slow-growing tumours such as those of breast and ovarian cancer. Eleutherobin is still being tested by researchers.

The future of the oceans

In the light of the Earth Summit held at Rio de Janeiro in 1992, as well as growing public awareness of the need for ecological conservation, it seems unlikely that the seas will be exploited as cavalierly as the land has often been. The developed nations are under ever-increasing pressure to ensure that new industry behaves in a way that is environmentally friendly. For the moment, however, it is unclear who will monitor and police this new 'rush to the oceans'. It seems likely that the United Nations will have a role.

Many countries use the ocean as a dumping ground for sewer sludge. More than 10 million tons are dumped into the sea each year by Britain alone. The sludge coats the seabed with toxins which are gradually released and kill vital microorganisms, whilst polluting the food chain. Agriculture and industry also create oceanic pollution. Pesticides and fertilisers permeate aquifers (lay-

SICK OCEANS A ship dumps the industrial by-product phosphogypsum off the coast of France (right). Marine pollution is causing visible signs of damage, such as ulcerated fish and sudden blooms of poisonous algae.

ers of rock that hold water) and contaminate rivers, which eventually feed into the sea. Industrial pollution, such as oil and tar-based derivatives, salt and metals, similarly pollute the industrial world's rivers and seas. The harbours of North America's Eastern Seaboard, especially those of Boston and New York, are so polluted after decades of sewage and industrial waste dumping that very little marine life can exist there. Environmentalists are seriously concerned by the rise in ocean pollution. They fear that it might be reaching a critical mass, as evidenced by deformed fish now found in the Atlantic Ocean and the frequency of algal blooms which starve the ocean of oxygen. International efforts may help to reduce the effects of ocean pollution, but fears persist that such efforts would be too little, too late.

Mankind's attitude to the oceans has changed during the 20th century. In 1900 skilled fishermen worked in traditional ways, taking mostly the fish they could catch in their locality. In the 1990s, the oceans are trawled by vast floating factories, taking virtually every fish in their path. The risk and hardship, so much a part of a fisherman's life at the beginning of the century, are now a reality for only a few. The mass extraction of mineral wealth locked beneath the waves – a process already begun in the oil fields of the North Sea – will no doubt define man's relationship with the sea in the 21st century. It is possible that the oceans hold the biotechnological keys to pharmaceuticals and chemical agents that will revolutionise medicine. Man's exploration of this alien environment on Earth has only just begun.

UNDERSEA LAND SLIP

Tsunamis, seismic waves caused by the collapse of coastal areas or by shock waves from an earthquake, are a well-known phenomenon in the geologically unstable Pacific Rim. They also occur in Europe. Recent studies by Colin Summerhays of the British Institute of Oceanographic Sciences and Dr Alistair Dawson of Coventry University suggest that tsunamis could have a dramatic impact, in particular, on north-western Europe, including the British Isles. As the sea defeats sea defences, waves wash away the supporting substructure of earth, causing land to tumble into the sea. Many villages and towns built on cliffs have already succumbed and fallen into the sea – along parts of England's east coast, for example. Tsunamis could exacerbate land erosion and threaten those who depend upon Europe's shorelines for their livelihoods.

Dr Dawson points to the devastation suffered by Portugal on November 1, 1755. An earthquake on the sea floor generated a massive seismic wave. Lisbon was swamped; 50 000 people died. One risky site is a geologically unstable zone on the continental slope of western Norway. This was responsible for a tsunami that devastated Scotland's north coast about 7000 years ago, and it could cause havoc again. Exploration of the North Sea oil fields since the 1970s could unsettle the bank of sediment there, resulting in a tsunami, virtually without warning.

HUNGRY SEAS On Yorkshire's Holderness coast homes and hotels have literally fallen into the sea, as the cliff face crumbled beneath them.

THE AGE OF THE ATOM

PHYSICISTS PROBED THE LIFE OF THE ATOM AND INTRODUCED MANKIND TO THE PERILOUS SECRETS OF THE NUCLEAR BOMB AND NUCLEAR POWER

The 20th century is defined, at least in part, by the quest to unleash the power of the atom. Four hundred years before the birth of Christ, a Greek philosopher, Leucippus, put forward the theory that all matter was formed out of imperceptible atoms moving at random through space. The theory has prevailed in science ever since, but it was not until the late 19th century that the idea of breaking an atom apart and releasing energy was discussed.

An atom is simply the smallest unit of matter recognisable as a chemical element. Because atoms are smaller than the wavelength of light, they must be observed using very advanced imaging processes – an electron microscope, for example, which uses electrons instead of light, and magnetic fields instead of lenses. This technology has been developed only in the latter half of the 20th century, so until then physicists had to rely on chemical reactions and complex mathematical predictions to learn about the structure of the atom. This almost mystical quest to understand the so-called quantum universe inspired some of the greatest minds of the century.

The world's most notable physicists formed a truly international community in the first three decades of the century, happy to share research and information. As it was a relatively small community, any radical new theory had a significant impact on the science as a whole. One such breakthrough came in

1913 when the Danish physicist, Niels Bohr, proposed a theory for the structure of the atom. According to the 'Bohr model', the atom consisted of a central nucleus with smaller particles known as electrons orbiting round it. Bohr's mentor was Manchester University's Ernest Rutherford, one of the most brilliant atomic physicists of the day. Building on his protégé's work, Rutherford speculated in his lectures on the existence of another group of subatomic particles, neutrons, occurring within the nucleus.

Meanwhile, in the field of radioactivity, other scientists had also been carrying out ground-breaking research. As early as 1896, the French physicist Henri Becquerel had discovered that uranium salts, a silver-white substance found in the mineral pitchblende, give off radiation. This was somewhat similar to the recently discovered X-rays and was capable of blackening a photographic plate even in the dark: Becquerel had discovered

FIRE GAZERS With their researches into atomic structure, Niels Bohr (right) and James Chadwick (far right) helped to usher in the atomic age. Background: Bohr's Copenhagen laboratory.

1913 Bohr's model of the atom

1932 Chadwick proves existence of neutron

1945 Bombing of Hiroshima and Nagasaki

ESCAPE ROUTE In 1939 Berlin Jews, anxious to escape Nazi persecution, queue for travel visas for the USA. Many German physicists were Jewish, and many left Germany, gladly pledging their services to the Allies during the war.

radioactivity. By 1902 his colleagues, Pierre and Marie Curie, had isolated another two radioactive elements, radium and polonium, also found in pitchblende.

By the 1930s atomic science was maturing, with astonishing breakthroughs following one another year after year. Another of Rutherford's protégés, James Chadwick, proved the existence of the neutron in 1932 during experiments in which he bombarded light elements with alpha particles, high-energy particles emitted by certain radioactive elements.

THEORETICAL INSIGHT

Niels Bohr was a 28-year-old assistant professor at the University of Copenhagen when in 1913 he published his model for the structure of an atom. It was a watershed in our understanding of the structure of matter. Within six years Ernest Rutherford had split an atom; Bohr's model also influenced the path of Einstein's research. In 1939 Bohr also first demonstrated the incredible energy potential of nuclear fission.

Chadwick's work enabled other physicists to experiment with neutrons. They developed an understanding of how bombarding the atoms of naturally radioactive materials, such as uranium, with neutrons might result in a release of energy. It was the Hungarian-born physicist, Leo Szilard, who first foresaw the possibility of using this process in a weapon.

Genesis of the A-bomb

Szilard's career was nomadic even by the standards of atomic science in the 1930s. He studied at Budapest University, then worked in Berlin, Oxford, London and finally emigrated to the United States in 1938. In an

age without sophisticated telecommunications and high-speed travel, Szilard's peregrinations had given him an exceptional insight into the state of world atomic research. In 1934, he filed for a patent for a process of neutron-induced chain reactions which could create massive explosions.

The fact that fission – the release of energy as a result of splitting an atom's nucleus – was not discovered until December 1938 makes Szilard's patent all the more remarkable. The fission breakthrough guaranteed the production of nuclear energy, and with war clouds looming over Europe it was more and more probable that the first use of nuclear power would be military. Within a year the Second World War had broken out, and the race to create a superbomb had begun.

Attitudes changed. Gone was the international cooperation of the 1930s. The war polarised physicists into two camps: those who worked for the Axis powers, and those who worked for the Allies. The

Nazis' anti-Semitic policies, however, had driven many of Germany's greatest physicists – and later those living in annexed countries such as Denmark – into exile in the United States and Britain. This exodus of leading minds probably prevented the Third Reich from creating an atom bomb.

Albert Einstein, perhaps the most revered scientist of the 20th century, had emigrated from Germany to the United States in 1933, the year Hitler came to power. In 1939 Leo Szilard persuaded him to write a letter to President Roosevelt. In spite of Einstein's pacifist beliefs, it urged Roosevelt to initiate research into the development of an atomic bomb, since Einstein was convinced that Germany was already engaged in such research. The eventual result was the establishment of the Manhattan Project in 1942.

Maud bows in

Somewhat ahead of the United States, British scientists had already begun a serious study of fission. The driving force here was the Maud Committee, a group that owed its name to a misunderstanding about a nanny. In April 1940 when Germany invaded Denmark, Niels Bohr sent a telegram from Copenhagen to a colleague in Britain, Otto Frisch, telling him about what had happened. At the end he asked Frisch to

MEN BEHIND THE BOMB The chemist Harold Urey (left) and the physicists Leo Szilard (centre) and Albert Einstein (right), all played key roles in the development of the atomic bomb.

1956 Calder Hall opens – world's first industrial-scale nuclear power plant

1968 Nuclear Arms Non-Proliferation Treaty

1986 Chernobyl disaster

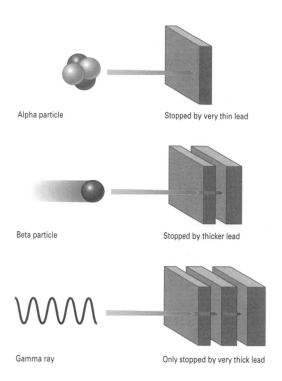

Alpha particle   Stopped by very thin lead

Beta particle   Stopped by thicker lead

Gamma ray   Only stopped by very thick lead

THREE WAYS TO RADIATE The nucleus of a radioactive atom emits three kinds of radiation: alpha, beta and gamma. Alpha and beta particles, though easier to stop than gamma rays, do more damage to living cells. Gamma rays are high-frequency electromagnetic waves.

tell John Cockcroft – another nuclear physicist – and Maud Ray. Bohr's colleagues thought that 'maud ray' was a cryptic reference to uranium radiation, and so chose Maud as an appropriate name for a committee being set up, under James Chadwick, to start research into an atomic bomb. Maud Ray was, in fact, a former nanny to Bohr's children.

By now scientists had an increasingly sophisticated understanding of the structure of the atom. They knew that the nucleus consisted of two kinds of subatomic particle, neutrons and positively charged protons. They also understood that the same chemical element can have two or more 'isotopes', in which the nuclei of the atoms have the same number of protons but different numbers of neutrons. The British chemicals giant ICI was called in to help to devise a method of providing the particular isotope of uranium that would allow a mass release of energy.

In essence, radioactivity is the way in which the nuclei of certain atoms disintegrate over time, emitting neutrons, protons and other forms of radiation. This process of decay will eventually transform the atoms of an unstable, radioactive element such as

uranium into those of a stable, nonradioactive element – lead in the case of uranium. For an element like uranium the process of transformation takes thousands of millions of years to complete; for the much rarer element radium it takes a few minutes – this makes radium more radioactive than uranium because it releases its energy and particles in a far shorter space of time. Radioactive materials include uranium, radium, polonium and certain isotopes of other elements.

In nuclear fission an atom of radioactive material is hit by a neutron, causing the nucleus to split. Each time a nucleus splits it releases stray neutrons and lighter atoms, which in turn collide with other atoms, splitting their nuclei and creating a chain reaction. The chain reaction results in an enormous release of energy.

The Maud Committee sought uranium-235, an isotope that is found in very small concentrations in uranium ore – only 0.7 per cent of the total. It is, however, one of the most useful of radioactive materials because it contains a high number of neutrons in its nuclei. This means that it releases many neutrons during fission and increases the likelihood of a chain reaction.

How, then, to extract the U-235 isotope? ICI helped to come up with the gaseous extraction method finally used to produce weapons-grade uranium. This exploited a

slight difference in weight between U-235 and the unwanted uranium material. A membrane with atom-sized holes – analogous to a sieve – would be made, and the uranium forced through it in gaseous form. Because U-235 atoms are lighter than other uranium atoms, they would pass through the membrane faster and the gas on the far side of the 'sieve' would have a higher concentration of them. If this process were repeated several times, the result would be a gas rich in U-235.

The Maud Committee's report in July 1941 concluded that an atomic bomb could be constructed by the end of 1943 and that it would deliver an explosion of unprecedented proportions. Finally, on September 3, 1941, Prime Minister Winston Churchill agreed to the development of a British atomic bomb.

In June 1942 the United States launched its own research initiative – what would become the Manhattan Project. This was to be one of the most singular scientific research programmes in history. Never before had

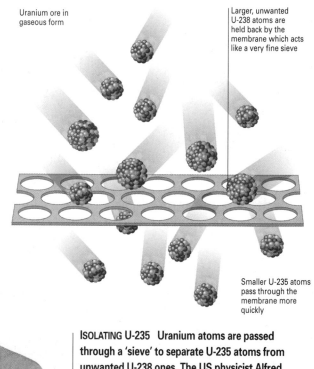

Uranium ore in gaseous form

Larger, unwanted U-238 atoms are held back by the membrane which acts like a very fine sieve

Smaller U-235 atoms pass through the membrane more quickly

ISOLATING U-235 Uranium atoms are passed through a 'sieve' to separate U-235 atoms from unwanted U-238 ones. The US physicist Alfred O. Nier (left) first isolated the U-235 isotope.

scientists from such diverse backgrounds worked together in harmony towards one goal. They were joined in November 1943 by Britain's researchers, including Niels Bohr (who had made a daring escape by fishing boat from occupied Denmark), Chadwick and another

producing a synthetic fissionable isotope of the element plutonium. To create this, the much commoner uranium isotope, U-238 –

LIGHTING THE FIRE The mushroom cloud forms after the first test at Alamogordo. Below: Oppenheimer and General Leslie Groves, military head of the Manhattan Project, inspect all that remains of the steel tower where the bomb was placed.

which makes up more than 99 per cent of uranium ore – is bombarded with neutrons, triggering a process of radioactive decay that will yield plutonium. In December 1942 a team led by the Italian-born physicist Enrico Fermi built a prototype plant for producing plutonium in a former squash court at the University of Chicago. A more sophisticated plant was later built at the Manhattan Project headquarters at Oak Ridge, Tennessee. Since then, plutonium has become one of the most important man-made radioactive isotopes – known as transuranic elements. It is used as a fuel source for modern nuclear reactors, particularly in the Russian Federation and

refugee from Hitler, the German physicist Klaus Fuchs. The Manhattan Project, headed by the US physicist Robert Oppenheimer became an unstoppable juggernaut.

Transuranic expertise

In the end, the difficulties involved in producing the U-235 isotope – otherwise known as enriched uranium – were almost prohibitive. So the scientists devised a method of

PLUTONIUM BOMB

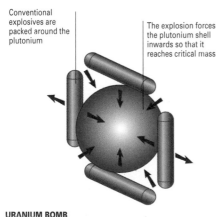

Conventional explosives are packed around the plutonium

The explosion forces the plutonium shell inwards so that it reaches critical mass

URANIUM BOMB

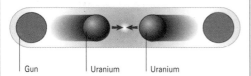

Gun | Uranium | Uranium

REACHING CRITICAL MASS The plutonium bomb worked on the basis of implosion. For the uranium bomb, the principle of explosion was used. Two pieces of U-235 were fired at each other in order to reach critical mass.

A GARISH DEATHLY LIGHT

Father John Siemes was a professor of philosophy at Tokyo's Catholic University. The morning of August 6, 1945, found him at a Jesuit-owned house just outside Hiroshima:

'Suddenly – the time is approximately 8.14 – the whole valley is filled by a garish light which resembles the magnesium light used in photography, and I am conscious of a wave of heat . . .

'Perhaps a half-hour after the explosion, a procession of people begins to stream up the valley from the city . . . More and more of the injured come to us. The least injured drag the more seriously wounded. There are wounded soldiers, and mothers carrying burned children in their arms . . . The wounded come from the sections at the edge of the city. They saw the bright light, their houses collapsed and buried the inmates in their rooms. Those that were in the open suffered instantaneous burns, particularly on the lightly clothed or unclothed parts of the body. Numerous fires sprang up which soon consumed the entire district . . .'

France, where nuclear power contributes heavily to national electricity supplies. In the postwar years natural plutonium was found in small quantities in uranium ore.

Because of the urgency of the project, all avenues of research were pursued simultaneously. As a result two entirely different types of bomb were developed, one based on uranium, the other on plutonium. For the plutonium bomb a technique called implosion was devised. A small spherical shell of plutonium was manufactured, with explosives packed around it. When the explosives were detonated the extreme pressure forced the plutonium into a critical mass – that is, it started to produce neutrons in sufficient quantities to trigger a chain reaction, resulting in an enormous explosion.

The uranium bomb reached the same state in a much simpler way. Two pieces of U-235, too small individually to trigger a chain reaction, were fired towards each other in a gun-like device. Having collided, they formed a single critical mass that exploded instantaneously.

Unholy Trinity

The first nuclear explosion known to man occurred at a test site named Trinity at Alamogordo in New Mexico on July 16, 1945. The test was of the more complex plutonium bomb. The uranium bomb was considered so unlikely to fail that the scientists never bothered to test it. As the nuclear mushroom cloud burst into the New Mexico sky for the very first time, most of the atomic scientists felt only relief. Their years of intensive research had produced a working bomb. A decisive victory in the war with Japan could, at last, be achieved.

Less than a month later, on August 6, a single uranium bomb, dropped from a B-29 Superfortress bomber, devastated Hiroshima. It detonated at a height of about 1800 ft (550 m). The resulting explosion destroyed an area of over 4 sq miles (10 km²), killing up to 100 000 people immediately after the blast and responsible for a futher 150 000 deaths due to radiation sickness by 1950. 'A RAIN

TIME STANDS STILL Hiroshima is still a scene of desolation nearly a year after the bomb was dropped (below). This charred clock is frozen at the fatal moment: 8.15 am, August 6, 1945.

BLAST PATTERN The destruction wreaked by a 1 megaton nuclear bomb ripples outwards, raising temperatures to unbelievable levels and creating a firestorm.

Severe damage to brick and reinforced buildings

Third degree burns from heat and radiation

Severe damage to wooden buildings

Second degree burns from heat and radiation

First degree burns from heat and radiation

Radioactive fallout causes death, cancer and birth defects over the long term

An electromagnetic pulse destroys circuits immediately after the blast

Ground Zero

4 km (2.5 miles)

10 km (6.2 miles)

14 km (8.7 miles)

16 km (10 miles)

24 km (15 miles)

FAT MAN'S WRATH The 10 000 lb (4500 kg) 'Fat Man' plutonium bomb (right) vaporised Nagasaki. Survivors later returned and built temporary wooden huts amidst the ashes.

OF RUIN FROM THE AIR', read the headline in the London *Times* as the Press reported that a secret research project had delivered an explosion equal to 20 000 tons of TNT.

Confusion followed the detonation. There were reports of a huge dust cloud covering

FROM THE ASHES This survivor of the Nagasaki bomb had been at the outer edge of its destructive reach. Even so, he received high doses of radiation and suffered burns to his body. By 1950, some 60 000 such survivors had died prematurely of radiation-related diseases such as cancer.

the area; this made it impossible, at first, to establish what the consequences of the explosion were. The cloud – a mushroom cloud – was a boiling mass of radioactive dust, sucked into the air by the force of the explosion. The falling dust (fallout) ensured the protracted deaths of those on the outskirts of Hiroshima and obscured the devastation from prying eyes for several hours. Only as the days passed did the world come to realise the full frightening power of the atomic bomb.

Japanese survivors were the first to realise the horror of it all. Those living several miles

TESTING TIMES

Between 1942 and 1996, 2044 nuclear weapons were test-detonated. Many of these detonations were carried out by communist states and countries such as France outside the NATO defence protocols, all of which had mastered nuclear technology despite the efforts of the USA to contain it.

During the 1950s thousands of US soldiers took part in tests, mostly in the Nevada desert. Men, wearing only combat fatigues, were told to turn away during the explosion. But once the bomb had created the familiar mushroom cloud, they were often ordered to close in on 'ground zero', the test site itself. The effects of radiation were little understood, so that soldiers were unwittingly exposed to life-threatening levels of radioactive fallout. Many later developed radiation-related illnesses such as leukaemia and cancer of the thyroid.

Nuclear weapons tests have been carried out all over the world and in every environment from underwater tests – 2000 ft (600 m) down – to high-level atmospheric tests, more than 200 miles (320 km) above sea level. Most recently, in 1995-6, France test-detonated nuclear weapons in the Pacific. Then in September 1997, Israeli intelligence agents accused the Russian Space Agency of assisting the Iranian government to design and test long-range nuclear weapons; Moscow denied the accusation. Tests carried out by India in 1998 triggered worldwide fears of a regional, South Asian nuclear arms race.

OPERATION 'DESERT ROCK'
US troops watch a bomb test at Yucca Flats, Nevada, in 1951.

away from the blast found their immediate surroundings totally changed – as though they had been transported to a different place without their knowledge. Trees and houses had been incinerated. Indeed, there was little to prove that humans had ever lived in Hiroshima. A shadow scorched into the earth by the searing heat of the blast was all that remained of one Japanese sentry.

As news of the Hiroshima devastation reached the Manhattan Project's scientists, their initial feelings of euphoria were replaced by dread. Already, at the time of the first test blast at Los Alamos, Robert Oppenheimer had memorably summed up his position as the 'midwife' to the A-bomb by echoing the words of the Hindu deity Shiva: 'I am become death, the destroyer of worlds.' Now the project's team realised increasingly that they had built a doomsday device. Henceforth, people would live under the shadow of possible nuclear obliteration. Mankind was no longer simply an inhabiter and exploiter of the Earth; it had the power to be the Earth's destroyer.

On August 9, 1945, three days after the Hiroshima bomb, a plutonium bomb destroyed Nagasaki. A little more than a week after that, Oppenheimer wrote to Henry Stimson, the US Secretary of War, warning him about the long-term consequences of nuclear weapons. He told Stimson that adequate defences against them could never be devised and that the United States would not be able to retain dominion over the technology. The reactions of the US military and political leaders, however, were quite different. President Truman and his staff had been only too aware that dwindling *Continued on page 49*

Continued on page 49

CLEAN SWEEP? After inspecting a test site in 1952, one US soldier sweeps radioactive dust off another. In fact, this measure made the particles airborne and so more easily inhaled.

SKYBURN The US army and navy carry out a joint bomb test at Bikini atoll in the Pacific in August 1946. Bikini was the site of 23 tests between 1946 and 1963.

MAD

**THE NUCLEAR STAND-OFF BETWEEN THE UNITED STATES AND THE SOVIET UNION
SEEMED TO MANY PEOPLE TO ENSURE PEACE OF A KIND**

Mutually Assured Destruction – MAD for short – describes the no-win scenario reached in the early 1960s, when Eastern and Western nuclear arsenals guaranteed destruction of equal proportions for both sides in a conflict. The term was coined by American strategists, who saw MAD as the level of destruction that the US nuclear arsenal had to be capable of achieving: 50 per cent of the industry and 33 per cent of the people of the Soviet Union had to be destroyed during a retaliatory strike, following a Soviet nuclear attack. MAD ensured that no state would win such a conflict – in other words, stalemate.

In many ways, the MAD scenario achieved what spies such as Klaus Fuchs wanted to achieve when they gave Western nuclear technology to the Soviets in the postwar years. They aimed at the speedy establishment of a nuclear impasse. Yet there were moments when the world held its breath. One such incident occurred in October 1962, after US military reconnaissance flights determined that the Soviets were building launch platforms for ballistic missiles on Cuba, less than 90 miles (150 km) from Florida. Cuba was ruled by a Communist government led by Fidel Castro. Castro had successfully fought off a US invasion the previous year – the so-called Bay of Pigs episode. The Soviets apparently intended to use their ally's proximity to the USA as a way of increasing political leverage.

On October 22, 1962, President Kennedy demanded removal of the missiles and ordered a blockade of Cuba until the Soviets complied. He was effectively threatening a nuclear strike against the Soviet Union if it did not fall in with his demands. For 14 days, the world was on the brink of nuclear war. Fortunately, the Soviet leader Nikita Khrushchev yielded and Kennedy agreed not to attempt to overthrow Castro's government.

The consequences of nuclear conflict in 1962 would have been serious for the rest of the

CRISIS OVER A Soviet freighter takes missiles away from Cuba after the crisis had been resolved. Right: Castro in mid-speech.

world. Nuclear material would have drifted around the Earth, eventually affecting every nation. Nevertheless, they would have been far less serious than in a similar situation using more modern devices, such as the neutron bomb. First developed in the 1970s but not assembled until 1981, this weapon can kill people by releasing lethal levels of neutron radiation without destroying any buildings.

Many experts believe that MAD was the only logical approach to the threat of nuclear war. Once the technological barrier had been breached, there was no turning back. Man could not forget such a technology. Ensuring mutual destruction was the only way of preventing its abuse. Today, without the counterbalancing influence of a Soviet superpower, the deterrent approach to nuclear weapons has collapsed. If a terrorist organisation, for example, detonated a series of nuclear devices on US soil, the threat of guaranteed retaliation – which proved so effective during the Cold War – would be useless. Unless the terrorist organisation admitted responsibility for the attack, the US military would have no sure target.

ON THE EDGE Khrushchev (left) and Kennedy (right) engage in face-to-face brinkmanship during talks at the US Embassy in Vienna in 1961.

political support and low morale within the USA would have ended the war with Japan long before a decisive victory could have been achieved by conventional means. The atom bomb had changed the course of history in the Americans' favour. The USA had become the only world superpower.

The worst-kept secret

In the postwar years, the United States began to stockpile atomic weapons. By the early 1950s, it had become obvious that Washington's attempt to preside over the world's only nuclear arsenal had failed. Largely due to espionage – but also as a result of what was probably a voluntary communication between Soviet and Western European scientists – the Soviet Bloc developed its own atomic weapons.

Many physicists at that time had a hidden agenda. They felt that as long as the Soviets could offer a retaliatory nuclear strike in the event of a Western aggressive launch, an atomic war would never happen. It seems that many took part in covert exchanges of information with the Soviet intelligence agencies. The only major nuclear scientist to be tried and convicted of espionage crimes, however, was the German-born Klaus Fuchs, now working in Britain as a British citizen. Fuchs revealed secrets about the implosion method to the Soviets and as a result the first Soviet nuclear device was completed in 1949. Fuchs was arrested the following year. Although seen as a traitor and sentenced to 14 years in prison, he – and others like him – had restored the balance of power. But for all his altruistic intentions, the result of Fuchs' action was political paranoia.

Because the Soviets had developed the atomic bomb, the US military were keen for even bigger and better weapons. Despite the protests of Oppenheimer, Einstein and others, the hydrogen bomb, more than 1000 times more powerful than the device detonated

over Hiroshima, was developed and, in 1952, tested on the Pacific atoll of Eniwetok. Mankind had finally reached the point of mutually assured destruction in the event of a nuclear war.

In 1954, nuclear technology was put to another, though still military, use. In January the US navy launched its first nuclear-powered submarine, the *Nautilus*, capable of staying submerged much longer than any

previous submarine. In 1958 it proved this when it made an unprecedented underwater journey from a harbour in Alaska to the Greenland Sea, passing beneath the ice cap at the North Pole.

UNDER STAIRS   Leaflets in the 1950s sought to reassure the public with dubious suggestions about how to survive a nuclear attack.

Many people, alarmed at the rapid proliferation of nuclear weapons, began to demand control. Pressure groups were established, such as Britain's Campaign for Nuclear Disarmament (CND), formed in 1958. In the 1950s, 60s and 70s, Switzerland and Sweden, in particular, set out to provide shelters for civilians. Most towns in Sweden have large underground shelters – nowadays, chiefly used as car parks – where citizens were supposed to be able to find refuge for up to a month in case of nuclear attack. Switzerland aimed to provide fallout shelters for its whole population; most homes built after the Second World War had provision for protection. On the other side of the Iron Curtain, shelters were built and stocked with essential supplies in all strategic Soviet cities.

Civil defence

Many governments also produced 'survival plans'. In 1973 the Canadian government produced a public information film entitled *Eleven Steps to Survival*, which explained

POWER FOR ALL   Britain's Calder Hall (right), built in 1956, was the first commercial nuclear power station. Today, France's La Hague Reprocessing Plant in Normandy (below) recycles spent fuels for re-use.

how to build a makeshift fallout shelter and how best to survive the days following a nuclear engagement. The film presented little that was of any practical help. The 11 steps were unlikely to prevent viewers from dying of radiation poisoning or starvation, though they might help individuals on the fringe of a nuclear blast to avoid flash blindness.

In the United Kingdom, the government published a booklet, *Protect and Survive*, in 1979. This was similar in tone and content to the public information documents released during the Second World War, and bore a

warning: 'Read this booklet with care. Your life and the lives of your family may depend upon it.' *Protect and Survive* explained that whitewashing windowpanes could reflect some of the heat of a nuclear detonation, while hiding beneath a table might block out some of the radiation during a blast. For those particularly keen to survive, it suggested ways of building semipermanent 'nuclear bunkers' using household materials.

The potential effectiveness of civilian shelters and other recommended measures was dubious at best. They were probably more important as a means of shoring up morale during the darkest days of Cold War tension. By the 1970s, the consequences of a sustained nuclear conflict were becoming apparent, particularly in the 'nuclear winter' theory. This predicts that smoke and debris thrown into the atmosphere by nuclear explosions would block out the Sun's rays for many months, causing severe global cooling in which average temperatures would plunge by as much as 20°C (36°F).

People came increasingly to accept that no amount of whitewashed windows or makeshift shelters would genuinely allow them to 'protect and survive' in a nuclear engagement. Even if they survived by hiding underground, they would emerge into a

world probably in the grip of a nuclear winter and the worst famine ever suffered by mankind – it was a nightmare prospect.

Sharing the atom

In 1953 President Eisenhower had announced that the world should share in nuclear technology and explore its peaceful potential. The USA's military allies had been demanding full access to atomic technology from 1945, and since the team of scientists responsible for splitting the atom were largely of European origin, they seemed to have a legitimate claim. Yet the USA was reluctant to share its information, chiefly because of fears arising from its intensifying stand-off with the Soviet Union. By the mid 1950s, however, it was clear that maintaining secrecy was not only impossible; it had also retarded the 'peaceful' exploitation of the atom.

By then, the Soviets had already constructed their first-ever nuclear reactor, completed in 1954. In the West, France and Britain were also keen to exploit nuclear power for civilian purposes. As Britain's Sir John Anderson, the government minister with responsibility for atomic research, put it in an interview with *The Times*: 'There are great possibilities, if energy on the scale represented by the bomb is made available to drive machinery, and provide sources of power. It might produce something that will revolutionise industrial life.' The French and British governments, their countries exhausted by the war, saw the energy yield of nuclear fission as a possible saviour of their faltering economies.

Overseen by the newly set up International Atomic Energy Agency, based in Vienna, Britain built the world's first industrial-scale nuclear power plant, Calder Hall, in 1956. Later renamed Sellafield, it was the first plant to supply electricity to domestic users. A degree of international regulation came with the Nuclear Non-Proliferation Treaty, agreed by the USSR, the United States and Britain in 1968. The treaty set out strict guidelines for non-nuclear nations wishing to build nuclear energy industries.

Despite Britain's nuclear advantage – a result of its wartime research – it was France

MELTDOWN IN THE UKRAINE

LEGACY OF DISASTER An aerial view shows the damaged plant. Below: Fish in the nearby lakes are tested for radioactivity.

At 1.23 on the afternoon of April 26, 1986, two explosions smashed through the roof of a nuclear reactor and spewed clouds containing thousands of tons of radioactive debris into the atmosphere. Reactor No 4 at the Chernobyl nuclear power station in the Ukraine had just become the worst nuclear disaster in history. The radioactive dust was carried away from the plant by the winds and drifted across Europe for two days before Swedish monitoring stations detected levels of radiation 20 per cent above normal. The Soviets had failed to warn their European neighbours of the danger. Caused by a managerial blunder – during an ill-advised test of the reactor's abilities, all safety mechanisms were disabled – the Chernobyl disaster has claimed at least 120 000 lives to date.

The area around Chernobyl was poisoned, yet 36 hours passed before the Soviet authorities began evacuation procedures. Television footage, shot several days later from a helicopter, revealed a gaping hole in the structure of the reactor. Radioactive material still poured from the destroyed core, which continued to burn for nine days. Soviet volunteers built a giant concrete sarcophagus over the reactor. Radiation levels were so intense that, although they worked only in one-minute bursts, the volunteers all died of radiation poisoning within 12 months.

The true consequences of the Chornobyl nuclear disaster are still emerging. More than a decade after the explosion, scientists predict 40 000 premature deaths throughout Europe within the next 20 years as a direct result of the accident. The radioactive dust that spewed out into the atmosphere eventually descended once more to the ground as 'fallout'. It often entered the food chain. Massive amounts of it are still being discovered; on September 4, 1997, for example, chemical analysts announced that they had discovered large quantities of radioactive caesium – a highly dangerous nuclear waste product – in a number of Hungarian fishing lakes. The Chernobyl explosion is seen as the only possible explanation for this contamination.

that took the new energy source to heart. Unquestionably the home of nuclear power, France had 55 reactors in service by 1996. It produces 77 per cent of its electricity by nuclear means; only Lithuania outstrips it, generating 83 per cent of its electricity in

FEAR IN KIEV

Kiev on April 29, 1986, was a city gripped by fear. Rumours were circulating that a terrible accident had happened 60 miles (95 km) away at the Chernobyl nuclear power plant. It was three days since the accident happened, but no official statement had been made. Rhona Branson, a 29-year-old Scottish teacher working in Kiev, described events:

'I was told that fleets of buses had been seen driving north to the area on Saturday night to evacuate people living close to the site. It has been very difficult to get any proper information about what has happened, but in the last 24 hours, reports of the seriousness of things have started to filter through. I have just heard . . . that all the French nationals in the city are being evacuated back to Moscow. I do not even know if I should be drinking the water anymore. My Soviet students said that there are pills to put in it to make it OK, but how am I to know if they are right?

'All day they have been telling me that we were lucky because the wind was blowing in the opposite direction when it happened. It is all very frightening. I just do not know if there are things I should be doing now to protect my health. I hope that soon I will be getting some official information.'

A radiation-monitoring centre was finally established on Wednesday, April 30. Despite reassurances, many of the city's residents were afraid that their bodies might bear hidden scars which would emerge with time and end their lives.

nuclear stations, compared with 52 per cent in Sweden, 34 per cent in Germany, 33 per cent in Japan, 27 per cent in Britain and 22 per cent in the USA. Taking an innovative approach, the Electricité de France (EDF) has constructed all of its nuclear reactors in an identical way, thus improving servicing,

productivity and safety. One of the few countries dedicated to the safe and clean use of nuclear power, France has made significant strides in reprocessing nuclear waste. Reactor fuel, usually the U-235 isotope, has a limited life because of the by-products of nuclear fission; these inhibit the chain reaction necessary to create power. Reprocessing removes the by-products, allowing the fuel to be re-used. So far only France and Britain are committed to reprocessing, even though it offers a potential 30 per cent reduction in worldwide demand for new uranium.

In the aftermath of the Chernobyl disaster (1986) and the collapse of the Soviet Union (1991), the European Union has engaged in two major campaigns to improve maintenance and security measures in the nuclear programmes of less economically secure countries. The former Soviet Union is of particular concern; the long-term stability of its nuclear installations and weapons is in doubt. Many Soviet nuclear vessels have been neglected, left to rot in dock, their nuclear reactors barely maintained and awaiting decommissioning. Such is the power shortage in the Ukraine that the remaining reactors at the Chernobyl plant are still operational.

Nano-cogs and fusion

After 50 years of nuclear threat, mankind is beginning to work towards a safer future in which atomic science is exploited for a variety of peaceful purposes.

One promising area is nanotechnology, a newly emerging science in which experts will engineer minuscule machines, so precisely crafted – literally atom by atom – and so small that they will be able to operate within human cells. Experts hope to use these devices to repair damaged cells or even kill unwanted ones – such as cancer cells – from inside. The same technology can be used to

GAMMA RAY BURSTS

A nuclear test ban treaty signed in 1963 inadvertently led scientists to one of the great unsolved riddles of present-day astronomy. The treaty was signed on August 8, 1963, by representatives of the US, British and Soviet governments, and outlawed the testing of nuclear devices in the oceans, the atmosphere and space. Before ratifying the treaty, however, the US Senate insisted that it must be monitored. Accordingly, the Americans launched a series of satellites carrying instruments that could detect pulses of neutrons, X-rays and gamma rays, all of which are produced by nuclear explosions. In the event, they never picked up evidence of illegal nuclear testing; what they did start to detect were brief bursts of gamma rays coming from space, usually lasting a few seconds, though sometimes a few minutes.

What are they? In 1997 scientists finally managed to get sightings of a gamma ray burst using an optical telescope. These confirmed what many had long suspected: the bursts are the results of explosions involving quite phenomenal amounts of energy at unimaginable distances from our own corner of the cosmos. What causes the explosions, however, remains a mystery.

make much larger machines, so precisely engineered that they would be very unlikely to break down. Nanotechnology may even lead to a machine that is virtually self-repairing, operating and 'healing' its structure in much the same way that living tissue does. Scientists have already succeeded in manufacturing working nano-cogs and wheels – micromotors – and hope to have practical industrial applications for this technology early next century.

In the field of nuclear energy, meanwhile, there is a desire to move beyond the dangers of the fission age. Research into fusion generation – the process which fuels the Sun and is the power behind the hydrogen bomb – could lead to a cleaner nuclear future. The two processes of fission and fusion are opposites. Where fission splits the nucleus of a 'heavy' element such as uranium (with 92 protons), fusion takes the nuclei of a 'light' element such as hydrogen (with just one proton) and fuses them; energy is released in the process. Unlike fission, fusion uses cheap and plentiful elements as fuel and they are not radioactive. Fusion may play a key part in man's quest for energy in the next century.

MINI REVOLUTION Each of these gears is smaller in diameter than a human hair. Such devices could be used inside the body.

DOMINION OVER NATURE

A GROWING GLOBAL POPULATION CREATED ITS OWN PRESSURES FOR THE ENVIRONMENT, NOT LEAST THE QUESTION OF HOW TO FEED THE WORLD. IN THE 1960S THE GREEN REVOLUTION MET THE CHALLENGE WITH ARTIFICIAL FERTILISERS AND HIGH-YIELD CROP STRAINS. SOME PEOPLE, HOWEVER, FAVOURED A RETURN TO 'ORGANIC' METHODS. GENETIC SCIENCE PROGRESSED IN LEAPS AND BOUNDS, AND A FEW EXPERTS DREAMED OF INFLUENCING THE PLANET'S WEATHER PATTERNS.

HUMAN HIVES

WHETHER AS SHANTY TOWN OR GARDEN CITY, THE METROPOLIS HAS GROWN STEADILY THROUGHOUT THE 20TH CENTURY

In 1926 the Berlin film studio UFA released *Metropolis,* directed by Fritz Lang. Still hailed as a masterpiece, this depicts a futuristic slave society based in a single monolithic city. It is a fantasy inspired by trends evident at the time it was made.

Ever since the start of the Industrial Revolution in the 18th and 19th centuries, the cities of Europe and North America had been sucking in more and more people. This population explosion continued through the 1920s. At the same time, although much had been done and was being done to improve the lot of urban workers, it was still an age when the bulk of the population had scant protection from the effects of poverty and poor health. Employees had little control over their working environment and even less over the conditions of their housing. Their work was often poorly paid, repetitive and dangerous. Workers were frequently seen as a resource, with little thought given to their emotional or mental well-being. Russia's Bolshevik Revolution of 1917 was still fresh in the minds of Western capitalists who feared that their own workers might revolt.

Lang had no left-wing political affiliations. Even so, these themes – the ever-expanding city, and within it the contrast between the relative powerlessness of the workers and the powerful position of the bosses – influenced his depiction of a capitalist metropolis. His vision was, to a large extent, based upon his first glimpse of the Manhattan skyline during a visit to New York in 1924. The great city, with its skyscrapers, had a huge emotional effect on this self-confessed visual obsessive. The film depicted disenfranchised labourers working until they died from exhaustion – driven on while the rich capitalists, living above the workers at the top of the monstrous city, enjoyed the good things of life.

New life in the new world

In the real metropolis of New York, it was a huge immigrant workforce that, above all, kept the city going. The more than 6 million New Yorkers were of disparate nationalities, religions and cultures, as the city continued to experience a mass immigration, particularly from eastern and southern Europe that had started in the previous century. This mass movement of labour from one country to

METROPOLITAN HADES Workers revolt against the bosses deep in the industrial bowels of Fritz Lang's nightmarish city.

SWEATSHOP Work seldom stopped in clothing factories like this one in New York. Ventilation was poor and safety of little concern. Far left: An Italian immigrant to New York carries a bundle of clothes between workshops in 1910.

workers would toil in filthy, poorly lit workshops for as much as 18 hours a day. Pay was poor – in 1904 an average family living in a tenement and working in the clothing industry earned just under $6 a week – but it was enough to subsist on. Many did not see their new lives as horrific or dehumanising. They knew that they had better prospects there than in their own countries.

IN ALL ITS GLORY For many, the Manhattan skyline in the 1930s embodied all that was modern and magnificent about the contemporary city. Its proudest, newest landmark was the Empire State Building (right), completed in 1931.

another – known as external migration – has been one of the driving forces behind the evolution and development of the Western city during the 20th century.

In part this was driven by better transport, which facilitated mass movements between countries. Violence and forcible attempts in many countries to assimilate disparate peoples within one national identity provided another

engine of change. In Russia, violent purges – pogroms – killed more than 600 000 Jews between 1881 and 1921. The Russian Jews escaped into Western Europe and then, attracted by the promise of liberty and opportunity, to New York and North America. Similar atrocities committed by the Turks against Christian Armenians in 1894-6 and again in 1915 forced many of the Armenian people to leave the lands of their birth. Italy was another source of migration. Between 1861 and 1965, a total of 26 million Italians sought to escape poverty at home by emigrating to the United States.

This diverse migrant horde needed work and often found it in clothing factories. New York's Lower East Side became notorious as a 'sweatshop' area, where mostly immigrant

For all that, their working and living environments were appalling. Streets were dark and crowded, houses devoid of power; 80 per cent lacked running water. By 1900 almost 40 per cent of New York's population lived in overcrowded tenements. Few streets were paved; most were earth paths rutted and pitted with use. Rubbish encouraged disease and harboured vermin such as rats; it was collected no more than once a month in many areas. Cholera and tuberculosis were frequent visitors. These conditions were not limited to New York but were common in all major Western cities.

Ever expanding

City growth has been an inescapable fact of life in the 20th century. New York's population exploded from 4 million at the start of the century to exceed 16 million people by 1990. During the 19th century, Western cities had already devoured swathes of their surrounding countryside, leaving unplanned and insanitary structures in their place. The Victorians had started to tackle these problems, but much remained to be done.

In Britain, the working man was not given the right to vote in elections until 1918 when the Representation of the People Act first

enfranchised non-homeowners. The same Act gave the vote to women over the age of 30. In this disenfranchised environment, working-class city-dwellers – invariably living in rented property – had limited means of influencing the conditions around them. To a large extent, many still depended on the mercy of philanthropic individuals. One such person was George Cadbury.

A British cocoa and chocolate producer, and a Quaker by religion, Cadbury was a visionary who wanted to revolutionise the way in which his workers lived and worked.

BOURNVILLE DELIGHT Cadbury's Bournville lies on the edge of a vast and sprawling city. Yet with its detached and semidetached houses, it has a distinctly village-like air.

To do so, he moved away from Birmingham city to a neighbouring semirural area. Cadbury hated the new cities of the Industrial Revolution. He knew that industry was the engine of future growth, but had a vision that it could thrive in a rural environment. In 1895 he established the Bournville Building Estate, which became the Bournville Village Trust in 1900. The trust bought 120 acres (50 ha) of land next to a new factory site and built mould-breaking housing for the workers. Dwellings had running water, comfortable

1900

1900 Bournville Village Trust
1903 Letchworth garden
city started

1923 Tokyo
fire
1926 Fritz Lang's *Metropolis* released
1927 Canberra becomes Australia's capital
1928 Berlin's Horseshoe Estate

1950

living rooms, private latrines and green areas for recreation. Yet despite his philanthropy, Cadbury did little to help those left behind in the city. More interested in starting a new community, he rejected the idea of improving the cityscape itself. A contemporary, Ebenezer Howard, a former clerk and shorthand stenographer, tackled that problem head on.

Garden city movement

Howard lived in London, the world's largest metropolis. Nearly 6.5 million people lived and worked within its boundaries, 3 million of them in terrible conditions. In his book, *Tomorrow: A Peaceful Path to Reform* (1898) – reissued as *Garden Cities of Tomorrow* in 1902 – Howard presented a study of problems in the expanding metropolis, but it was more than just that; it also presented a whole new doctrine for the development and building of towns and cities. Howard understood the production potential of the city: a place where resources might be massed and products manufactured and distributed on a vast scale. But his book also recognised the need for the people who lived there to be physically and emotionally fulfilled.

Howard laid down a series of principles which helped to push the Western city into its next phase of evolution. Even established metropolises such as New York would try to embrace his theories in the subsequent development of suburban areas. His basic principle was that cities attracted people because of good employment opportunities and cultural activities such as music halls and theatres. On the other hand, cities also repelled people because of overcrowding, a lack of free space, smog and the difficulty of commuting to work. For their part, rural areas repelled people because of low wages and poor work opportunities, while they also attracted them because of the clean air and a healthy environment. Howard's aim was to exploit the advantages of both city and rural environments. The garden city idea was based around a planned urban centre, a micro-economy in its own right, surrounded by a ring of farmland and open countryside, called a green belt, that was protected from any future development. The city itself would be free of slums, have good sewerage and sanitary provision and, above all else, be an

GROWING YOUR OWN

The United Nations Development Programme encourages people in urban areas to grow their own fruit and vegetables. This not only provides food, but helps to solve sewerage and atmospheric problems. Sewage is used as fertiliser, while the plants absorb some of the carbon monoxide produced by industry and cars. The UN estimates that nearly 20 per cent of the world's food is grown in urban plots.

attractive place in which to live. In 1903 Howard, backed by industrialists and other sympathetic individuals, started the town of Letchworth in Hertfordshire.

His example led to the adoption of systematic town planning across much of the globe. During the 20th century, more than 30 'new towns', as they became known, were built in Britain alone, including Welwyn Garden City and Milton Keynes. Continental Europe also

EBENEZER'S GARDEN British enthusiasts for Ebenezer Howard's ideas founded the Garden City Association in 1902. The following year they started building Letchworth (below), promoting it with booklets (left) that extolled the delights of its 'urban cottages'.

1960 Brasília becomes Brazil's capital
1961 Jean Gottman coins term 'megalopolis'

1967 Islamabad becomes Pakistan's capital

1989 Mexico City imposes limits on car use

THE LEGACY OF MEXICO'S LOST PIONEER

When the *Lusitania* was sunk by a German torpedo in May 1915, among the 1198 people who drowned was Frederick Pearson, the engineer who pioneered one of the world's first great hydroelectric dams. At the turn of the century, Pearson had a notion of exploiting the Nexaca waterfall, about 100 miles (160 km) east of Mexico City. He believed that developing countries should be encouraged to adopt a new approach to industrialisation, particularly by exploiting what he saw as cleaner and less wasteful methods of energy production. The river at Nexaca fell more than 3000 ft (910 m) in 10 miles (16 km) over a series of large steps.

With the approval of the national government, Pearson designed and built a hydroelectric plant beneath the first fall. At the top, he built one of the largest earthwork dams in the world, which diverted water through pipes and down onto a series of turbines in the power plant below. The rotary motion, produced by the turbines, generated electricity, which was fed along a 100 mile cable – at that time one of the longest transmission lines in the world – to Mexico City.

Although Pearson did not live to see his project completed, it succeeded in establishing a model for the rest of Latin America. Today, 73 per cent of all electrical power used in South America is generated by hydroelectric means.

embraced the plans laid out in his book. New towns were built around Paris, Grenoble, Helsinki and Stockholm, as well as places such as Radburn, New Jersey, in the USA.

For different reasons, the century also saw new capital cities built in countries such as Australia, Brazil and Pakistan. In each case, these were laid out as expressions of their nations' newly won independence or confidence. Australia's new capital, Canberra, was inaugurated in 1927, Brasília in 1960 and Pakistan's Islamabad in 1967. Of the three, Brasília is probably the most remarkable. Planned by the urban designer Lúcio Costa, with Oscar Niemeyer as the chief architect, the city was built in what had previously been a wilderness. With two great axes, running north-south and east-west, it includes features that would have been familiar to Ebenezer Howard and other town-planning pioneers from the start of the century – a huge artificial recreational lake and copious green belt areas.

Howard's influence on modern towns and cities has been immense. The concept of the green belt, in particular, has become a commonplace. Yet Howard's ideas did not lead to the demise of the old city in favour of the new town. For as planning and the orchestration of refuse collection, electrification and better sanitation improved conditions within cities, so they became more, rather than less, attractive places in which to live and work. Moreover, industry has proved less than willing to relocate out of the big cities, which have a major advantage over rural or semirural locations: a large skillbase. Distribution networks are also well developed around cities. In Britain, generous incentives, such as cut-price rents, had to be offered to encourage companies to relocate to new towns such as Milton Keynes. Even Brasília, impressive though it is as a place to visit, has never been much loved as a place to live in. As a city started from scratch in the middle of 'nowhere', it lacks the vibrancy

DARING TO INNOVATE These tower blocks were built in the new town of Créteil in the southern suburbs of Paris. The rounded balconies were intended to soften their lines.

TWO CITIES IN ONE Calcutta's leafier suburbs (left) stand in marked contrast to its shanty towns (above).

of Brazil's older coastal cities, such as Rio de Janeiro.

Calcutta in India is one of the world's largest cities, with a population in the greater metropolitan area of more than 10 million people. It displays many of the problems faced by cities in the developing world. Only 90 years ago, its population amounted to little more than a million, so that its growth represents a 1000 per cent increase. In this, Calcutta reflects a new trend; the cities of the developing world are growing faster than their Western industrial counterparts, as thousands of impoverished workers pour off the land in the hope of finding prosperity.

With a population density of 85500 people per sq mile (33000 per km²), Calcutta is now one of the most crowded cities in the world. The situation is highly polarised: Calcutta's

THE WORLD'S FIFTEEN MOST POPULOUS CITIES

Population in thousands

1900	Pop	1990	Pop
London	6 480	Tokyo	25 013
New York	4 242	New York	16 056
Paris	3 330	Mexico City	15 085
Berlin	2 707	São Paulo	14 847
Chicago	1 717	Shanghai	13 452
Vienna	1 698	Bombay	12 223
Tokyo	1 497	Los Angeles	11 456
St Petersburg	1 439	Beijing (Peking)	10 872
Manchester	1 435	Calcutta	10 741
Philadelphia	1 418	Buenos Aires	10 623
Birmingham	1 248	Seoul	10 558
Moscow	1 120	Osaka	10 482
Beijing (Peking)	1 100	Rio de Janeiro	9 515
Calcutta	1 085	Paris	9 334
Boston	1 075	Tianjin (Tientsin)	9 253

Population statistics for cities are inevitably somewhat arbitrary, depending on where boundaries are drawn. In 1991, for example, the population of Greater London – its 32 boroughs and the City – was 6.4 million. But if the entire metropolitan region of London is taken into account, its population stood at 12.5 million. Bearing such warnings in mind, the table above – using statistics drawn up by the International Institute for Environment and Development – nonetheless shows a trend away from the developed towards the developing nations.

population of university undergraduates exceeds a quarter of a million – making it one of the world's foremost centres of learning – and yet this is matched, almost exactly person for person, by people who live in shanty towns. The educated population live in modern housing, while the poor struggle to survive in the shanty towns.

In the shanties

Built from waste materials on rented land to the north of the city, the shanty towns are not some removed, dislocated satellite; the area is very much a part of the metropolis itself. Small, single-storey shacks stand in a haphazard fashion one beside another. The streets, if they can be called streets, are little more than mud tracks, winding between the homes. Yet the shanties are a hive of activity. In one house a man may make crude sandals from old car tyres, while in another a woman will look after the elderly members of her 'street'. The air is heavy with smoke; small fires are the main source of power. Water is available from standpipes, as the government has instigated sewerage schemes and

provided basic amenities in the older, more established areas.

Historically, those who live in the streets tend to work, if they work at all, in the black market economy. This hidden economy undermines the government by cheating it of tax revenue, thereby weakening its ability to effect changes. The story is similar throughout the developing world. A rapid growth in urban population can rarely be matched by a corresponding growth in housing. House construction takes time and responds relatively slowly to changing trends. At the same time, there is not enough economic growth within cities to finance cheap housing. It is a dilemma repeated across the globe, from São Paolo and Lima in South America to Jakarta in Indonesia.

In Calcutta, country people are still pouring in from the largely agricultural province of Bengal and beyond. Like their predecessors, these people find city life hard to adapt to; nothing in their previous existence has prepared them for this highly specialised world. But standards have improved over the last two decades – thanks in part to international schemes, sponsored by organisations such as the United Nations. Resulting changes in attitude have helped to ease the problems of the shanty-dwellers. Indeed, all across the developing world, shanty towns are increasingly seen as buffer areas for newly arrived rural immigrants as well as young people who were born in the city but are having difficulty in finding a permanent job. In Calcutta and elsewhere, many inhabitants have been encouraged to make their shanty homes more permanent by offering them vacant plots of land with amenities already provided.

In 1961, the French geographer Jean Gottman completed

NO OPTION An unused concrete cylinder is the best home this young mother in Calcutta can find for herself and her child.

an intensive 20-year study of US cities. In his book *Megalopolis: The Urbanised Northeastern Seaboard of the United States*, he noted that an almost continuous strip of urban and suburban development had emerged between New Hampshire and northern Virginia. His studies revealed a trend apparent in various parts of the world, including the English Midlands and the Parisian region in France. It is a trend in which cities grow and often merge at the edges, creating a less centralised environment based around a number of large population centres, each with several million inhabitants of its own. In Japan, the Tokyo metropolitan area epitomises this development.

Megalopolis

In 1923 Tokyo's 2 million inhabitants endured a terrible fire. Caused by an earthquake, the fire swept across the city – built mostly of wood – leaving few structures intact. After 20 years of reconstruction, Allied air raids during the Second World War once again razed the city to the ground. Yet, within a few decades, Tokyo had bounced back. It has emerged from the shock of earthquake, bombings and fire with a population growth over the century of nearly 2000 per cent. Its mass is all-consuming: a huge 'population island' stretching

YESTERDAY AND TODAY Tokyo in 1900 (above) would have been familiar to Japan's medieval inhabitants. By contrast, modern Tokyo (right) is the ultimate megalopolis.

along the western shore of Honshu Island, encompassing smaller satellite cities including Yokohama. It is not so much a city as a megalopolistic semiurban human hive, a society and economy in its own right.

A time traveller from the start of the century, familiar with the streets of Tokyo in 1900, would be astonished at the transformation. The open, leafy streets have vanished; the formal lines of traditional Japanese houses, boxy in appearance with low curved roofs, have been abandoned. The ornate garden, such a strong part of Japanese culture and an extension of the interior of the home, is now a luxury. Instead, an agglomeration of glass and concrete structures, many of them hundreds of feet high, covers the ground with

BROWN NOT GREEN

By the 1990s, the need for new housing was putting the green belts around many cities under threat. This led to a movement to clean up and exploit 'brown field' sites – derelict or even polluted land and buildings, often in inner cities – rather than encroach on the green belt.

little space for leaf or tree. Elevated roads sweep past tower blocks, home to millions of Tokyo's residents. The once-tranquil streets now seethe with a swarm of workers, residents and tourists. The distinctive Japanese culture has in many ways been cast aside in favour of a Western, largely US, hybrid. The Tokyo of the late 20th century might frighten our time traveller; it would be an experience quite alien to him – a place so unlike any city in 1900 that it could be a different world entirely.

In cities that are still able to cope with an expanding population – typically old Western European conurbations such as Munich and

A MATTER OF PARISIAN SEWAGE

AS CITIES HAVE GROWN, SO HAVE THE PROBLEMS OF HOW TO GET RID OF WASTE. PARIS WAS USING AGE-OLD, BUT EFFECTIVE, METHODS UNTIL WELL INTO THE 20TH CENTURY

T he problem of removing human waste from the world's great cities was not easily solved until the beginning of the 20th century. Yet it was a problem that had to be tackled because of the dangers of disease. In 1894 cholera swept through Paris – killing 12 000 people – and led in 1899 to a ban on the dumping of untreated human excrement in the River Seine.

For hundreds of years the Parisian authorities, like their counterparts in many other cities, had dealt with most human waste by the process known as 'circulus'. Excrement was collected from each house, and transported by horse and cart to the edge of the city, where it was spread on the land. In this way, the waste could be 'reclaimed by nature' and the nutrients would nourish the soil. It was an extremely smelly process – the odours wafted across the entire city on some days – and required an army of men to collect and transport the sewage. Nonetheless, it was effective, good for the soil and continued to be practised in certain quarters of Paris until the 1920s.

By then water closets – as opposed to the 'privy', essentially a seat with a collection bucket beneath it, which had to be emptied by hand – had become more normal in most parts of the city; there was on average one toilet for every 20 people. Yet there had been considerable resistance to these 'new-fangled' devices. Rather than rely on WCs and sewers, notable figures, including the world-famous chemist Louis Pasteur, had preferred the option of dumping excrement at sea. They

UNBLOCKING THE DRAINS In a subterranean world beneath Paris's Place de la Concorde, workers prepare to lower a huge ball to clean out a sewer.

felt that the sewers would not allow the waste to be flushed away fast enough to the treatment works outside the city. They feared that waste would fester in the sewers and harbour disease.

Nowadays, artificial fertilisers are used when the soil is depleted of nitrogen, while sewage is treated using a process that involves sedimentation (to separate out the solids), filtration and then the biological breaking down of the effluent in order that the water may be recycled. The old practice of circulus was smelly, but it did have a certain simple efficiency.

CIRCULUS DISPOSAL Carts wait to offload their cargoes of human waste at a plant at Issy on the outskirts of Paris in 1908.

the major cities of the United States – rising population density has definite economic advantages. The greater the population density, the more viable public transport becomes. Public transport is generally twice as fuel-efficient as private, which means that the better the public transport system, the greater the saving in pollution and fossil fuel use. At the same time, the larger the population using and paying for public transport, the better it is likely to be.

Pollution

Yet petrol and diesel-powered vehicles are still the mainstay of transport in cities, pumping often dangerous levels of pollutants into the atmosphere. In January 1998, a British government report estimated that air pollution hastened the deaths of as many as 24 000 people in Britain every year and was responsible for as many hospital admissions. Industry was a major cause, but road traffic was more important, particularly in towns and cities, where motor vehicles were the principal source of nitrous oxides and hydrocarbons. These interact in sunlight to form ozone, which exacerbates asthma and causes other serious respiratory problems.

Even where there is good public transport, the habits of city-dwellers can be difficult to change by planning alone. On October 1,

1997, the French Environment Minister Dominique Voynet took exceptional measures when she ordered traffic restrictions in Paris after air pollution – especially nitrous oxide fumes – hit maximum levels. Only vehicles carrying three or more people and with registration numbers ending in an odd digit were allowed into the city between 5.30 am and midnight.

A similar scheme has long been in permanent operation in Mexico City. The Mexican capital sprawls across a valley that traps pollution, making it also one of the most contaminated cities in the world. According to a scheme set up in 1989, every car is banned from the streets one day a week – this is determined by the car's licence plate. In this way, about 20 per cent of vehicles are kept off the streets on any one day. Heavy fines and high-profile policing make sure that the ban is enforced. When air pollution rises to exceptionally dangerous levels, the restrictions are tightened still further, raising the proportion of vehicles

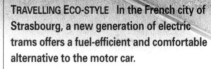

TRAVELLING ECO-STYLE In the French city of Strasbourg, a new generation of electric trams offers a fuel-efficient and comfortable alternative to the motor car.

banned to 40 per cent. In addition, petrol stations and some of the city's most polluting industries are temporarily shut down.

Massed advantage

Through most of the 20th century, cities have continued to grow. And throughout the century, from the time of Ebenezer Howard onwards, planners, architects and reformers have pondered their future. Between the wars, this produced some remarkable experiments in working-class housing, notably in the cities of Germany and Austria – projects such as Berlin's modernist *Hufeisensiedlung* (Horseshoe Estate), built in 1928. Post-war reconstruction brought sweeping new powers for many urban authorities as they set about rebuilding badly bombed cities such as Coventry in England and Rotterdam in The Netherlands. Later came the often ill-fated experiments with high-rise residential blocks in the 1960s.

By the end of the century, one thing was clear: the logic behind a properly managed massing of resources remained irrefutable. The city has been with mankind since the emergence of the first civilisations. It will stay with us, though regularly reinventing and renewing itself.

GRIDLOCK Parisian boulevards, conceived for their elegance in an age when traffic was less of a problem, are now the setting for rush-hour jams.

FOOD ON DEMAND

FERTILISERS AND IMPROVED CROP STRAINS HAVE INCREASED FOOD PRODUCTION, BUT WITH SOME COST TO THE ENVIRONMENT

The rise of industry and the growth of Western cities brought a changing relationship between town and country, the consumers of food and its producers. Where their villager parents and grandparents had grown or raised at least some of what they ate, the increasing numbers of city-dwellers at the start of the 20th century had to buy it. Traditional towns and cities had lived chiefly from the surrounding countryside, with farmers bringing in their produce to sell in the markets. In many regions, even of Western Europe, such links would survive right through to the end of the century, but by 1900 they were already fast disappearing in the big industrial conurbations.

Here, food came from shops, and consumers had little contact with its producers. In a country like Britain, a meal might include lamb imported in refrigerated ships from New Zealand or beef from Argentina and bread made from wheat grown on the prairies of North America or the steppes of Russia. More and more, agriculture was

becoming an industry like any other; it had to supply the goods to meet a growing demand. And demand grew spectacularly through the century as world population expanded from 2 billion people in 1900 to 3 billion by 1950 to 6 billion in 1996.

Production rose and brought a new agricultural revolution. In developed countries, this was reflected in farm sizes. In the USA, the average farm was 200 acres (80 ha) in 1900; by 1990, it was 500 acres (200 ha). Larger-scale production meant increased output per acre. It also meant a drop in the number of small individually run farms. In the USA, the number fell from an estimated 12 million in 1900 to 2.4 million in 1980.

New techniques

Increasing amounts of land have been brought into cultivation during the course of the century. Yet population levels have grown so fast that by the beginning of the 1990s, there was only about 1.7 acres (0.7 ha) for every human being. Some 12 billion acres (5 billion ha) of the Earth's landmass, roughly a third of all dry land, are fertile and potentially cultivable. However, this includes areas hidden beneath the dense canopies of the tropical rain forests of equatorial Asia and South America. Such

land is often inaccessible, and clearing the forests has damaging consequences. The dangers of burning off were demonstrated in 1997-8 by protracted fires in Indonesia, while clearing by cutting is rarely economically viable for small farmers. So, it seems that most future food production will have to be achieved using existing resources. Farmers

ECONOMICS ON THE HOOF Gauchos with prime cattle on an Argentine ranch in the mid 1950s. Beef exports have been the backbone of Argentina's economy for much of the century.

1909 Haber creates synthetic ammonia

1929 Eijkman receives Nobel prize for discovering thiamine

1939 Müller discovers DDT

fertiliser. But they also had to be groomed, fed and housed. The horse's food intake, in particular, was significant; historians estimate that 100 million acres (40 million ha) of land were needed to grow the hay to feed Europe's horses. The motorised tractor required less

PICK OF THE CROP

Potatoes are the world's most popular vegetable. Their total production is exceeded only by the cereal crops (such as wheat and rice) which account for 70 per cent of all human food. Europe, Russia, China and the USA are the largest producers and consumers of the potato. It is high in vitamin C and in energy-rich carbohydrate, making it nutritionally one of the most crucial of foodstuffs in the world.

time and effort to maintain. Early tractors offered the equivalent of 16-20 horsepower, while releasing millions of acres of arable land for the production of commercial crops.

Fertilisers were another key component of improved productivity. They have been used since the time of the ancient Egyptians, at least, when farmers depended upon the rich silt from the Nile to make their soil fertile. The Egyptians even redirected the river to make sure that it flooded arable areas during fallow months. In the centuries since

GOLDEN FIELDS Wheat farms spread for thousands of acres in Palouse, Washington State (above). The Mogul motorised tractor (below) was in common use on large US farms in the interwar period.

at the end of the 20th century face similar problems to those confronting their ancestors in 1900. They have a limited amount of land and need to improve its productivity.

In the first three decades of the 20th century one factor more than any other contributed to better productivity: mechanisation. The motorised tractor was embraced across the Western world as the most useful agricultural innovation since the plough. For millennia, the horse and ox had provided motive power on farms. They were flexible and had the added benefit of generating natural ammonia-rich

1960 International Rice Research Institute, Manila
1962 Silent Spring
1966 International Maize and Wheat Improvement Center, Mexico City
1971 The Farm founded at Summertown, Tennessee
1985 First case of BSE reported
1997 Forest fires in Indonesia

ERADICATE THE INSECTS Insecticidal sprays have greatly increased the yield of sugar cane in production areas such as Mauritius (above).

then, human and animal fertilisers have been used almost universally and still are today, although they have been overtaken to an increasing extent by artificial fertilisers.

These were made possible by the German chemist Fritz Haber, who in 1909 perfected a process for creating synthetic ammonia by subjecting nitrogen and hydrogen to high pressure and temperatures of around 1000°C (1800°F). The process was adapted for industrial-scale production by another German chemist, Carl Bosch. It was initially used during the First World War to manufacture explosives; the Germans were obliged to resort to it after an Allied shipping blockade cut off their supplies of natural ammonia from Chile. Only later was the Haber-Bosch process – which won Haber the Nobel prize for chemistry in 1918 – used to manufacture the first artificial fertilisers.

The result was another revolution. Farmers could give their plants additional nutrients which enhanced the plants' rates of growth and their hardiness in the face of disease. Since the 1940s a variety of nutrients vital to healthy crops have been synthesised and developed as artificial fertilisers. Among them, phosphate and nitrate fertilisers have been of particular importance. The use of inorganic (synthesised) fertilisers increased from about 18 million tons in 1953 to 60 million tons in 1969, and reached a peak of 120 million tons in 1980.

New pesticides have been another weapon in the 20th-century farmer's arsenal. Metals were initially used, chiefly potassium permanganate and lead derivatives. Unfortunately, after prolonged use, these chemical agents poisoned the soil and so killed the plants they were used on. Chemists strove to create an organic pesticide – one without metallic elements – and in 1939 Paul Müller, a Swiss chemist, made a major breakthrough, when he noted the insect-killing quality of the chemical compound DDT (dichloro-diphenyltrichloroethane).

World governments and chemical manufacturing giants saw DDT as a potential wonder pesticide. In 1944, civilians and Allied soldiers entering Naples were sprayed with DDT powder to help to control a typhus epidemic. By 1946 DDT was being used in the tropics in an effort to exterminate mosquitoes and eradicate malaria. It was deadly to most insects, and although it proved to be toxic to some bean, barley and young tomato crops, it was embraced as a true victory of science. Mass spraying programmes began in the USA and Europe. Developing nations still use it today. The success of DDT led to the creation of other pesticides and herbicides such as Zineb – a fungicide developed for use on vines, onions, lettuces, tobacco and other plants.

Green revolution

In the 1940s, as researchers were developing new pesticides, the Rockefeller Foundation in the USA began a programme to study and enhance wheat crops. The intention was to develop a hardier 'superwheat' which required less tending than traditional strains, produced more prolific crops and could help to feed the developing nations. The research

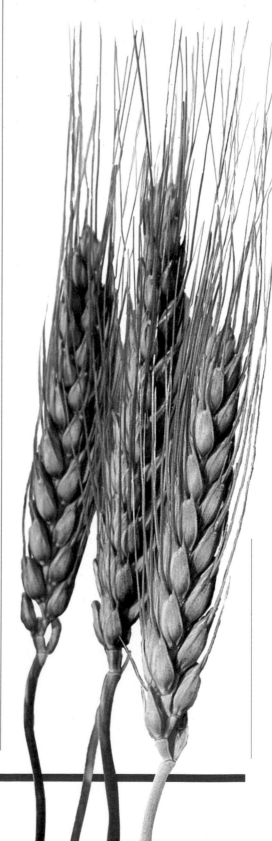

FINE BREEDING This wheat was grown in Rajasthan, India. Although it produces high yields, it also demands a greater degree of irrigation and fertiliser than indigenous crops.

led to the establishment in 1966 of the International Maize and Wheat Improvement Center (CIMMYT), based in Mexico City and partially funded by the Mexican government, which conducted revolutionary research into new crossbreeds. Similar investigations were already being carried out by the International Rice Research Institute, established in Manila in 1960 with aid from the Rockefeller Foundation and the Philippines government. It produced highly productive, hardy rice crops, later distributed throughout Asia.

These initiatives fostered a so-called Green Revolution in the late 1950s and the 1960s. Developing nations were encouraged to use the new superbreeds, with their vastly increased yields, to feed their people. It was seen as a way of helping these countries to avoid famine and to trigger a new form of 'instant' agricultural revolution, the Green Revolution – without the need for protracted periods of learning and change as in the agricultural revolution of the West.

Large-scale farms, mechanisation and new breeds of crops have combined with the use of artificial fertilisers and pesticides to achieve what would have seemed impossible in 1900. In just 40 years between 1955 and 1995, the world grain harvest soared by 124 per cent.

LONG-LIFE TOMATOES

Most developed nations have now accepted the irradiation of foodstuffs as an acceptable way of reducing bacteria infestations as well as larger pests and of extending shelf life. Tomatoes, potatoes and other vegetables exposed to bursts of low-level radiation can have shelf lives twice that of non-irradiated foods. Many popular canned foods, such as baked beans, are also irradiated. In the USA, the irradiation of poultry has become common since 1990 in an effort to reduce the incidence of salmonella-related food poisoning. Even so, despite the apparent benefits of irradiation, there is a certain amount of consumer resistance to irradiated foods. European consumer groups and nutritionists have campaigned to have all irradiated foods clearly labelled in supermarkets, though their efforts have met with only limited success. Concerns that irradiated food may lead to long-term increases in the incidence of cancer are probably unfounded; on the other hand, the destruction of bacteria in some vegetables may have detrimental effects, as the body uses bacteria to break down foodstuffs in the stomach. Moreover, irradiation does not kill viruses and it reduces some of the vitamin content of food – for example, levels of vitamin E.

AS CRUDE AS THE CAVEMAN'S CLUB

Rachel Carson concluded *Silent Spring* by expressing her doubts that people would move beyond their obsession with trying to control, rather than work with, nature:

'As crude a weapon as the cave man's club, the chemical barrage has been hurled against the fabric of life – a fabric on the one hand delicate and destructible, on the other miraculously tough and resilient, and capable of striking back in unexpected ways. These extraordinary capacities of life have been ignored by the practitioners of chemical control who have brought to their task no "high-minded orientation", no humility before the vast forces with which they tamper.

'The "control of nature" is a phrase conceived in arrogance, born of the Neanderthal age of biology and philosophy, when it was supposed that nature exists for the convenience of man. The concepts and practices of applied entomology for the most part date from that Stone Age of science. It is our alarming misfortune that so primitive a science has armed itself with the most modern and terrible weapons, and that in turning them against the insects it has also turned them against the earth.'

VOICE OF CONSCIENCE Carson (above right) provoked controversy with *Silent Spring*, but helped to increase environmental awareness.

The developing nations now account for half of the world's grain production.

But less comforting evidence has also emerged. By the early 1960s, some scientists were rejecting the idea of science 'conquering' nature. It was the use of pesticides that caused most concern. DDT had been used for nearly 20 years to banish pests in both agricultural and urban areas – in one case, a million acres (400 000 ha) of Florida real estate were exposed to DDT simply to eradicate the Mediterranean fruit fly. No thought had been given to the long-term consequences. By 1972, evidence had accrued that DDT was harming desirable flora and fauna and the public was demanding action. A fledgling movement, which would later blossom into the environmental lobby of today, succeeded in securing a ban on the use of DDT in the Western world.

A pioneering figure of the new environmental concern

was US biologist Rachel Carson. Alarmed by what she saw as a dangerous abuse of science, she had written *Silent Spring*, published in 1962. This was the first work to attack modern farming methods and the use of chemical pesticides. Carson's use of hard data and lyrical phrasing proved irresistible. *Silent Spring* became a bestseller.

She had grown up in Pennsylvania, whose natural beauty encouraged her interest in biology. Despite a retiring personality, she was passionate about the world environment,

LIVING EXPERIMENT At a research station in Ouagadougou in Burkina, experimental crops are tested for their viability in the semiarid tropical regions of West Africa.

a passion that drove her to write two best-selling books, *The Sea Around Us* and *The Edge of the Sea*. Then came *Silent Spring*. This focused on the dangers of pesticides; the title referred to her fear that chemical sprays would eventually kill all bird life, ending the music of the songbirds. Carson believed that pesticides such as DDT would build up in the environment and have a cumulative effect; one creature infected with DDT would pass it on to its offspring and so on. Once such pesticides entered the food chain, she foresaw massive increases in the incidence of cancer. *Silent Spring* was hugely influential in making people reconsider a number of modern farming methods and in encouraging international legislation against the use of DDT. Carson died on April 14, 1964, after a protracted battle against breast cancer, a reluctant figurehead for the environmental movement she had helped to foster.

Much of what Carson feared about DDT proved to be true. The compound does not break down quickly in the soil and it can remain for long periods in human body fat. As a result, it persists decade after decade, working its way through the food chain, including the human food chain. Evidence of the extent to which it had penetrated came in the 1970s when environmental groups across the USA revealed the presence of dangerous levels of DDT in the breast milk of most mothers. The milk was so contaminated that had it been agriculturally produced, it would have been deemed unsafe for consumption. Nearly 30 years later, in 1997, a study conducted in the UK showed that the breast milk of thousands of women had traces of DDT that were more than 20 times the established permissible levels.

Concerns about DDT launched the environmental movement, but all other artificial pesticides are now the focus of research by scientists and pressure groups alike. Research conducted by the United Nations in the early 1990s brought home the severity of the problem. Pesticides poison as many as a million people, and kill up to 20 000 of them, every year.

Questionable benefits

Since the mid 1970s, the successes of the Green Revolution have increasingly been thrown in doubt. It has become apparent that the dependence on 'supercrops' has resulted in a loss of natural bio-diversity; plants indigenous to particular agricultural areas have been crowded out by the new breeds. Moreover, modern artificial fertilisers are essential for growing the 'supercrops' successfully; with developing nations increasingly dependent on the new crops, the world-wide use of artificial fertilisers has increased considerably. This in its turn poses problems for many Third World farmers who find the expense of buying them well-nigh prohibitive. At the same time, salt levels in soil have risen, due to the increased need for irrigation. The irrigation water draws up salt from below, which then accumulates in the topsoil when the water evaporates, thus actually reducing fertility.

THE PRESERVATION GAME

Refrigeration and artificial additives have played a pivotal role in improving the quality and availability of food this century. Additives, commonly referred to in Europe by their 'e-numbers', are used, among other things, as preservatives, to add colour and nutrients and to alter texture. Virtually unknown before the 20th century, they have been adopted as a way of replacing nutrients commonly found in traditionally grown foods. Since the 1960s breakfast cereals, milk products and the like have had synthetic vitamins added to their chemical make-up to increase their nutritional value.

At the same time, the growth in consumerism along with the development of mass transportation and storage systems has resulted in ever-larger shopping outlets. In 1945 the average food shop stocked fewer than 1000 items; by 1996 the average supermarket carried tens of thousands of goods. This growth in volume brought a corresponding demand for foods with longer shelf lives. Synthetically produced chemicals such as sorbates, for example, are used to delay fungal and bacterial growths. Derived from sorbic acid, commonly known in Europe as E200, sorbates are often used to coat cheese.

In the late 1970s child psychologists postulated the theory that food additives might be partly responsible for aberrant behaviour in children. Irritability, insomnia and disruptive behaviour typified a syndrome known as attention deficit hyperactivity disorder. Since the early 1980s environmental groups have backed calls to encourage children, and their parents, away from the consumption of highly processed foods, and to return to traditional foods including five helpings of fruit and vegetables every day. Similarly, nutritional groups warn that the mass production of foods which depend upon pesticides, herbicides and artificial fertilisers may also cause behavioural problems in children; these chemical agents become, in effect, unwanted additives

HALF THE PRICE, TWICE THE CHOICE By the 1940s mass farming techniques were one factor that had greatly increased the choice of foods available at low prices to consumers, like this shopper in Princetown, Massachusetts.

GROWING TREND Organic farming has been growing in popularity for the last two decades. Many farms in the UK now produce vegetables without the use of artificial pesticides, herbicides or fertilisers.

Studies in Antarctica, among other places, have revealed how complex and interconnected our world's ecosystem is. Pesticides washed off the land in Europe, Asia and the Americas are absorbed by plankton which are in turn eaten by shrimps. These have carried the pesticides to the Antarctic seas and infected penguins with DDT. It is clear that the problem of pesticide persistence will not be an easy one to resolve. DDT has been used for only 60 years; yet it has already affected the global food chain.

These concerns have led to a debate among experts and the public at large. Many consumers and some farmers demand a return to more traditional methods. They prefer the approach known as 'organic farming' which uses naturally derived products to control pests and fertilise the soil. A British agriculturalist, Sir Albert Howard, was a founding father of the modern organic movement. In the 1930s he encouraged the use of excrement from towns as a natural fertiliser, the planting of naturally hardy crops and the breeding and release of infertile male insects as a natural pesticide. He had been influenced by watching Indian farmers at work, and essentially he was calling on farmers in the developed world to return to some of the traditional methods their own forebears had practised until about 100 years or so earlier. Few farmers in the 1930s and 40s favoured his approach, however, preferring the 'high tech' modern techniques – in Britain during the the Second World War, the need to be self-sufficient encouraged farmers in this choice.

It was not until the 1970s that the organic approach began to gain ground. One key populariser was a 'community farm', established at the height of the Vietnam War in May 1971 at Summertown in Tennessee,

THE BSE CRISIS

A DISEASE THAT HAD LONG AFFLICTED SHEEP SEEMED TO CROSS THE SPECIES BARRIER TO CATTLE – AND THEN HUMANS

Bovine spongiform encephalopathy (BSE) was first discovered in England in 1986. It affects cattle in their brains, which develop microscopic holes so that the tissue resembles a sponge. This results in spasms in the limbs, aberrant behaviour and finally death as the nervous system fails. BSE (dubbed 'mad cow disease') is believed to be triggered by the presence of a protein known as a prion (proteinacious infectious particle), probably ingested by consuming infected meat. Sheep have long suffered from a version of the disease known as 'scrapie'. Between 1978 and 1988 sheep offal, some of which may have been scrapie-infected, was included as extra protein in the cow feed used on some farms. Prions may have crossed the species barrier, causing more than 150 000 cows to develop BSE between 1986 and 1996.

Humans suffer from a similar disease, named Creutzfeldt-Jakob Disease (CJD) after its German discoverers and first diagnosed in 1920. On average, there is one case per million people each year. It affects men and women, usually between the ages of 50 to 75. The possibility that such a disease could pass between species was ignored

OUTDOOR PYRE In the early days of the BSE outbreak, farmers often had to burn infected carcasses in their fields.

until a new variant of CJD was diagnosed in Britain in 1996. The new variant differs from previously discovered forms and was clustered in Britain, suggesting a common cause. The British government acknowledged a possible link between BSE and the new variant CJD (nvCJD) after ten people, the oldest of whom was 42, had been diagnosed as suffering from nvCJD. Half of them worked in the livestock and meat industries. By 1998, 20 cases had been diagnosed in Britain and one in France.

What really caused BSE and its human crossover is debated by scientists. Experiments conducted in Iowa since 1990 showed that cows infected with scrapie became ill, but did not go on to develop BSE. Some scientists suggest that BSE was a new form of spongiform encephalopathy that arose naturally in cattle, but grew to epidemic proportions because bovine carcasses were reprocessed and fed to cattle, herbivores by nature. This forced cannibalism spread the disease throughout the cattle population.

Whatever the cause, measures to remove cows older than three years from the food chain are likely to halt any further cross infection and bring the crisis to an end. But doctors still fear more cases of nvCJD, which is believed to have an incubation period of 5 to 15 years.

AWAITING SLAUGHTER The crisis meant that many cattle met a premature end, while a European ban on the export of British beef brought hardship to many farmers.

developing countries had risen on average by 32 per cent (though many get more than the average, and many much less). The proportion of the world's population that was malnourished fell from a high of 35 per cent in 1961 to a low of 21 per cent in 1994. For all its drawbacks, the Green Revolution had helped to increase the amount of food available in North Africa, Asia and the Americas.

However, population growth continues and will increase the demand for food. At the same time, doubts about modern pesticides and fertilisers and the results of mechanisation mean that many of these may not be available to the farmers of tomorrow. The UN predicts that if the world is to provide enough food to meet demand, the amount of land under cultivation must increase by 27 per cent by the year 2015. But with an estimated 740 million acres (300 million ha) of land severely degraded and overworked, future generations will have to manage newly cultivated land much more carefully.

A LIFE IN HARD LABOUR Battery chickens are forced to live in confined cages, often resulting in disease, loss of feathers and the spread of salmonella bacteria to their eggs.

USA. Its founders were young people idealistically committed to community living and self-reliance. By the early 1980s, 'The Farm' had attracted more than 1500 members and had pioneered the production and sale of organically grown produce. Today, as much as 20 per cent of fresh vegetables sold in European supermarkets are produced using organic techniques.

At the same time, other aspects of modern farming have been questioned. For example, there is much discussion among European Union ministers about 'factory farming', in which thousands of animals are kept in confined areas. Here, they are encouraged to grow fat due to inactivity in the case of, say, pigs, to lay eggs in the case of chickens. Chicken farms are the most common kind of factory farm. As many as 100 000 birds can be housed on one farm, maintained in groups of 10 000. Their conditions are poor; often a chicken is born and lives its entire life in a cage measuring 4 sq ft (0.4 m²) shared with up to eight other birds. The risk of infection and the rapid transmission of disease, especially salmonella, causes concern. In the 1980s outbreaks of food poisoning in Europe and the USA resulted in calls by consumer groups for an end to factory farming. In 1997 the British government openly stated that it was considering outlawing the sale of eggs from factory farms.

The organic movement also has its critics, meanwhile. If organic methods were adopted globally, they ask, where would the land come from to rear cattle that produce organic fertilisers? In 1990, the Washington-based Worldwatch Institute estimated that food output would decrease by 40 per cent if all farmers stopped using chemical fertilisers; this would leave about 2 billion people to starve.

A world of plenty

A report published by the United Nations in 1997 revealed that global production of food could now easily meet world demand. Between 1961 and 1994 the food available per person in

DEFICIENCY AND DISEASE

A Dutch physician, Christiaan Eijkman, first recognised the link between vitamin deficiency and disease. In 1929 he received the Nobel prize for medicine for the discovery of thiamine (vitamin B_1). His work was furthered by Casimir Funk, a Polish-American biochemist, who coined the word 'vitamin'. Thiamine deficiency causes one of the commonest vitamin-related diseases, beriberi, a debilitating and potentially lethal ailment which attacks the nervous system. Another is rickets, caused by a vitamin D deficiency, usually as a result of a poor diet and a lack of sunlight (which enables the body to synthesise its own supply of the vitamin). Sufferers tend to be children and suffer from malformation of the bones. Education programmes and cheap vitamin supplements have virtually eradicated vitamin-deficiency diseases in the West.

A VITAMIN A DAY Starting in the 1940s, many schools provided vitamin supplements and regular examinations to prevent childhood diseases.

EXPLOITING LIFE

THE SCIENCE OF GENETICS, BORN WITH THE CENTURY, HAS UNFOLDED INTIMATE SECRETS OF WHAT MAKES EACH OF US WHAT WE ARE

The birth of a sheep does not normally hit the headlines, but Dolly's did. On February 23, 1997, the world woke up to a remarkable and unprecedented announcement. A sheep had been born by the process known as cloning. Life had been artificially stimulated in an unfertilised ovum, after genetic material drawn from six-year-old cells was inserted into the egg.

Does the creation of Dolly, only a century after the inception of genetic science, mean that mankind has developed the ability to create human life? Dr Ian Wilmot heads the research programme at the Roslin Institute near Edinburgh, Scotland, that produced her. During a British parliamentary inquiry, he was asked if his technique could be applied to the cloning of human beings. Although he did not advocate human cloning, he made it clear in his reply that it was possible: 'It would

be my belief, that if you really wanted to do it, it could be done.'

The science of genetics traces its origins to the mid 19th century in an Augustinian monastery at Brno in what is now the Czech Republic, then part of the Austro-Hungarian Empire. One of the monks, Gregor Mendel, was ordained as a priest in 1847 and then went to the University of Vienna to train as a teacher of natural sciences and mathematics. After his return to the monastery, he became fascinated with the concept of creation: how plants and animals develop their individual characteristics. He studied garden peas (*Pisum satium*), which he crossbred by artificially pollinating them. Mendel kept meticulous records of the shape and colour of the pods and seeds, how frequently the plants flowered and their height. In 1865, he presented his findings to the Brno Natural History

Society and the following year published an essay entitled 'Experiments with Plant Hybrids' in the society's journal. Later, Mendel became abbot of the monastery, and he died in 1884, his work having gone largely unnoticed. It was not until 1900 that this changed.

Three scientists – Erich von Ischermak-Seysenegg from Vienna, Hugo de Vries from the Netherlands and Carl Correns from Germany – each independently discovered Mendel's work while engaged in similar studies. Some 35 years after the publication of Mendel's essay, each realised that one of the secrets of nature had already been solved. The three scientists gave the monk's findings wider publicity, so that a new science, genetics, could be said to have been born in the first year of the 20th century.

The work was furthered by an American zoologist, Thomas Hunt Morgan. Morgan had a deep-rooted interest in the origins of species and after 20 years of work in the field was offered the chair of experimental

LEARNING FROM PLANTS Two of the founders of genetics: Carl Correns (below left), a botanist at the University of Tübingen in Germany, and Hugo de Vries (below), professor of botany at the University of Amsterdam.

1900

1900 Mendel's
work rediscovered

1926 Morgan's *The
Theory of the Gene*

1935 Butenandt and Ruzicka
synthesise testosterone

1950

MORGAN'S QUEST The US zoologist Thomas Hunt Morgan experimented with fruit flies to try to understand the mechanism of heredity. His *The Theory of the Gene* (background) became a 'bible' for experimental geneticists.

zoology at Columbia University in 1904. Over a period of ten years, he conducted a number of experiments with fruit flies (*Drosophila melanogaster*), and in 1915 presented his findings in *The Mechanism of Mendelian Heredity*. Mendel had originally proposed the theory of genes as carriers of genetic information from each parent. It was Morgan who conceived the theory of chromosomal heredity. According to this, genes are arranged inside the nucleus of cells in lines or joined strips, which he called chromosomes. In 1926, Morgan published *The Theory of the Gene*, in which he explained how to make 'maps' of chromosomes indicating the position of different genes. In recognition of his work, he was awarded the Nobel prize for medicine in 1933.

Enhancing human performance

In the 1930s biochemists also began to seek answers to the problems of foetal development, puberty and the reduction of vitality in the old. They conjectured – correctly – that these stages of human development have a common link. As early as 1889, a French physiologist, Charles-Edouard Brown-Sequard, had suggested that chemicals extracted from the testicles of animals could have a rejuvenating effect. Over the next four decades scientists attempted to isolate the chemicals – now known as hormones – that control body functions, including the key stages in a person's development. A breakthrough came in 1931 when the German biochemist Adolf Butenandt distilled a tiny amount of androsterone, one of the male sex hormones, from 26 400 pints (15 000 litres) of male urine. Shortly afterwards, other scientists established beyond doubt that a still more powerful male sex hormone (or steroid) existed in the testes. The race began to isolate and synthesise the hormone we now know as testosterone.

A female with white eyes (a recessive characteristic) and grey wings (dominant) is mated with a male with red eyes (dominant) and yellow wings (recessive).

GENERATING GENERATIONS Morgan bred pairs of fruit flies with different characteristics (some 'dominant' and some 'recessive') and observed how these were passed down to later generations. Dominant characteristics prevail even when their genes are paired with dissimilar ones; recessive characteristics prevail only when their genes are paired with similar ones.

The daughters inherit the dominant characteristics of each parent – red eyes and grey wings.

If one of the daughters is mated with a male with white eyes and yellow wings (both recessive characteristics), their offspring will combine the parents' characteristics in four different ways (below).

Female with red eyes (dominant) and grey wings (dominant).

Female with white eyes (recessive) and yellow wings (recessive).

Male with red eyes (dominant) and yellow wings (recessive).

Male with white eyes (recessive) and grey wings (dominant).

CREATING HORMONES Adolf Butenandt who first synthesised testosterone. It was an important step towards understanding human sex hormones, such as oestrogen, the female sex hormone – shown magnified through a microscope (background).

Research on animals had already proved that testosterone was responsible for aspects of body growth and promoted the development of certain sexual characteristics. In 1935 two research teams made simultaneous breakthroughs. On August 24, Butenandt's team published details of how to produce testosterone from the naturally occurring chemical cholesterol. One week later a Swiss team led by Leopold Ruzicka published a paper outlining a similar method for synthesising testosterone. Within two years researchers were conducting clinical trials on humans, beginning with adult males who suffered from underdeveloped sexual organs and impotence.

In 1939 tests were carried out in which testosterone was injected into women suffering from breast cancer. An excess of the female hormone oestrogen had long been linked with certain kinds of breast cancer, and the aim was to suppress the effects of the oestrogen. Results were promising, although the therapy had various side effects which included increased sexual desire in the women, the growth of unwelcome facial hair and lowering voices. It was becoming clear, though, that testosterone might be used to stimulate changes in the human body for specific ends: in particular, enhancing sporting performance in athletes or perhaps producing superior soldiers.

Butenandt and Ruzicka were jointly awarded the Nobel prize for chemistry in 1939. With the outbreak of the Second World War, scientists began to experiment with testosterone as a muscle restorative for the injured, and by 1941 several groups had realised that testosterone enhanced the ability of men to do physical work. This performance-enhancing feature – which has made the illegal use of testosterone irresistible to some athletes – was explored by Germany's Nazis in an effort to create an Aryan 'superman'.

The same quest led the Nazis to twist the new science of genetics to their own ends. In this attempt a key figure was Josef Mengele. He was born in the village of Gunzburg on the banks of the Danube in 1911. He was socially ambitious and drawn to right-wing politics. In October 1930 he enrolled at Munich University to study philosophy and life sciences, and fast became involved with the Nazi Party. Lecturers at Munich University were key proponents of a theory that would later find favour in Nazi Germany – that it was necessary to destroy life which 'was not of value' to society, such as the lives of the disabled and mentally ill.

In pursuit of the master race

Munich was a Nazi stronghold, and Mengele readily absorbed Nazi theories, such as the need to achieve racial purity and further Hitler's dream of a master race. He became a member of the SS. Then, in 1937, he was appointed to work as a research assistant at the Third Reich Institute for Heredity, Biology and Racial Purity at the University of Frankfurt. He worked with one of the world's leading geneticists, Professor Otmar Freiherr von Verschuer, another keen supporter of Hitler's racial policies, who was using twins to try to understand how the human body develops from egg and sperm. Mengele received his doctorate the following year. Later he was posted to the SS-run concentration camp at Auschwitz in Poland. It is possible that he asked for this job, since it offered him an almost unlimited supply of human guinea pigs.

DEAD MAN'S ISLAND

Bacteria or viruses can be turned into weapons – biological weapons. An early example of their use was by Napoleon who tried to spread swamp fever among his enemies. During the Second World War, the British government conducted secret biological warfare experiments on Gruinard Island off the west coast of Scotland. Tiny amounts of the anthrax bacterium were produced and then released on the island. They were enough to kill all animal life and make Gruinard uninhabitable for 40 years. Biological weapons cause special concern because they are so easy to make and spread. Anyone with a biochemistry degree and the right raw materials can brew them up. They are airborne, and one tiny dose released into the air can kill thousands. In the hands of terrorists, they could be used to appalling effect.

PUBLIC WARNING It took two years' extensive cleaning in the 1980s to make 'Anthrax Island' safe again.

Mengele conducted his experiments without any regard to suffering, operating on live subjects without anaesthetic, removing organs and injecting drugs to see their effect. Yet for all his dreadful diligence, his work did not lead to the development of a superhuman race and did remarkably little to further the science of genetics. As with the work of many Nazi scientists it left a body of data that is questionable both ethically – because of the way in which it was acquired – and scientifically because so many of the ideas behind it were ill-founded.

It is believed that Josef Mengele died in 1979 in Brazil where he probably sought refuge after the Second World War. His 'experiments' may have led to a deepening of the general public's fears about genetics. Certainly,

IN THE NAME OF SCIENCE Mengele (left) saw his cruel experiments with twins (above) as a means of learning more about human genetics.

'SUPER RACE' Nazi propaganda promoted images like this of super-fit Aryans.

Many witnesses testify to the atrocities Mengele committed against camp inmates in the name of genetic research. He carried out experiments on people with growth impairments; he also continued the research on twins begun by his mentor, von Verschuer, using Jewish children as though they were animals. Twins were pivotal in his research, since identical twins are, in fact, clones, perfect genetic copies of one another. If he introduced a poison into one of the twins, he might kill the other by shooting, and then compare the two bodies, one affected by poison and the other not. In this way, he could develop an understanding of how the poison damaged the body. His aim was to garner an understanding of human heredity, and after further research to improve the German race until it became 'a superhuman species'.

CRUCIAL RESEARCHER Rosalind Franklin (below) provided the X-ray diffraction images which offered vital clues to the structure of DNA. Her colleague Maurice Wilkins (left) showed her findings to Crick and Watson.

after the war there was an attempt by the world's scientific community to demystify genetics, leading to its inclusion in most school syllabuses by the mid 1970s.

Models and games

Born at the start of the century, genetics truly came of age in 1953, when two young researchers at the Cavendish Laboratories in Cambridge won a race to understand the complex structure of DNA (deoxyribonucleic acid), the chief constituent of chromosomes. Earlier, Rosalind Franklin, a scientist working at King's College, London, had made important progress in the field, using a technique called X-ray diffraction. In this process X-rays are directed at an object's atoms; they scatter when they hit the atoms and project the structure of the object onto an X-ray plate. Franklin's work proved that the DNA molecule was shaped like a spiral or helix. Franklin would undoubtedly have gone on to win great acclaim had she not died prematurely in 1958, aged only 37.

One of Franklin's colleagues at King's, Maurice Wilkins, shared Franklin's results with two Cambridge scientists, also studying the structure of DNA – Francis Crick, an English physicist and biochemist, and James Dewey Watson, an American biologist. Franklin's findings gave them the key information they needed to make a breakthrough. The structure of DNA appeared nonsensical

when studied in two dimensions. Logic told them that if they built a three-dimensional model, which fitted together all of the known components of DNA, they would surely arrive at the molecule's structure. Some of their colleagues baulked at this idea, but Watson and Crick were unperturbed. They were aware that other colleagues were close to a breakthrough and so worked long hours. Before she died, Rosalind Franklin gave them important help by carrying out essential research to confirm their findings.

Watson and Crick built and rebuilt their model several times, and yet they still had not solved the puzzle. Eventually, they realised that the DNA molecule must create a replica of itself when new cells are created. If the molecule had two helical (spiral) strands of genes, the strands could unwind, produce identical copies of themselves and then recombine, leaving an entirely new copy of the original DNA. They had solved the riddle. The DNA molecule is shaped like a double helix, one spiral winding around the other. The molecule coils round itself in this way, like the strands of a rope, so as to store vast amounts of genetic information within

each cell. We now know that each human cell – except those involved in reproduction – contains a double chain of genetic data consisting of 23 paternal chromosomes and 23 maternal ones. Together, the chromosomes contain about 100 000 genes.

Watson, Crick and Wilkins received the Nobel prize for medicine in 1962. By then Franklin had died and for various reasons, notably the fact that she was a woman working in what was still a very male-dominated scientific world, her contribution was overlooked – only in the 1990s did she begin to receive the recognition she deserved. With the double helix structure and function of DNA determined, genetic scientists could begin to use their knowledge to develop practical techniques for manipulating life.

Transferring genes

In the 1960s geneticists took another step forwards, when they transplanted genes into a donor egg and created exact duplicates, or clones. Dr John Gurdon of Cambridge University oversaw the cloning of tadpoles in an effort to understand how a single cell – an egg – can develop into a complex creature with a head and tail and separate organs.

His team took undifferentiated intestine cells – intestine cells that were alive but had yet to divide and become adult – from tadpole embryos. Using pipettes as small as a human hair, approximately 0.004 in (0.1 mm) wide, they then extracted the DNA and transplanted it into other cells, from which the nuclei had been removed, to produce clones. The resultant tadpoles grew to lead normal lives, in the process revealing that there is nothing specific about the DNA found in eggs. If an intestine cell transplanted into an empty ovum can produce a complete tadpole, then clearly the genetic information needed to 'make' a creature exists in every cell. The technique failed, however, when Gurdon's team attempted to transplant genetic material from adult cells. Indeed, cloning of adult cells appeared to be an impossibility.

In the 1980s genetic research was driven by giant pharmaceutical companies, who saw in genetic manipulation the possibility of new medicines and treatments for human ailments. Gene splicing – the movement of genetic material from one organism to another – became important as a means of producing synthesised drugs. For this, DNA from an organism known to produce a useful protein

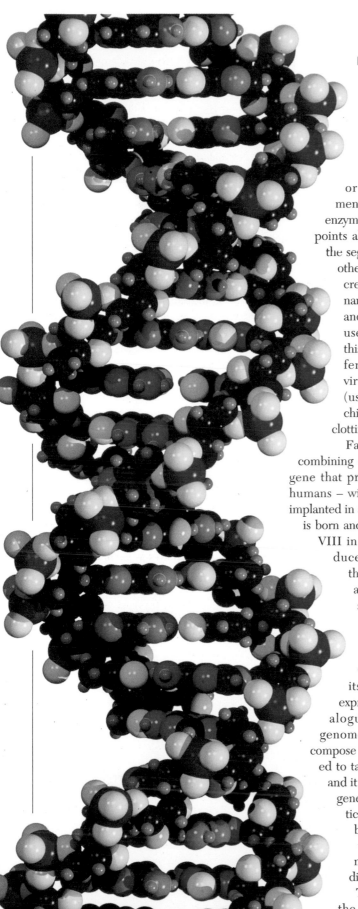

DNA This model shows the double helix structure of the DNA molecule. Its component atoms are nitrogen (coloured blue here), phosphorous (red), oxygen (yellow), carbon (green) and hydrogen (orange).

or chemical is sliced into segments; this is done by introducing enzymes that break down the bonds at points along the DNA strand. Parts of the segments are then introduced into other cells, such as bacteria cells, to create what is known as recombinant DNA. When these cells divide and proliferate, they produce the useful chemical. Geneticists use this technique to synthesise Interferon (used to fight cancer and viruses), human growth hormone (used to treat stunted growth in children) and factor VIII (a blood-clotting agent for haemophiliacs).

Factor VIII is usually produced by combining one part of human DNA – the gene that produces factor VIII in healthy humans – with sheep DNA, which is then implanted in a sheep's ovum. When the sheep is born and matures, it will produce factor VIII in its milk. This procedure produces a 'transgenic' animal: one that carries a gene from another animal. The first commercially successful use of recombinant DNA was in the synthesis of human insulin in 1982.

In 1989, the Human Genome Organization was set up, with its headquarters in Geneva. Its expressed aim was to develop a catalogue of the complete human genome – the totality of genes that compose a human. The project is expected to take 15 years of intense analysis, and it is hoped that it will identify the genes that are responsible for particular diseases. These could then be removed or corrected, potentially eradicating inherited illnesses such as Huntingdon's disease and cystic fibrosis.

The research philosophy behind the Human Genome Project has fostered other projects with more commercial motives. Many groups have emerged who seek to patent genes. They find a gene, sometimes in DNA taken from blood samples given by indigenous peoples in parts of the developing world. They then patent it, hoping that the gene will be useful in the production of medical treatments in years to come. Sometimes called 'genetic pirates', these groups have been accused of acting with colonial disregard towards people in developing nations who freely give their blood samples, without knowing the potential financial benefits that could accrue to the 'pirates' in the future. Genetic material is also, however, taken from people in the developed world, especially those suffering from diseases such as inherited Alzheimer's. Any research group that found a medicine for diseases like this could make enormous profits.

The British Medical Council abandoned the practice of gene patenting in 1993 on the grounds that it was morally reprehensible. The fear that large companies might restrict any future benefits of genetic research – by demanding high prices for their patented products – now preoccupies many humanitarian groups. Another tricky question is that of ownership of human material: do companies have the right to patent a person's genetic material, especially without the person's full permission? Public opinion seems

PANDORA'S BOX

Australia is overrun by an alien invader: the rabbit. Introduced by European settlers, the rabbit has thrived and now threatens to crowd out many of the continent's natural inhabitants, while destroying cash crops. Scientists offered the Australian government a possible solution: a virus, the rabbit calicivirus, which they believed would wipe out the rabbit population within months. The government was hesitant to use it, however, for fear that it might cross the species barrier and decimate other – indigenous – animal species. In the event, the virus escaped anyway, in 1995, from the island off South Australia where it was being tested. It was also illegally released in New Zealand. It has now infected and killed millions of rabbits around the world. Although it has not fulfilled the direr predictions of some experts by crossing the species barrier, it is still a warning of how microorganisms – a naturally occurring one, in this case – can escape laboratory conditions, with potentially lethal consequences.

HENRIETTA LACKS

Breakthroughs achieved in cancer research since the 1950s would have been held back without the unwitting assistance of one cancer victim, a black American woman, Henrietta Lacks. Cancerous cells taken from Lacks' cervix have been cultured and transported around the world since her death in 1951. They even penetrated the Iron Curtain at the height of the Cold War. HeLa cells, as they became known, are the foundation of most modern cancer research, but the cells were exploited without Lacks' knowledge or consent.

Her surviving family discovered in the early 1990s that her cell line was still being exploited. Indeed, it is now so established across the globe that it would be virtually impossible to locate and withdraw all the cells. Yet her family has received no recognition, let alone remuneration, from the pharmaceutical industry or the government.

The situation of the Lacks family reinforces many people's views about the exploitation of living material. Gene patents have become commonplace in the 1990s. Astonishingly, they have often ignored altogether the right of donors to have a say in how their DNA is used.

to be building against these practices. Yet it is also apparent that only the pharmaceutical giants have the resources to fund large-scale genetic research. Without their input the potential benefits of genetic engineering might be considerably delayed.

A new responsibility

Dolly the sheep unwittingly ushered in a new era of responsibility for mankind. The research team at the Roslin Institute wanted to find an efficient way of creating animals which would produce chemicals, such as factor VIII, without having to use recombinant DNA techniques. Gene splicing, although practicable, is laborious and invariably requires many attempts before a transgenic animal is produced; the combining of two different DNA elements often fails. Dr Ian Wilmot's team wanted to take an unfertilised ovum from a ewe, remove the cell nucleus and replace it with another nucleus from a specifically chosen animal cell, a process known as nuclear transfer. When planted in the womb of a host ewe, this egg would mature into an exact copy of the animal: a clone – in effect, an artificially produced twin, since twins are natural clones of one another.

Their problem was how to prevent the abnormalities experienced by other researchers when attempting to clone adult animals. Cloned creatures, such as sheep, would often grow abnormally large in the host mother's womb, endangering the mother and the cloned foetus. Others died prematurely or developed illnesses.

Wilmot's team thought that the answer lay in the state of the chosen cells before nuclear transfer. If the cells were in a state known as 'quiescence' – a condition of low activity, performing only a minimum of 'housekeeping' functions to stay alive – it might be possible to transplant them successfully into ewes' eggs. To achieve this state the team placed the cells in a specially formulated gel, and then starved them of food. Like all organisms in these circumstances, the cells shut down to conserve energy.

They took a cell from the mammary gland of a ewe, and an ovum from another donor ewe. Then they removed the nucleus of the ovum and inserted the cell, using a pipette. The combined egg was placed between two fine wires and 'fused' by 25 volts of electricity. This egg was then implanted in the ewe that had donated the egg. It took 277 attempts, but finally the team were successful and Dolly was the result.

The announcement of Dolly's birth was made months after the Roslin Institute filed for a patent on the technique. They delayed

BAA BAA CLONED SHEEP Dolly was the first clone of an adult animal. Researchers at the Roslin Institute used a cell from the udder of an adult sheep to create a viable embryo, which they implanted in a surrogate mother.

breaking the news in order to be sure of secrecy and of Dolly's survival beyond infancy. The response was overwhelming, and often hostile. The Vatican declared the technique to be a dangerous infringement on God's domain; Italy and Argentina banned cloning within days of the announcement. The Press speculated about the application of cloning, wondering if the dead could be returned to life, or individuals cloned without their knowledge or consent. Dr Wilmot spent the remainder of 1997 fielding questions from the public and legislators. He travelled the world in response to fears that his technique would be applied to clone human beings.

Many of his international colleagues have no doubt that this will now happen. Some are openly supportive of such an eventuality, pointing to the process as a way of helping infertile couples. Although the resultant child would be a clone, it would develop a totally separate personality from that of its 'originator', as seen in identical twins.

Another fear is that we might see the development of specifically engineered children, perhaps born to rich 'parents'. They might have enhanced intelligence or resistance to disease, while those less fortunate would be born with human weaknesses; there would literally be a genetic division between classes of people.

NUCLEAR TRANSFER In essence, nuclear transfer involves taking the genetic material from one cell (the 'donor cell') and transferring it into an unfertilised egg whose own genetic material has been removed. An embryo, with the genetic characteristics of the donor cell, results.

INSULIN: LIFE SAVER

The Canadian biochemists Frederick Banting and Charles Best first isolated insulin in 1921. Biotechnology laboratories now splice human genes into the DNA of bacteria, and then breed the bacteria to synthesise 'human' insulin for diabetics – a technique first used to produce medication in 1982. Previously pig or beef insulin was used, extracted from the pancreas. It was a life saver, but it does have drawbacks. It often triggers an antibody response in human diabetics, reducing the effectiveness of the insulin. Also, worldwide demand is set to outstrip the supply of animal insulin.

Before insulin was prescribed as a controlling medication, diabetics suffered the full effects of this illness. In 1900 a diabetic would suffer regular and violent mood swings, while poor circulation often resulted in diabetic gangrene in the extremities. Amputation was common, as were blindness and loss of skin sensitivity. In some cases diabetics fell into comas and died. By comparison, diabetics in the 1990s lead relatively normal lives. Regular daily injections of insulin enable

them to maintain constant levels of sugar in the blood. They can work and enjoy recreation like other people. Some now have automatic injectors. Worn close to the skin, this device provides an appropriate dose of insulin at timed intervals, giving diabetics complete freedom from worry about their condition while at work or play.

STEADY FLOW An electronically managed pump (left) delivers a continuous supply of insulin. Above: Banting (on the left) and Best (right) tested their insulin on diabetic dogs.

Although these topics preoccupy politicians across the globe, most scientists see the development of a human clone as a remote and unlikely, though possible, eventuality.

Any woman wishing to participate in such a scheme would have to be prepared to donate a significant number of eggs – a lengthy and often painful procedure – and undergo numerous, equally difficult, implantation operations. Nevertheless, it could be done.

Unanswered questions remain. As cells age, 'faults' occur during the reproduction of DNA when they divide to replenish our bodies. No one knows whether nuclear transfer causes cells to revert to their initial state, or whether the effects of ageing are carried across to the newly born clone. Consequently, Dr Wilmot's team are uncertain about Dolly's age. She could be one or seven years old – the donor cells used to create Dolly were six years old. If she is the equivalent of seven years old, Dolly may have a greatly reduced life span or may soon become susceptible to disease. Answers to these questions would, of course, have a bearing on any future attempt to clone a human being.

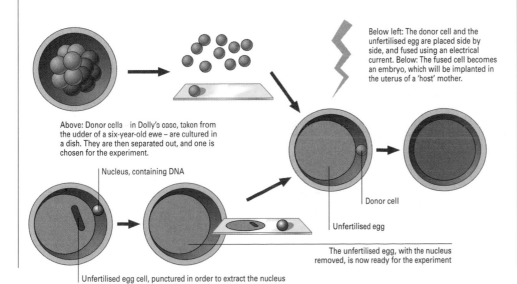

Below left: The donor cell and the unfertilised egg are placed side by side, and fused using an electrical current. Below: The fused cell becomes an embryo, which will be implanted in the uterus of a 'host' mother.

Above: Donor cells – in Dolly's case, taken from the udder of a six-year-old ewe – are cultured in a dish. They are then separated out, and one is chosen for the experiment.

Nucleus, containing DNA

Donor cell

Unfertilised egg

The unfertilised egg, with the nucleus removed, is now ready for the experiment

Unfertilised egg cell, punctured in order to extract the nucleus

MANIPULATING THE WEATHER

SCIENCE HAS ENHANCED OUR UNDERSTANDING OF HOW THE WEATHER WORKS, AND MAY ONE DAY GIVE US A DEGREE OF CONTROL OVER IT

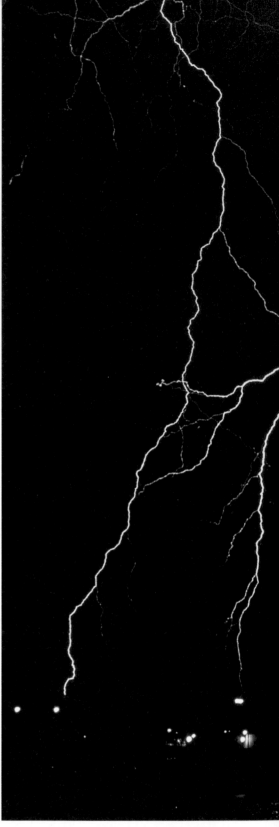

The weather dominates our world. It is the single most powerful natural force on Earth, one that both fosters life and destroys it. Every minute 2000 thunderstorms are in progress, pummelling the Earth. Lightning, creating a current of 300 000 amps (a household electrical system usually handles tens of amps), strikes disparate parts of the planet's surface 100 times a second. Experts estimate that around 100 people die in the United States every year because of lightning strikes. Other destructive phenomena include tornadoes, great vortexes of swirling air and energy that tear tracks through settlements, sucking debris and earth into their cores at speeds sometimes exceeding 250 mph (410 km/h).

The American author Mark Twain once said: 'Everybody talks about weather, but no one does anything about it.' Since the Second World War mankind, for the first time in its history, has developed tools that enable people to achieve at least a measure of control over the weather – to do something about it.

Weather in any given area is determined by the constantly changing properties of the local atmosphere – its temperature, humidity and air pressure at different altitudes. These properties have been at the centre of mankind's attempt to understand, predict and control weather patterns. Meteorology has advanced so much this century that experts can now give significant warnings of the arrival of many dangerous weather conditions. By using complex computerised radar technology, they predict with great accuracy

NATURE'S AWESOME POWER   A 'twister' or tornado (below) photographed in Kansas. Right: Forks of lightning streak across the night sky over Tampa Bay, Florida.

the incidence and paths of tornadoes and hurricanes. Thanks to satellite images of cloud formations, highly skilled forecasters warn of impending snow or rain storms.

Nowadays, radar and television images are beamed down from man-made objects that orbit the planet on the fringes of the atmosphere. These influence decisions about matters as varied as the planting of expensive cash crops, the construction of buildings, the transportation of sensitive equipment and

1900

1950

1902 Teisserenc de
Bort discovers
stratosphere

1921 Vilhelm Bjerknes'
theory of polar fronts
1922 Richardson's *Weather
Prediction by Numerical Process*

1927 Radiosonde invented

1946 Schafer and
Langmuir discover
principles behind
cloud seeding

the launching of rockets. Yet one question still dominates: if we can achieve a true understanding of the weather in all its complexity, will we be able to manipulate it?

Developing the tools

In the mid 18th century the American Benjamin Franklin tried to discover more about lightning by sending a kite into the heart of a storm cloud. Since then, unmanned balloons have been used to investigate the upper atmosphere. They were fitted with crude instruments (called meteorographs) which recorded the pressure and temperature patterns of the atmosphere at various heights. In 1902, Leon Teisserenc de Bort, a French meteorologist, was using this crude technology when he discovered the stratosphere – the layer of the atmosphere between about 9 and 30 miles (15 and 50 km) above the Earth's surface, where temperature increases rather than decreases with height.

Experiments using balloons continued into the 20th century. Then, in the 1920s, meteorologists in Western Europe, the USA and the USSR simultaneously developed methods of carrying information-gathering instruments in small packs underneath meteorological balloons. Thermometers and barometers were connected to a small radio transmitter, which relayed the data to the ground. These devices, known as radiosondes, allowed meteorologists to come to grips with

1950

1962 Rainbow tests –
nuclear bombs detonated
in ionosphere

1992 Work
starts on
HAARP

2000

the nature of winds and atmospheric activity. The radiosonde is so cost-effective and efficient that it is still the most common means of gathering high-altitude data. Many are

OLD AND NEW In 1923 meteorologists at Le Bourget airport, Paris, use a balloon to check wind direction (bottom). Below: By the 1980s, computers were projecting models of storms.

able to climb to a height of 30 miles (50 km). Radiosonde stations are located above sites all over the Earth and data is collated internationally twice daily, at noon and midnight (Greenwich Mean Time).

Prediction

In 1922 an English mathematician, Lewis Fry Richardson, thought of a way of interpreting and using this new influx of data – a weather 'forecasting factory'. He described this in a pamphlet entitled *Weather Prediction by Numerical Process*. Envisaged before the age of the microcomputer, the 'factory' would occupy a vast room with circular walls to imitate the shape of the Earth. Each region of the world would have a number of mathematicians collating and interpreting data that had been received via radio

JELLYFISH IN THE SKIES Today's weather balloons carry electronic instruments into the skies. Here, meteorologists at the European Space Agency's launch site in French Guiana, use a French-designed 'meduse' (jellyfish) balloon to calculate wind speed.

in a central area. At the epicentre of this factory a tall pillar would carry a 'conductor'. His job would be to gather the information worked out by the mathematicians and direct it to four senior clerks – representing the points of the compass. They in turn would dispatch predictions about 'future weather'

PUNISHING INACCURACY

In 1964 the Director of the Provincial Weather Bureau in Taiwan was arrested, charged with giving an inaccurate weather forecast and tried. He had predicted that Hurricane *Gloria* would avoid the island. He was wrong and nearly 300 people died. Although he was found guilty, the director was not imprisoned for his fatal mistake.

via radio around the world. Richardson's vision was realised in several features of the modern meteorological office, although in place of a circular room with an army of subordinates working to a 'conductor', individual meteorologists use computer terminals to process and distribute information relayed to them via satellite.

At the same time, a group of Norwegian meteorologists had been pushing back the frontiers of our knowledge about the weather. Indeed, throughout the 1920s, they dominated the science, thanks mostly to the work of the Bergen-based father-and-son team, Vilhelm and Jacob Bjerknes, who produced an explanation for the movement of air masses over the surface of the globe.

It was the son Jacob who put together the final pieces in this research when he set up a network of weather monitoring stations across Norway between the end of the First World War and 1931. This network, probably the most comprehensive in the world at the time, allowed him to test and elaborate ideas he had already put forward in 1918 about the relationship between polar air masses and the creation of storms. He realised that the atmosphere is composed of warm tropical air masses and cold polar ones which are divided by precise boundaries, which he related to military battle lines: fronts. Disturbances in these 'fronts', he noted, create cyclonic vortexes of air, resulting in storms.

Jerome Namias, an American meteorologist, added to these breakthroughs while working at the Boston Institute of Technology in the 1930s. He began studying the possibility of a mathematical averaging process which would enable forecasters to determine the most likely development of weather patterns, based on numerical data, for a 30-day period. The long-range weather forecast was born.

Jule Charney, another American, further developed numerical prediction by devising complex mathematical models which could predict the movement and interaction of weather fronts. After successful tests in 1950, Charney's techniques became the standard for weather forecasting. His work is still used as the basis for complex models of weather, now constructed in meteorological computers.

The quest for control

These developments coincided with an accidental discovery in a chemical laboratory. In 1946 Vincent Schafer and Irving Langmuir, working in the General Electric Company Laboratory in Schenectady, New York, accidentally discovered that frozen carbon dioxide (dry ice) creates ice crystals similar to those found in rain clouds when dropped in a canister at $-40°C$ ($-40°F$). Throughout the next decade Schafer, Langmuir and a third

WIZARD OF THE WEST

The Croatian-born inventor Nikola Tesla (1856-1943) emigrated to New York in 1884. He predicted the advent of faxes, radar, missiles and even radio-guided aircraft. As the inventor of alternating current, power lines and electrical grid systems, he could claim to be the man who first illuminated the world. He had well over 700 technological patents to his credit – many of which are still classified, for military eyes only.

In 1901 Tesla began an experiment to harness the ionosphere – which at that time had not even been discovered by orthodox science. He convinced his backers to finance a scheme that would enable wireless communication between New York and London – one was the financier J. P. Morgan, who wanted to exploit information about London Stock Exchange prices ahead of his US competitors. But Tesla wanted more than he dared to say. He believed in the existence of an electroconductive sheath in the atmosphere, capable of carrying power around the world without wires. He had visions of illuminating the Paris Exposition with hydroelectric power generated at the Niagara Falls. He also believed that the ionosphere could be used to manipulate the weather and even generate a defensive electromagnetic shield over the USA. In the end, Guglielmo Marconi beat him in the race to transmit across the oceans. Marconi's radio signals exploited the ionosphere in much the same way that Tesla had planned to, bouncing radio waves off it. Morgan was furious. Tesla had to reveal the full extent of his plans for the ionosphere. His energy transmission scheme was too outlandish, and his financiers deserted him.

AHEAD OF HIS TIME Nikola Tesla was regarded as an eccentric by many contemporaries. Today, however, his inventions are taken seriously.

colleague, Bernard Vonnegut, carried out experiments across the USA in which light aircraft flew over clouds and 'seeded' them with crushed dry ice. The dry ice froze water vapour in the clouds, turning it into ice crystals. These fell to earth as snow or rain.

Cloud seeding is a controversial subject. The process is expensive; it costs millions of pounds to staff and equip a team of cloud seeders, and many people believe it is ineffective and a waste of tax revenues. On the other hand, it can save crops and thereby huge amounts of money. Despite difficulties

in quantifying rates of success, many commercial companies exist (particularly in Australasia) that specialise in cloud seeding and frequently sell their expertise to other nations. The Indonesian and South African governments both employed cloud seeders in the 1990s to augment natural rainfall; they claimed increases in precipitation of as much as 30 per cent. The South Korean government enlisted the help of Tasmanian cloud seeders in October 1997. They wanted the seeders to try to reverse the effects of the meteorological phenomenon known as El Niño, which

SOWING RAIN SEEDS A Malaysian technician checks the equipment on a plane to be used for cloud seeding in September 1997. Rain was needed desperately to help clear the haze created by forest fires in Indonesia.

threatened to cause severe drought in the area. Tasmania has used cloud seeding since the mid 1960s because of its reliance on hydroelectricity; seeding helps to maintain water levels in reservoirs that feed the hydroelectric dams.

A US government research programme investigating weather modification began work in the late 1940s. Largely basing their research on the work of Schafer, Langmuir and Vonnegut, its teams experimented with cloud dissipation, hail suppression and fog dispersal. Using silver salts (particularly silver iodide), they attempted to neutralise storm clouds that were capable of creating dangerous hail stones, sometimes as large as golf balls. They used the silver iodide to change all the water vapour in the clouds into ice crystals before the clouds reached metropolitan areas where the hail could prove dangerous to humans. This process proved so effective – some claim that it can reduce the incidence of hail in built-up areas by as much as 40 per cent – that it has since been used all around the world, in places such as the former Soviet Union, France, Switzerland and Italy. The scientists were able to dissipate cold fogs and clouds using a similar process. Many airports now use this technique to prevent fog and clouds over runways.

This form of manipulation has become commonplace, but it is still very crude. In the 1950s another, more ambitious, programme was initiated, the results of which might one day lead to mankind having true control over the planet's weather.

In the ionosphere

Victorian scientists noted that turbulence on the Sun's surface creates forces of immense magnitude that eject matter out into the solar system. Our magnetosphere – the region around the Earth in which its magnetic field dominates the behaviour of charged particles – is buffeted by this so-called 'solar wind'. Where it penetrates our planet's upper atmosphere, it creates a field of charged particles, or plasma. This is the ionosphere.

In the 1950s the US military initiated a study of the ionosphere in an attempt to understand it for military purposes – how it affects the trajectory of rockets and missiles, for example, and the passage of radio waves.

In this task they were helped by the new rocket technology, spearheaded by the former Nazi scientist Wernher von Braun, who had masterminded the wartime V-2 rocket missile and was now employed by the USA. Rockets were used to explore the upper atmosphere and led to the discovery of radioactive zones on its upper fringes. These 'Van Allen belts' – named after the scientist in charge of the research, James Van Allen – protect our world from deadly solar radiation.

DEATH IN A CLOUD

Hail is created when crystals of ice circulate within a thundercloud. In 1930 five Germans in a glider experienced this when they had to bail out over a thundercloud. Updraughts caught their parachutes and carried them to the top of the cloud. One was thrown clear and survived; the others dropped through the cloud and froze to death.

Thirty years later, scientists developed a range of technologies for manipulating the ionosphere as part of President Reagan's Strategic Defence Initiative (SDI). Dubbed Star Wars by the Press, this was a large research programme initiated with the express aim of constructing an energy defence shield. Pivotal in this research was the ionospheric heater. This machine could transmit a beam of radiation directly at the ionosphere to heat an area of the plasma field. Just as a microwave oven functions by vibrating water molecules to generate heat within food, so the electromagnetic wave of an ionospheric heater hits the plasma and causes electrons and neutral particles to move, which in turn causes friction and heat.

The development of ionospheric heaters coincided with a problem on the gas fields of Alaska. Arco (Atlantic Richfield Company) had billions of cubic yards of excess gas to dispose of, produced whilst drilling for

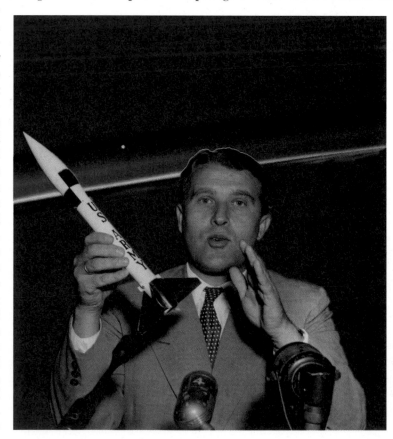

BRAUN TECHNOLOGY Werner von Braun headed the US Ballistic Missile Agency at Huntsville, Alabama, which gave the US military the ability to penetrate the ionosphere (background).

LAUNCHING TIROS: APRIL 1, 1960

The world's first weather satellite, TIROS 1, was launched on April 1, 1960. The Television and Infrared Observation Satellite (TIROS) was the first of ten experimental meteorological spacecraft. They had been developed to test the notion that orbiting craft could monitor our planet's weather patterns and relay more accurate information about them than could be gleaned from any number of observation posts within the atmosphere. Each satellite was fitted with two video cameras, one with a wide-angle and the other with a telephoto lens, which offered a close-up view of meteorological events. The images were stored on videotape and were then relayed to monitoring stations on the ground by radio links – more reliable microwave links are used today.

The TIROS experiment proved to be a tremendous success. Just one day after the launch, the satellite was successfully sending back pictures showing the cloud cover over the north-eastern corner of North America. It led to the development of the highly sophisticated meteorological and other satellites that now play an essential part in our everyday lives.

Alaskan oil. It was not commercially feasible to build gas pipelines leading direct to the rest of the USA. So they turned to a well-known plasma physicist, Bernard Eastlund, in the hope that he would think of a way of putting the gas to use.

Alaska lies close to the Earth's magnetic pole. Arco's surplus gas would provide the

PLAYING AURORA ON THE HAARP For all its spectacular beauty, the aurora borealis (northern lights) interferes with satellite communications. One of the purposes of HAARP in Alaska (inset) is to prevent this.

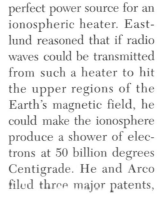

perfect power source for an ionospheric heater. East-lund reasoned that if radio waves could be transmitted from such a heater to hit the upper regions of the Earth's magnetic field, he could make the ionosphere produce a shower of electrons at 50 billion degrees Centigrade. He and Arco filed three major patents,

which caught the attention of the US military because of the range of uses they could be put to. They included the creation of an energy shield, communication jamming, the destruction by remote control of enemy electronics and weather control.

Fear of weather change

In 1992, construction started in Alaska on the High Frequency Active Auroral Research Program (HAARP), funded by the US navy and Air Force. The US Defense Department insists that HAARP's main function is to monitor the weather and to attempt to control the effects of the aurora borealis on satellite communication and electronic equipment – the electrically charged field of an aurora can cause system failures in electronic equipment and even corrode power lines. Officials claim that any other abilities the system may have are merely by-products. Yet the first experiment conducted with it was to image a disused

SPRITES AND JETS

Red sprites and blue jets are phenomena first observed in 1994 by a pilot flying at a height of 43 000 ft (13 000 m). Previously unknown to science, they were recorded by chance on a high-speed camera aboard an aircraft. They are, in fact, large vertical discharges of gas, thrown out from storm clouds during a lightning strike.

mine near Fairbanks, Alaska. It could do this because heating the ionosphere generates extra-low frequency (ELF) waves which can penetrate the ground or sea – they are used to communicate with submerged submarines. ELF signals can be processed, much like radar signals, to create an image. It seems that HAARP's ability to operate as a covert 'tool' was appreciated from near the start.

HAARP has already faced heavy criticism from environmental groups. They claim that by heating the ionosphere, the US military is

THE POLLUTION EFFECT Smog hangs over western Tokyo. The world's cities contribute significantly to greenhouse gas emissions.

running the risk of permanently altering weather patterns. They point to the fact that one of Bernard Eastlund's original patents for the project stated that the ionospheric heaters could be angled to hit the jet streams – narrow 'rivers' of high-speed winds which circle the Earth and influence global weather patterns – and so alter their course, changing global weather at will.

It is impossible to predict whether an operational upgrade for HAARP – planned for the late 1990s – will enable it to exercise some kind of control of the ionosphere, or even if the US Defense Department intends to try to exercise such control. What is clear is that the effects of ionospheric heating are too little understood for anyone to be certain of the long-term consequences of HAARP's use, either as a weapon or to attempt weather control. It is possible that HAARP or some larger future project may produce beneficial results, offering us the ability to improve our weather patterns and control them for industrial and agricultural gain. Artificially induced rainfall would certainly be welcome in countries that frequently suffer drought.

A warm globe

Mankind may yet learn how to control weather formation deliberately. What many experts are increasingly convinced of, however, is that we have manipulated the climate unwittingly. Global warming, first proposed by scientists in the mid 1980s, is believed by many to be a result of industrial activity and

OPERATION 'DOMINIC'

In 1962, after four years of planning, the US military launched Operation *Dominic*, the simultaneous detonation in the Pacific of large thermonuclear bombs under water, on land and in the ionosphere. Anticipating favourable media coverage, they went public. They dubbed the devices 'rainbow bombs' because they were expected to create artificial aurorae. In the event, the detonation in the ionosphere had a much greater effect than was expected. It created an artificial electromagnetic storm which knocked out Hawaii's power supply and generated a massive synthetic aurora. There were great fears about radioactive contamination. Many non-US military satellites were destroyed by the explosion and long-wave radio communication was impossible in certain parts of the globe for many hours.

the use of motorised vehicles. Carbon dioxide released by burning fossil fuels, such as oil and coal, has accumulated in our atmosphere. The Sun warms the Earth's surface during the day, and this heat radiates into space at night. But the carbon dioxide gases act like an insulator, trapping the heat within the atmosphere, like a greenhouse.

The result is climate change. Higher global temperatures could lead to the melting of polar ice sheets and a rise in sea levels, swamping some lowland countries. Harsh winters would be followed by terrible summer droughts. If this catastrophic theory is correct, our attempts to gain mastery of the climate may prove essential if we are to survive the harsh realities of a 'post-global warming' era.

ECOLOGICAL CRISIS

FAMINES HAVE BEEN A FEATURE OF THE 20TH CENTURY AS OF ANY OTHER, AND MOST OF THEM HAVE BEEN MAN-MADE – THE RESULT OF WAR, REVOLUTION AND SOCIAL EXPERIMENT. HUMAN DEVELOPMENT HAS CAUSED THE LOSS OF PLANT AND ANIMAL SPECIES, AND THE WORLD MAY NOW BE FACING GLOBAL SHOCK AS THE RAIN FORESTS, THE PLANET'S LUNGS, CONTINUE TO BE DECIMATED, AND THE STABILISING ICE OF ANTARCTICA BEGINS TO ERODE DUE TO A RISE IN GLOBAL TEMPERATURE.

FAMINE AND DISEASE

**THE APPLICATION OF SCIENCE HAS IMPROVED AGRICULTURAL YIELDS.
BUT WARS AND REVOLUTIONS HAVE REDUCED MILLIONS TO STARVATION**

Technology in farming is nothing new. Ever since the first human agriculturalists devised the first farming implements and started selecting and sowing particular plants and plant varieties more than 10 000 years ago, people have 'interfered' with nature. In the 20th century we have used technology to increase crop yields and obtain animal products on demand. These attempts have led to many successes. But the century has also seen famine and the destruction of soil, creating at different times vast tracts of near-desert in the Great Plains of North America, Ethiopia in Africa and the Aral Sea in Central Asia.

At the end of the century, we increasingly appreciate the delicate balance that exists in the relationship between humans and their environment. With the benefit of experience, we have started to learn how any shift in that balance, sometimes the result of

HUNGER! A Russian mother feeding her child in 1924. Peasant families subsisted on meagre plots of land, while struggling to meet new taxes.

a new technology, can cause unforeseen harm – in some cases undermining genuine advances that have been made in the struggle to feed the world's population.

A century of famine

Death caused by famine can result either directly from starvation or from diseases that attack the malnourished. If the calorific intake of someone on a normal healthy diet is halved over a period of months, his or her body weight will drop by around a quarter. Despite much pain and lethargy for the victim, survival is entirely possible at that level for many months. Further drops in calorific intake, however, bring additional losses in body weight. The body's immune system stops working as effectively as it should do, and diseases set in. Among the billion people all over the globe who are currently undernourished, many die from quite commonplace ailments, such as influenza and measles. If they can start eating again at normal levels, most people will make a full recovery.

There have been more than a dozen major famines in the 20th century, at least

11 of which had one cause: mankind. Harmful effects are a nearly inevitable consequence when prudent farming methods are abandoned in pursuit of war or the fanatical imposition of a political doctrine (such as the collectivisation of agriculture in communist Russia and later communist China) or just plain greed. Figures are unreliable; even so, it is clear that lives lost in the 20th century as a result of man-induced famine number in their tens of millions.

In the October Revolution of 1917, the Bolsheviks seized power in Russia, leading to a bloody civil war that lasted until 1922.

1920 Famine in Armenia, Ukraine and Crimea
1921 Lenin's New Economic Policy in Russia

1928 Stalin introduces collectivisation in Soviet Union

1941-3 Some 400 000 people starve in Greece during German occupation
1945 UN Food and Agriculture Organization founded

МЫ КОЛХОЗНИКИ на БАЗЕ СПЛОШНОЙ КОЛЛЕКТИВИЗАЦИИ
ЛИКВИДИРУЕМ КУЛАКА как КЛАССА.

ПОМНИ о ГОЛОДАЮЩИХ!

Two seasons of drought after the revolution compounded an existing problem in Russia of underproduction. War made things still worse, and by 1920 famine gripped Armenia, the Ukraine, the Crimea and regions of the Volga river valley.

The US government refused to acknowledge the new communist regime in Russia. But by August 1920 the situation was so bad that Washington and Moscow agreed a US aid package amounting to US$20 million. Hundreds of American aid workers flooded into Russia, with Herbert Hoover, a senior American statesman and future president,

EQUAL DRUDGERY 'Liquidate the *kulaks* as a class' reads the banner held aloft by workers on a Soviet collective farm in 1930. Right: Posters like this promoted the supposed benefits of collectivisation – enough for everyone.

orchestrating the relief effort. This campaign probably saved as many as 10 million lives.

The Bolshevik leader, Lenin, however, had his own agenda for change. This included the introduction of 'scientific socialism' into Russian agriculture. Policy here took a number of twists and turns. In the immediate aftermath of the revolution the new

1950

1958 'Great Leap
Forward' launched
in China

1969 Paul
Ehrlich's *The
Population Bomb*

1984 Famine in Ethiopia brought
to world attention
1985 Live Aid concerts

2000

Bolshevik authorities instituted the enforced collection of food produce from peasant farmers and its redistribution to the rest of the population. In his New Economic Policy, however, introduced in 1921, Lenin changed tack and started collecting taxes rather than produce from the farmers, allowing peasants – who worked on allocated land – to sell their produce in free markets. This had mixed success. Many peasants, unable to produce surpluses, faced starvation; those who did manage to achieve more than a meagre subsistence from their land often failed to sell their produce for the best price – their traditional village commune system had left them with no experience of a free market economy. Many failed to earn

enough to meet Lenin's tax, let alone buy food and other provisions for their families. Experts in post-communist Russia now estimate that nearly 6 million people starved to death between 1921 and 1923 as a result of these enforced changes.

And there was more to come. In 1928 Soviet Russia's next ruler, Stalin, introduced collectivisation, the forced grouping of individual farms into large state-run organisations. The private enterprise initiatives of Lenin's New Economic Policy were revoked under a series of five-year plans. Stalin's aim was to create a grain surplus that could be exported in exchange for machinery which would be used to develop a modern industrial base for the Soviet economy. Already farmers had been forced to switch from the old Russian communal system to working their land as individuals; in another upheaval they now had to give their all to the state. Many peasants revolted, destroying valuable farm property. The managers of the new collective farms were frequently inexperienced, while the richer *kulak* farmers (those who had formerly worked the larger acreages)

were forcibly removed to be replaced by untrained peasant workers.

In the event, what resulted was a catastrophic drop in production. In 1928, some 73 million tons of grain were produced in the Soviet Union, with the state taking 10.6 million tons. By 1933 the grain harvest had fallen to 67.3 million tons, with state procurements rising by more than 200 per cent to over 22 million tons. Between 1928 and 1934 the number of cattle in the Soviet Union fell from 67 million head to 33 million; half the country's livestock died in the lifetime of Stalin's first five-year plan. Similarly, goat and sheep populations plummeted from 115 million to 37 million over the first five years. Food was forcibly procured from the collectivised farms, often meaning starvation for agricultural workers. Grain shortages, resulting from poor working

MAO'S NEW CULTURE People working for 'the good of all' on a collective farm in the wheatlands of China's Heilongjiang Province. Mao's version of collectivisation was part of an attempt to purge the country of elites.

practices and inexperience, exacerbated the problems of collectivisation. Five million people died of famine in the Caucasus and Ukraine between 1933 and 1938. It took 22 years of real hardship after the introduction of the first five-year initiative for grain production to return to pre-1914 levels.

Great leap forward?

Mao Zedong, who founded the Communist People's Republic of China in 1949, followed the collectivist precedent set by Stalin. He announced that all remnants of privately owned farms should be eradicated in favour of a new communalism. The policy, known as the 'Great Leap Forward', was meant to prove that China could catch up with the USA within 15 years and become the next agricultural and industrial giant.

Although Mao had established close links with the USSR, he wanted to surpass it and create the first truly communal society. He foresaw a great collective state which would banish hunger, providing for everyone according to their need. Farmers would work together on large agricultural compounds, each with its own community, eating and sleeping in communal housing.

This policy was launched in 1958, with workers exhorted to achieve superhuman levels of work. But the truth was that the forced collectivisation of land and animals left the people with virtually no incentive. Without the spur of self-interest, peasant farmers – as in Stalin's Russia – were indifferent to the task of tending the land. Experiments with new systems for planting crops were unsuccessful as they ignored the need for fallow land and fertilisers, and mismanagement became the norm. The Great Leap Forward was a catastrophic failure. Many millions died, though the true numbers may never be known.

War and starvation

War has precipitated starvation since ancient times. In the 20th century hundreds of thousands have died in this way – for example, during Nazi Germany's invasion of the Soviet Union in 1941-4 and the starvation of some 400 000 people in Greece (1941-3) after the Germans took control and stripped the country of food to feed their army. But the most severe episodes of war-induced famine took place in pre-communist China and in Indochina and Africa.

In China, Chiang Kai-shek's Nationalists and Mao Zedong's Communists had been intermittently fighting each other since the start of the 1930s. A ruthless and bloody Japanese invasion began in 1937 and temporarily eclipsed the civil conflict, but with the ending of the Second World War the two sides were back at each other's throats; the Communists eventually drove the Nationalists from the mainland in 1949. Drought, meanwhile, coupled with the effects of war had pushed grain and food production to an all-time low in the late 1940s. No accurate figures exist, but it is believed that as many as 5 million people died as a result of the final stages of the Chinese civil war.

Similarly, war in Nigeria (especially Biafra in 1967-70), Cambodia (in the 1970s), Uganda (from 1979 to 1980) and Ethiopia and Somalia (1983 to the present day) have cost untold lives. Conservative estimates suggest that at least 6 million people have died in Africa in the 20th century as a result of war-induced famine and disease; other figures suggest a total closer to 20 million. In a continent where malnutrition affects 40 per cent of the population, any additional shock – such as war – can destroy the delicate agricultural balance and generate a famine. War also closes borders and interrupts communications, preventing the rapid redistribution of food in times of need.

Leaders of military groups often use the food supply as a means of bludgeoning opposition or potential opposition. Pol Pot, the leader of the Khmer Rouge which took control of Cambodia in 1975, enforced a policy of evacuating the cities – the strongholds of the Western-influenced middle classes whose influence he was determined to wipe out – and making people work on the land. In the process, he sanctioned mass deaths (as many as a million) and freely allowed the people of Cambodia to die – even ignoring the existence of famine after forcibly introducing the collectivisation of farms.

In Ethiopia, it was the BBC's groundbreaking reporting in 1984 that for the first time brought home to Western viewers the

FEED THE WORLD

A 16-hour rock concert, broadcast simultaneously from Britain and the USA, starting at midday local time in London's Wembley Stadium and finishing at midnight local time in Philadelphia's JFK Stadium, and including along the way every conceivable member of the rock and pop firmament, from Tina Turner to Freddie Mercury, Madonna to Elton John – it was all the brainchild and extraordinary achievement of 32-year-old Dublin-born rock musician Bob Geldof, lead singer of the Boomtown Rats. And it started with TV images of starving people in Ethiopia. Geldof was so distressed that he decided to raise funds to help them. In 1984 he organised the charity Band Aid, which on November 25 recorded a single, *Do They Know It's Christmas?*, featuring dozens of leading rock stars. It became an instant bestseller, raising £8 million. Bolstered by the record's success, Geldof conceived an even more ambitious plan – the Live Aid concerts, to be held on July 13, 1985. Musicians gave their talent free in front of capacity audiences, including the Prince and Princess of Wales. In the words of Geldof: 'We were for a few hours no longer obsessed by ourselves . . . It was so pathetically obvious that in a world of surplus, starvation is the most senseless death of all.'

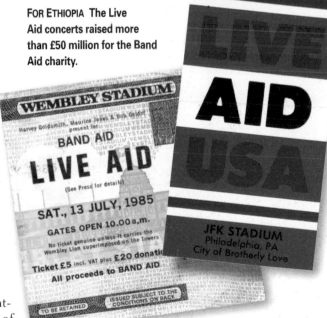

FOR ETHIOPIA The Live Aid concerts raised more than £50 million for the Band Aid charity.

suffering of famine victims. Images of starving children with bloated stomachs and wasted limbs broadcast live from Ethiopia forced the West to help. Pop stars and thousands of ordinary people united in charitable fund-raising events to achieve unprecedented levels of public support for international victims of famine and disease.

Foreign aid poured into Ethiopia in 1984 and 1985, but much of it was prevented from reaching the famine victims by mismanagement and the refusal of the Ethiopian government to accept that a state of famine existed in the first place. Indeed, much of the foreign relief was spirited away and sold for personal profit by government officials, while their people starved. It was proof that the problem of feeding the world is not limited to production, as the British nutritionist John Boyd Orr had pointed out as early as 1947. The experience of the 20th century suggests that we are capable of producing more than enough food to feed everyone in

MAKESHIFT RELIEF Korem relief camp gave tented shelter to tens of thousands of Ethiopians. Butter oil was one of the high-energy, low-bulk foods distributed to refugees (right).

the world. It is the problem of distribution rather than production that has bedevilled so many international attempts to solve the scourge of famine.

One – controversial – way of dealing with famine is to control the number of births. Many authors, now mostly regarded as false prophets of doom, have predicted excessive population growth and mass starvation by the end of the 20th century because of spiralling population levels and inadequate

LORD BOYD ORR'S FOOD FOR ALL

John Boyd Orr (1880-1971) was one of the 20th century's greatest nutritionists, the man who spurred a generation into action against the horrors of famine. He was born in Ayrshire in Scotland and gained an insight into the problems of malnutrition at the turn of the century when he was a trainee teacher in Glasgow. Although little more than a young man intent on enjoying a Saturday night frolic, his experiences of the Glasgow slums led him to the utopian thought that world governments could eliminate famine and disease if they took an active role in the production and distribution of food.

Quitting the teaching profession, he became a nutritionist. When the United Nations Food and Agriculture Organization (FAO) was set up in 1945, he was given the job of heading it. He wanted to establish a comprehensive food plan, which would not only see a constant redistribution of food from the developed to the developing nations, but would also assist in the spread of modern agricultural methods across the world. In 1947 Britain and the USA rejected his plans for a World Food Board, but Boyd Orr was already paving the way for the Green Revolution of the 1960s. He was one of the first international figures to draw attention to the problem of famine and to suggest ways for governments, working together, to abolish it. In 1949 Lord Boyd Orr, as he now was, received the Nobel peace prize.

BOYD ORR'S WISDOM Boyd Orr called on leading agriculturalists to control pests, which destroy 10 per cent of the world's food supply.

food production. The 18th-century father of this 'catastrophist' school was the English economist Thomas Malthus who in 1798 published the cumbersomely titled *An Essay on the Principle of Population, as it Affects the Future Improvement of Society.* For Malthus, mass starvation was inevitable: 'The power of population is indefinitely greater than the power of the Earth to produce subsistence for man.'

Controlling births

In the 20th century, his successors have convinced many governments to consider the introduction of birth control. One of the most eminent of these experts is the biologist Paul Ehrlich of Stanford University in California, who reinterpreted the Malthusian doctrine in response to the population explosion of the 1960s. His book, *The Population Bomb* (1969), warned that people would starve in their hundreds of millions if the population continued to expand at the rate of 2.2 per cent every year while agricultural growth remained static. Ehrlich's logic was in many ways sound, but ignored the possibility of technological advances.

In the late 1960s and throughout the 1970s, an agricultural revolution took place:

the 'Green Revolution'. It was the result of an effort to introduce scientific advances into agriculture in order to boost food production, particularly among the developing nations. Initial research into superior crop strains had been conducted by the Rockefeller Foundation as early as the 1940s. In 1941, researchers managed to produce mutations in crops such as wheat and maize by exposing them to X-rays. Although crude, these experiments paved the way for a revolution which by the 1960s would allow scientists to customise crops for specific areas. They chose plant strains that seemed to offer superior qualities and then crossbred

them with other strains to create high-yield crops. By the mid 1970s grain production levels worldwide were increasing by 3 per cent a year, far outstripping population growth. Yet these encouraging statistics took a long time to make any impact on the world's politicians. Ehrlich's Malthusian doctrine continued to influence international policy for decades.

After 1974, when the first World Population Conference (sponsored by the United Nations) was held in Bucharest, many governments adopted a policy of actively encouraging lower birth rates. India, for example, instigated a mass contraception and sterilisation programme in 1975 – despite strong cultural and religious resistance to the notion of birth control. In fact, evidence from India – with 950 million people, the world's second most populous nation – suggests that literacy is a far more effective measure. At present, only a third of all Indian women are literate. Yet in areas where literacy levels are at their highest – such as the communist-ruled state of Kerala in the south, where 90 per cent of women can read – birth rates have stopped escalating. Around 65 per cent of women in Kerala use birth-control methods; the average for the rest of India is around 40 per cent.

Karan Singh, India's delegate to the 1974 World Population Conference, stated the position clearly: 'Development is the best

MOBILE PROPAGANDA An elephant carries the family planning message down India's west coast. The government used familiar cultural emblems to lend weight to its campaign.

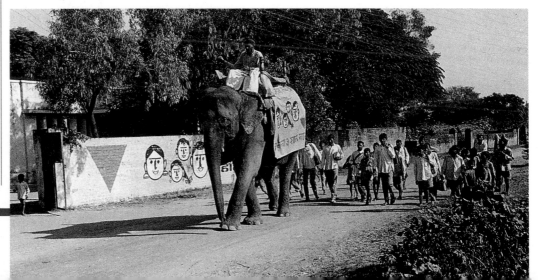

A TRAIL OF FIRES: 1997

In the summer and autumn of 1997, fires, lit to clear land in the rain forests of Indonesia, covered South-east Asia in ground-level clouds of smoke. Burning back the forest is an age-old practice, but in 1997 the fires raged out of control because of a prolonged drought, attributed to the effects of El Niño, a seasonal ocean current off the coast of Peru. In a complicated chain of cause and effect, the current can alter global weather patterns. In 1997 it caused drought in Australia, resulting in a ring of bush fires around Sydney, while across North America and Europe it resulted in higher than average rainfall. The monsoon rains finally arrived over South-east Asia in November, dousing the fires and washing smoke from the atmosphere. Victims will probably suffer from long-term health effects, particularly bronchial problems.

LOSING BATTLE This fireman came from Malaysia to help the Indonesians try to control their fires.

introduction of intensive farming methods. As a result, the world's grain harvest grew 20 per cent faster than its population.

Illustrating this point was China. Under Mao Zedong, who died in 1976, it had ignored all calls to control its population growth. Mao once said: 'Another mouth to feed is another pair of hands to work.' However, memories of mass famine and disease in the 1960s – thanks largely to Mao's policies – probably fuelled the Chinese government's decision in 1979 to implement aggressive population controls. The Chinese population was edging towards a billion people when the government introduced a one-child policy: women were encouraged to give birth to only one child. Old women, often referred to as the 'Granny Police', would cajole women into having an abortion if they conceived a second child.

In the event, the birth-control tool was blunt and ineffective. Moreover, subsequent statistics have revealed that fertility rates had already fallen in China by 1979. Indeed, the biggest drop had occurred in the 1970s, from 34 live births per thousand people in 1970 to 18 per thousand in 1979. In the 1980s, by contrast – after the adoption of the one-child policy – there was a slight increase to around 21 live births per thousand. The Chinese agricultural sector, meanwhile, had improved radically – to the extent that the country was a net exporter of rice by 1979. China could feed itself; the Malthusians had been wrong.

Ecological collapse

Worldwide, however, there is no room for complacency. Scientific farming methods increased world production of food, but this growth has started to slow down – from 3 per cent per year in the 1970s to just 1 per

contraceptive.' He knew, even then, that contraception is only viable in certain contexts. If women are seen as being replaceable and men's right to have sex more or less on demand is seen as sacrosanct, women will continue to suffer from regular and often unwanted pregnancies. In these circumstances, contraceptives are unlikely to have much effect. For all that, India decided to engage in an unpopular, even ruthless, mass birth-control scheme.

A failed experiment

By 1990, it was clear worldwide that such attempts to limit population had failed – and caused great misery into the bargain. The agricultural revolution of the 1960s, on the

other hand, had achieved a far more radical and beneficial effect. Indeed, without it the prophecy of world famine outlined in Ehrlich's book might well have come true, since the global population had dramatically increased – over the 40 years from 1955, it grew by more than 100 per cent, reaching almost 6 billion people in 1995. What really saved the day were new pesticides and the

DEADLY PARTICLES A farmer in the African republic of Niger, just south of the Sahara, sprays his crops against grasshoppers. In 1986 overuse of pesticides in parts of Niger came close to destroying a season's crops.

NITRATE PROS AND CONS

Scientific farming techniques have doubled the amount of nitrogen spread on land since 1900. The first synthetic nitrates were manufactured for use in explosives during the First World War; after the war they were used as fertiliser. Later, the Green Revolution encouraged the use of artificial fertilisers, especially nitrogen. Nitrate fertilisers are nothing new. Farmers have always put organic nitrates on the soil – they are contained in animal fertilisers. In any nitrate fertiliser, organic or artificial, the active ingredient is exactly the same: NO_3. It encourages plant growth. Nitrates do, however, present problems. Overuse can lead to a decline in the fertility of arable land and the poisoning of rivers and lakes as the nitrogen is washed out of the land by rain. After nearly a century of intensive farming, nitrogen-rich fertiliser has reduced the quality and fertility of much soil around the globe. New methods of fertilisation are currently being developed.

cent in the 1990s. The Green Revolution has come to an end. With population growing by an average of 80 million people across the globe year on year, new ways have to be found of keeping food production ahead of population growth.

Experts are also increasingly aware of the drawbacks of the Green Revolution. There was, for example, the expense. The poorest farmers, who most needed to benefit from it, did not have the money to buy the pesticides and fertilisers necessary to rear the new crop varieties. Furthermore, these varieties were hybrids: their seeds were the result of crossing two strains to achieve a desired set of characteristics. To make seeds with the same traits the original strains have to be crossed time and time again. So the farmer has to buy new seeds every year, adding to the costs.

The other great cost was the environmental one, which throws doubt on the possibility of a second Green Revolution. For example, the hardy crops introduced into developing nations in order to take advantage of higher yields and easier harvesting have resulted in a decline in biodiversity. Fewer strains of plants now predominate, with indigenous crops 'crowded out' by artificially introduced alternatives. The result can be catastrophic because of vulnerability to disease – for example, in 1943 brown spot swept through the Bengalese rice fields, causing a famine in which 1.5 million people died. If a disease like this takes hold in an area, it kills all plants of a similar strain, so reduced biodiversity increases the risk of famine. If, however, there are diverse strains of rice or wheat under cultivation in the area, the diseased crop can be discarded in favour of other

disease-resistant ones. People may still go hungry, but at least some of that year's production will have survived.

No answers, only questions

Another problem is highlighted by a growing number of experts, including Ehrlich. It is our overconsumption of natural resources and the resulting damage to our environment and global climate. Scientists argue that we must find a way of maintaining growth in both agriculture and industry without increasing the damage already inflicted on our environment.

One bright spot was pointed out by the US space agency NASA as part of its long-running programme, Mission to Planet Earth. In 1997, it revealed that plant growth in northern latitudes had increased by 10 per cent during the 1980s. This suggests that nature has responded to the higher levels of carbon dioxide in our atmosphere, growing more plants to absorb the gas and replenish oxygen supplies – trees 'breathe' carbon dioxide and 'exhale' oxygen. It is one example of the resilience of nature, and although this does not absolve us from our responsibility for the environment, it does suggest that the ecological collapse predicted by some experts is not inevitable. Given increased vigilance by humankind, the Earth can almost certainly continue to provide for us.

ENCOURAGING CHANGE
Modern scientific techniques include micropropagation, in which plants are grown in sterile jelly in test tubes. Right: In Nepal children take part in an educational tree-planting scheme.

HABITATS UNDER THREAT

AS HUMAN POPULATIONS SPREAD, SO NATURAL HABITATS AND THEIR SPECIES COME UNDER THREAT OF EXTINCTION

Writing in 1933, the historian of the Sioux people of North America, Luther Standing Bear, gave an eloquent description of his nation's traditional relationship with the natural environment: 'We did not think of the great open plains, the beautiful rolling hills, and the winding streams with tangled growth, as "wild". Only to the white man was nature a "wilderness" and only to him was the land infested with "wild" animals and "savage" people. To us it was tame. Earth was bountiful and we were surrounded with the blessings of the Great Mystery.'

Mankind's relationship with nature has been of growing concern during the 20th century. Already at the start of the century, some people in Western nations were worrying about the spread of industrial civilisation and the threat it posed to the survival of the Earth's 'wild places'. The first international treaty to protect an endangered animal – the northern fur seal – was signed in 1911, followed by another agreement to protect migratory water fowl in 1916. These accords were groundbreaking steps forward in international relations; the major industrialised nations, Japan and the economic powers of Europe and North America, had agreed on a matter of natural conservation. Unfortunately, these early treaties opted only to limit the effects of hunting and did not seek to address the problem of habitat loss.

A habitat is defined as a place where specific species of plant and animal live. Many of Europe's unique habitats, such as hay and water meadows, contain rare plants and animals that now have little chance of survival. Between 1900 and 1985, 80 per cent of Britain's hay meadows were ploughed up to make way for cash crop cultivation. The loss of hay meadows means an end to many breeds of butterflies and small mammals, such as field mice, which depend on these areas for survival. This situation is echoed across the world, with unique environments and their inhabitants lost for ever under the march of commercial agriculture and urban development. Time and time again, the Earth's most destructive species has proved to be *Homo sapiens* – mankind.

In Japan, for example, a rapid growth in the human population along with the expansion of cities such as Honshu and Tokyo in the decades since the Second World War has been particularly damaging. Urbanisation and an increase in demand for food resulted in the destruction of many wetland habitats. Marshlands were 'reclaimed' for agriculture, and many creatures became extinct, including the *toki* bird (Japanese crested ibis). By the 1970s the damage inflicted on these habitats was virtually irreversible. Although the Japanese government introduced strict anti-pollution guidelines, the habitats had collapsed and the population of many species had fallen below the level needed to prosper – generally accepted to be some 10 000 mature adults.

Invaders

The introduction of alien species can also throw natural habitats out of equilibrium. In Hawaii, habitats have been destroyed through logging and farming, but just as important has been the introduction of foreign mammals, such as horses, cattle and sheep, after the United States annexed the

SEALED FATE Northern fur seals on the Pribilof Islands off Alaska. In 1911 they became the first species to be protected by an international agreement.

1908 Roosevelt establishes Muir Woods, California
1911 Treaty protecting northern fur seal

1916 Treaty for conservation of migratory water fowl

1936 Su-Lin, the first panda exhibited in the West, at Brookfield Zoo, Chicago

STRIPPED BARE An invasion of gypsy moth caterpillars left many trees in this forest in the Shenandoah National Park, Virginia, almost completely leafless.

mussel, will come to threaten the majority of the USA's forest and wetland habitats by the middle of the 21st century. The gypsy moth (*Lymantria dispar*) is a native of Europe and Asia, introduced to North America in the late 1860s by Leopold Trouvelot, a Frenchman living in Boston. Trouvelot was an artist by trade, but he had become interested in trying to breed a strain of silk moth that would be resistant to disease. He imported the first gypsy moth caterpillars for his experiments, and some of them escaped, establishing themselves in the suburb where he lived. The moth did not begin to spread across the rest of the continent until the 20th century,

CHOKING THE LAKES The zebra mussel builds large colonies around river outlets, limiting the amount of free-flowing water for irrigation schemes and agriculture.

islands in 1898. Among the creatures to suffer were the Hawaiian honeycreepers.

Over the centuries honeycreepers, which are highly prized for their bright plumage, have developed a diversity of species, each living in differing habitats. Some, for example, have long thin bills which help them to obtain nectar, while others have shorter bills which make it easier to forage for insects. In the 20th century, however, eight species have passed into extinction. Researchers at the University of Texas have identified four causes for these extinctions: competition for food from ants and wasps introduced to Hawaii; the human destruction of their forest habitat; the introduction of predators such as dogs and pigs; the faster spread of disease due to their higher population density – the

honeycreepers are now living in a smaller area.

The spread of agriculture and industry across North America has wrought terrible damage to habitats. Since the start of the 20th century more than 3000 species of plant and animal have been introduced into the USA. It has been calculated that just under 100 of these species have been responsible for more than $100 billion-worth of environmental damage to habitats. The single most destructive is the boll weevil (*Anthonomus grandis*), a beetle that feeds on cotton plants and caused more than $50 billion-worth of damage between 1900 and 1950.

Scientists now predict that two arrivals from Europe, the gypsy moth and the zebra

however, when the burgeoning cities of the Midwest and West created a growing demand for wood. Gypsy moth caterpillars eat the leaves of pines and deciduous trees, and as logs were transported across North America so were the larvae. Between 1900 and 1990 the gypsy moth inflicted an estimated $100

1959 Kariba Dam
completed

1992 International treaty
to preserve biodiversity

million-worth of damage on the US forestry industry. The zebra mussel (*Dreissena polymorpha*) came much later, in 1988, expelled from the ballast water of ships. It builds large communities around flowing water, and is beginning to choke the Great Lakes, crowding out other species and preventing the flow of water to irrigation pipes.

Similar tales come from New South Wales in Australia, where foreign fish were introduced to restock rivers during the 1960s and came to dominate them within five years of their introduction. Although many indigenous species of fish still thrive in the area, at least 16 species seem to have dwindled to virtual extinction, probably victims of new disease variants for which they had no resistance. Indigenous fish such as the bony bream (*Nematalosa erebi*), the eastern mosquitofish (*Gambusia holbrooki*) and the flat-headed gudgeon (*Philypnodon grandiceps*) are now

threatened by alien 'pest' species, especially the highly adaptable common carp (*Cyprinus carpio*). The invading carp now have a population density of about one carp per yard (roughly a metre) of the Murray River. A report published in 1997 by the New South Wales Fisheries Research Institute blamed the introduction of irrigation and damming schemes, which changed the habitat so that it now favours the alien species.

MUIR'S EXAMPLE John Muir (far right) had the ear of President Theodore Roosevelt (right). Together they initiated conservation schemes, such as the Muir Woods National Monument, near San Francisco, California (below).

Ocean habitats have fared little better. Ninety-five per cent of the world's coral reefs have been damaged since 1900. There have been several causes, including the build-up of sediment washed into the reefs due to logging and farming inland, pollution from sewage and fertilisers (again washed into the reefs from inland) and pollution by petrol and chemicals from boats. Another factor has been the practice of 'explosive fishing' – literally explosive, since fishermen use dynamite to kill fish and then bring them to the

THICK BLANKET Without regular fires, the forest floor becomes smothered with debris, impeding seed germination.

surface. Tourists collecting coral for souvenirs have also inflicted significant damage.

The reefs of the Indian and Pacific oceans have been worst affected. Since 1900 Asia's human population has risen by an average of 2 per cent a year. This has led to a corresponding increase in demand for the more accessible reef-dwelling fish, and in the amount of pollutants pumped into the sea. Although sea-floor pollution has been brought under better control in recent years, global warming now poses a new threat.

Taking the initiative

The dangers of the mass disruption to Earth's natural habitats were recognised by several key figures at the beginning of the 20th century. Among the most influential was Theodore Roosevelt, US president from 1901 to 1909, who had a passion for the wilderness and believed strongly in the need to preserve it. (In his case, as in many others at the time, a concern for natural habitats went hand in hand with a love of hunting.)

In 1903 Roosevelt established one of the world's first major wildlife refuges when he decreed that a large tract of land on Pelican

NATURE'S BALANCING ACT Great steps have been taken in the 20th century to preserve wildernesses such as those of the American West. But mankind can be overprotective. Forest fires, for example, are often an essential part of nature's system of checks and balances.

NATURE RETALIATES

The natural habitat of North America's indigenous pollinating insects was stolen long ago by the *Apis mellifera* (honeybee), introduced by European colonisers. Today, nature is fighting to reclaim the habitat for native species as the honeybee comes under attack from the deadly varroa mite. These microscopic creatures reduced North American colonies of man's most compliant pollinator from a high of 6 million in 1940 to less than 3 million in 1996 – the mites have now also made their way to the British Isles.

The honeybee is kept by farmers in carefully managed hives and used to pollinate crops, such as apples, which are collectively worth at least $9 billion a year to the US economy. Since the varroa infestation started to make itself felt in the 1980s, farmers have tried to limit its spread using pesticides, though fears about environmental damage and consumer preference for organically grown crops mean that pesticides are now a less attractive option. To make matters worse a disease known as 'foulbrood' is also rife in the North American honeybee population and can only be treated with a course of antibiotics. Selective breeding experiments may yet result in an 'Apis superior' which would be resistant to attacks from both the varroa mite and foulbrood.

ALIEN INTERLOPER North American populations of the honeybee have been devastated by the varroa mite.

Island, Florida, should be set aside for brown pelicans, an endangered species. He encountered opposition, but carried on with this and similar schemes all the same. In 1908 he set up a more ambitious reserve, this time on the west coast: Muir Woods National Monument, north-west of San Francisco. Covering more than 500 acres (200 ha), this includes ancient redwood trees, some of which may be more than 1000 years old. Roosevelt named the reserve after one of his greatest friends, the Scots-born pioneer conservationist John Muir, who had spent his adult life touring America, studying habitats and the diversity of life they harboured. Muir particularly loved the Yosemite Valley, California, and it was partly as a result of his lobbying that the US government had established it as a

LITTLE AND OFTEN Frequent fires pass rapidly across the floor. Inset: Rare fires will explode destructively up the tree trunk.

LIFE-GIVING FIRE In the ponderosa pine forests of the US West, regular fires – every 5-25 years – clear the undergrowth without killing the trees. Inset: If the undergrowth grows up too much, fire will burn too strongly and kill the trees.

❝ LUCKY'S FOOT

Paul F. Salopek, an American writer and conservationist, spent several weeks in the spring of 1994 roaming the Virunga National Park in Zaire. There he met a ranger named Kambale who had found a three-year-old male gorilla, whose foot had become infected in a hunter's snare:

'The injured gorilla eyes us warily and limps off, trailing the frayed, snapped end of the wire behind. We follow. As the trackers begin circling, holding their old army coats out like matadors, I notice a shadow, very big and very still, in a nearby bamboo thicket.

' "Silverback," I hiss to Kambale, who pauses, his own coat already shrugged half off. "Le grand chef," he mutters, squinting through the feathery bamboo.

'It's the big chief all right, an ape named Ndungutse – or "benefits", as in ecotourism dollars – that dominates this local band of 30 gorillas. At about 400 pounds [180 kg], Ndungutse has a head as big as a bull's and a back the size of a door. The stricken youngster had been keeping close to the burly patriarch the whole time.

'In the end – to my enormous relief and the trackers' clear disappointment – Kambale calls off the rescue. We slip and skid down the mountain to Bukima village, where Kambale radios for help at the ranger station.

'Weeks later I hear that a veterinarian based in Rwanda has darted the youngster, saved his foot, and christened him Bahati – Swahili for "luck".' ❞

national park in 1890. He also founded one of the world's first conservationist organisations, the Sierra Club, in 1892. By the early 20th century, this had established itself as an influential body – thanks in part to Theodore Roosevelt's support.

Another leading conservationist of the early 20th century was Aldo Leopold, a US parks ranger who became a pioneering advocate of sustainable exploitation. Leopold had a pragmatic approach to environmental protection. His belief was founded in what he called the 'land ethic', which required people to use and exploit the land but not to damage it. He realised that human population would continue to increase, but saw no harm in this, feeling that the Earth was ours to use. He was also aware, however, that we share the land with billions of other creatures and live in a community together. Leopold was appointed an early advisor to the United Nations on matters of conservation. Although he died before his views received widespread international support, his book, *A Sand County Almanac* (published in 1949, a year after his death), did eventually inspire another generation and help to bring about the changes he desired.

Protection and regrowth

A number of organisations have been monitoring habitat loss since 1900. Many of them were established in the 19th century – such as the United States' Bureau of Biological Survey, set up in 1885. Most, however, came into their own only in the 1940s when the pace of habitat destruction increased. They compile catalogues of 'endangered' plant and

MONITORING BIODIVERSITY Biologists regularly monitor the health of specific species. Here a biologist in Canada's Yukon Delta checks the nest of a brent goose.

animal species. Notable among these bodies is the International Union for Conservation of Nature and Natural Resources (IUCN), based in Switzerland. It compiles a definitive list of endangered species and publishes its findings annually in the *Red Data Books*. Sadly, the list grows longer every year, mirroring the dwindling population of Earth's rarest habitats.

A true breakthrough was achieved in 1972 when 91 governments agreed to end the dumping of toxic chemicals into the seas. This achievement was followed by an even more impressive agreement in 1973, when 80 of the world's leading nations signed a guarantee to protect all animal species listed as endangered in the *Red Data Books*. Although there have been some contentions among the signatories, with a few developing nations accused of mismanagement and lax policing, the agreement has been remarkably

TURTLE REFUGE The green sea turtle has lived on Earth for more than 130 million years. Now, although protected by an international convention, it is an endangered species, thanks to human demand for turtle soup, turtle oil in cosmetics and turtle-skin leather.

PANDAS IN PERIL

THE GIANT PANDA, SO POPULAR IN ZOOS, IS COMING UNDER THREAT IN ITS CHINESE HOMELAND AS BAMBOO FORESTS ARE CLEARED FOR FARMING

The moist temperate bamboo forests which cover the mountains of central China are getting smaller every year, due to overlogging and clearance for farming. In the process, the giant panda (*Ailuropoda melanoleuca*) is losing its only habitat. First observed by Europeans in 1913-15 during an expedition led by the German Walther Stötzner, the giant panda stands 4½ft (1.5 m) tall and weighs 220-330 lb (100-150 kg). Some experts place it in the bear family, others among the raccoons. The familiar black and white markings and humorous antics, frequently displayed in captivity, have led to the giant panda being embraced as an international symbol for animal conservation.

It is particularly vulnerable to human destruction of its natural habitat. Bamboo, which constitutes both a living environment and a food source for the panda, is highly marketable and has been harvested for export throughout the 19th and 20th centuries. The giant panda must consume approximately 44 lb (20 kg) of bamboo leaves a day to garner enough calories to stay alive. As a result, the loss of bamboo stocks can be life threatening. Furthermore, for a long time land cleared of bamboo was generally used for agriculture, making inroads into the giant panda's home as well as its diet.

SAFE FOR NOW A giant panda in the Wolong Panda Preserve, Sichuan. The Chinese government has established reserves in areas where giant pandas live. The Wolong reserve also has a panda breeding centre.

Giant pandas mate only once a year, between March and May, and usually give birth to no more than two young. A panda can take six years to reach sexual maturity and so the species cannot rapidly repopulate after periods of decline. The combination of a dwindling habitat and the giant panda's protracted and limited reproductive cycle is a near-fatal one. It makes it unlikely that a species already reduced to a population of less than 1000 will survive without some kind of dramatic intervention.

In the 1960s the Chinese government recognised the danger of losing one of its most beloved species, and established 12 reserves for giant pandas in the mountain forests of Sichuan province. Any poachers caught with panda hides were severely punished. At the same time, the government established innovative breeding centres through which they are trying to repopulate the species. So far attempts have met with little success, largely because of the limited period during which pandas are fertile and because of the lack of diverse genetic stock from which to select mates.

Long-term hopes are placed in the use of cloning technology. If cloning does provide an answer, the 100 giant pandas currently in captivity around the world may act as surrogate mothers for cloned offspring created in the laboratory. Many scientists have advocated a giant panda gene bank, in which a collection of panda genetic material would be frozen, stored and used at a later date to re-establish the dwindling wild community of this unusual creature.

effective over three decades. Many wildlife preserves have been established, or enlarged, around the world, and the future of many species has been made much safer.

Other organisations have sought to protect the world's natural habitats. In the 1980s, the European Union devised a system for Co-ordinating Information on the Environment (CORINE). This was a response to growing concern about the loss of hedgerows on farms and the reduction of wildlands due to the explosion of road-building schemes.

Eco-warriors in action

Forests, woods and wetlands are under threat in the West and East alike. In Britain, the building of an 8 mile (13 km) bypass around the town of Newbury triggered fierce opposition from late 1995 on-wards. Opponents pointed out that the proposed route would cross areas of archaeological and ecological importance, including three government-designated Sites of Special Scientific Interest – a heath-land and two rivers. The protesters eventually built encampments in the tree canopies, creating mini-communities and acting as human barriers in an effort to prevent the trees from being felled; some even chained themselves to the trees. The 'eco-warriors' secured many delays and much publicity, and claim to have cost the developers and government more than £15 million

WAGING TREETOP 'ECO-WAR' Protesters against the Newbury bypass in Britain built elaborate communities in the treetop canopies of the Newbury Forest.

for policing and security. In 1996 the British government agreed to consider the long-term impact of the car on the environment, but refused to cancel the Newbury bypass.

One of the most important wetland habitats in the world is the Okavango Delta in Botswana. This 3860 sq mile (10 000 km²) swamp, fed by the Kavango river, is now endangered by pollution as more and more of it is drained for irrigation and domestic water supplies. Part of the Kavango river flows through neighbouring Namibia, and in 1996 the Namibian government announced plans to redirect 710 million cu ft (20 million m³) of water from the river to residential and agricultural areas. Many environmentalists feared that the pipeline would destroy the Okavango Delta. On the other hand, the

THE KARIBA DAM

The Kariba Dam (completed in 1959) was a breakthrough in hydro-electric power production for Zimbabwe and Zambia. But the artificial lake created behind the dam destroyed thousands of acres of habitat and killed untold numbers of animals. Built across the Kariba Gorge on the border between Zimbabwe and Zambia, the dam lies about 240 miles (390 km) downstream from the world's widest waterfall, the Victoria Falls. It provides cheap electricity for both countries, including 99 per cent of all Zambia's electricity. Power from the hydroelectric plant made a sig-

TAKING SHAPE Construction work on the Kariba Dam in 1958. The dam is still one of the largest in the world, providing hydroelectric energy to Zimbabwe and Zambia.

nificant contribution to the development and mechanisation of the copper-mining industry in Zambia.

As the newly created Lake Kariba took shape, however, the world media focused on the plight of the animals for which the gorge was their home. Millions died despite the efforts of park rangers to rescue them from the encroaching flood. Funds were raised by volunteers in Europe in an effort to support the work of the rangers, but they failed to achieve much. There has been one benefit, however. As well as the dam providing cheap electricity, Lake Kariba is now an important fishery for the local community.

Namibian people were desperately short of fresh water. There were protests from Botswana, where people saw the pipeline proposal as a threat to a common environment; those protesting included tour operators who value the Okavango wetland as a lucrative tourist draw. The swamp's origins as a prehistoric lake and its diversity of wildlife – including the vicious tigerfish, a voracious carnivore with knife-like teeth – give it a special environmental importance. But the needs of the Namibian people are important, too. After good rains in 1997, Namibia announced that it no longer regarded the pipeline as a 'crisis project', but it still intended to carry on with it, aiming to complete the scheme by 2003.

In Siberia, the region of Lake Baikal has one of Asia's most beautiful wetland

ANCIENT WETLAND Many local people, like the fisherman on the right, depend on the fish in Botswana's Okavango Delta (left), now threatened by a scheme to pipe water from the Kavango river.

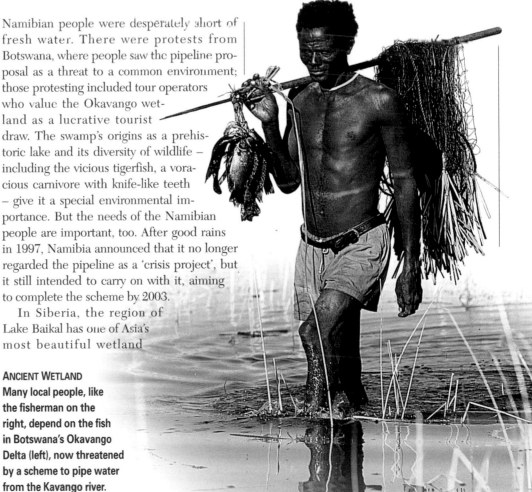

INDUSTRIAL POISON The Baikalski paper mill (right) on the south side of Lake Baikal (far right). Baikal Watch, an environmental group, intends to lobby for the long-term protection of the Baikal Wetland Habitat before irreparable damage is done.

sites, but this is threatened by industrial pollution. Fed by more than 300 rivers, Lake Baikal is drained by just one, the Lower Angara. As a result, it has accumulated the largest body of fresh water in the world, approximately one-fifth of the planet's freshwater reserves. The lake influences the weather patterns of the surrounding region, moderating the climate in much the same way that the sea moderates the climate of coastal regions. Baikal's plant and animal life include the sturgeon fish and the world's only freshwater seal.

In 1995 the environmental group Earth Island launched Baikal Watch to protect the lake and lobby for better conservation of its habitat. The group is particularly keen to see it registered with the United Nations as a World Heritage Site. Unfortunately for the environmentalists, 96 per cent of Russia's uranium reserves are located around Lake Baikal; there are also important gold reserves. Waste from the uranium mines has percolated into the water table, poisoning the lake with radioactive deposits. Similarly, paper-producing plants flood the lake's feeder rivers with pollutants. Baikal Watch hope for a closer collaboration between Western corporations and the Russian authorities on the future extraction of gold and uranium. This could lead to investment in new mining

WORKING TOGETHER

The 1992 UN Earth Summit in Rio de Janeiro saw the largest gathering of world leaders this century, meeting to establish principles that would guide economic growth and environmental policy. The Treaty for Biodiversity, first drafted in 1990, was finally ratified by 153 nations, though the United States was not one of them. It abstained on the grounds that the treaty enforced an unworkable limitation upon US industries and agriculture. Even among the countries that did sign, negotiations were often heated. The developing nations argued that they should be allowed to benefit more from the exploitation of natural resources in their territories. This included chemicals and genetic material extracted from plants and animals, including humans. Developing nations believed that the country of origin should share in the income generated. Similarly, they argued that if the industrialised nations wished to protect biodiversity and prevent species loss in the Third World, they should transfer important technology to the poorer nations in order to redress the balance between them and the richer countries. This would reduce high levels of pollution and loss of habitat in poor countries.

TREE OF LIFE Sculptor Peter Avery designed the 'Tree of Life' for the Rio de Janeiro Earth Summit in 1992.

technologies and environmental measures to clean up the entire habitat.

In the last 25 years there has been growing opposition to the destruction or damaging of natural habitats for the sake of commercial gain. Other activities, too, such as hunting, have become less environmentally respectable. Environmentalists are now less likely to be hunters than they were at the start of the 20th century; those fascinated by wildlife prefer to fire off frames of film rather than bullets. Zoos, by contrast, have become much more respectable than they were long considered to be. Once regarded as animal

prisons and criticised for encouraging the trade in exotic creatures and removing them from their natural environments, zoos now act as biological preserves and may give some species their only hope of survival. They may offer geneticists a way of restocking depleted natural habitats with indigenous species.

Sustainable development

At the UN Conference on the Environment and Development, held at Rio de Janeiro in 1992, most countries of the world signed an agreement in which they committed themselves to environmentally friendly economic growth, or 'sustainable development'. This would have been familiar to Aldo Leopold, for the idea that the environment can be replenished while also being exploited owes much to his vision. It is now being implemented around the world. During the course of the 20th century, many of the Earth's natural habitats have been irrevocably eroded by mankind. Fortunately, it seems that we are beginning to learn from our mistakes, and starting to pay as much attention to replenishment as to exploitation.

SAVING THE FISH Large aquaria, such as the Chattanooga Fish Aquarium in Tennessee provide refuge for some of the world's most exotic and endangered fish species.

GLOBAL SHOCK

TWO VERY DIFFERENT ENVIRONMENTS, THE TROPICAL RAIN FORESTS AND ANTARCTICA, HAVE COME UNDER INCREASING THREAT

Since the dawn of history people have sought out exploitable resources, and they have frequently inflicted damage on their environment in the process. In the 20th century, this quest has left its mark on a new and unprecedented scale, in particular on two of the Earth's great wildernesses, Antarctica and the rain forests.

Antarctica, the least-known continent on the planet, has attracted explorers and industrialists alike. Blanketed with ice, with ambient temperatures of –30°C (–22°F) and 30 knot (55 km/h) winds, this icy wasteland could hold a key to the future stability of our climate. It helps to regulate the planet's weather system, influencing levels of precipitation around the globe and playing a vital role in temperature regulation; it does this by contributing to the Earth's ability to reflect heat energy back into space.

The tropical and temperate rain forests of Central and South America, Africa and Southeast Asia operate like vast reverse lungs, transforming carbon dioxide into oxygen. They are vital for maintaining our atmosphere, yet between 1900 and 1990 almost 50 per cent of the world's rain forests were destroyed by the logging and mining industries or in order to open up land for grazing or growing cash crops. How long the Earth's environmental patterns can continue unchanged while deforestation carries on is unknown. Once the planet's rain forests fall below a certain minimum mass – we do not yet know where this minimum lies – our climate and atmospheric patterns may be irrevocably changed.

Forest rubber boom

As biological science has developed over the century, so has our appreciation of the importance, both environmental and economic, of the flora and fauna of the rain forests. The economic emphasis has shifted from one group of plants – those producing rubber – to a much wider spectrum, as pharmaceutical companies have come to see the rain forests as a source of new wonder drugs.

Many tropical plants exude the white latex that contains rubber. Of these, by far the most productive is the *Hevea brasiliensis*, native to Brazil. In 1839 the US inventor Charles Goodyear discovered the technique of vulcanisation, a way of heating rubber with sulphur to make it stronger and more elastic. After that, rubber established itself as a new wonder material, used in waterproof garments, in machinery and, increasingly, in tyres. By 1900 it was a valuable commodity.

For a long time the Brazilian government imposed limitations on the

FOREST DIVERSITY
The Amazon rain forest (left) is home to millions of species of plant and animal. A worker on a Burmese plantation around 1900 cutting grooves into a rubber tree to drain the latex.

1906 Brazil rubber exports near their peak at 11 500 tons

1911 Amundsen reaches South Pole

1928 Byrd becomes first man to fly over South Pole

rubber trade, ensuring an effective monopoly. But in 1876 an Englishman, Sir Henry Wickham, brought some seeds of *Hevea brasiliensis* from the rain forests of Brazil to Kew Gardens in London. From there seeds were taken to Sri Lanka and Malaysia (both then British colonies), where substantial areas of rain forest were destroyed to make way for rubber plantations. Today, 90 per cent of the world's natural rubber is produced in Asia from plants descended from the trees first propagated using Wickham's seeds.

Despite competition from Asia, Brazil at the start of the century was still prospering from its rubber exports, which by 1906 had reached 11 500 tons a year. But such high levels of supply were not met by corresponding levels of demand. The world market had become saturated, and the motor car – today, by far the largest user of rubber, consuming 70 per cent of world production – was still in its infancy. Prices plummeted, ruining rubber businesses around the globe and throwing plantation workers out of work. By 1912 capital investment into both Asia and Brazil began to dry up. Brazil defaulted on its national debt and the threat of a war in Europe did not bode well for Latin America. Consequently Brazil turned to other industries – logging and agriculture, in particular – in an effort to redress the balance. The best-known rain forest product had lost much of its importance.

Undiscovered treasures

Today, the world's rain forests are still largely unknown to science. They harbour an estimated 30 million species of animals and plants – half of all living organisms on Earth. They cover 6 per cent of the Earth's surface and make up 50 per cent of all growing wood. But this diversity is threatened by the seemingly remorseless process of deforestation.

Between 1979 and 1990, loggers alone were consuming the Amazonian rain forests at a rate of 5.4 million acres (2.2 million ha) a year. The decline in the Brazilian forests' human population has also been dramatic. It is estimated that between

NATURAL CURES Over countless generations, the indigenous peoples of the rain forests have built up an encyclopedic knowledge of the forest plants and their special properties. Here, a Brazilian market seller offers some of the healing riches of the Amazon Basin.

6 and 9 million indigenous people inhabited them in 1500; by 1900 only 1 million lived there, and in 1997 fewer than 200 000 Indians still lived in their dwindling habitat. Western diseases and social attitudes and impinging industry have all played their parts in decimating the forest peoples.

But the forests and their peoples have acquired a new importance in the eyes of outsiders. Aware of the rapid deforestation, leading pharmaceutical companies are currently engaged in a race to exploit the rain forests' flora and fauna. They are keen to expose and patent any useful agents concealed in the lush vegetation before it is totally destroyed. This activity, known as bioprospecting, is particularly active in the Amazon region. Amazonian Indians have

1950   2000

1959 Antarctic Treaty

1985 British scientists discover thinning of ozone layer
1987 Montreal Protocol

1994 Antarctic Ocean designated whale sanctuary

1997 Kyoto summit

long practised their own forms of medicine, deriving all their drugs from natural sources within the forest. Now, in an era when bacterial diseases are evolving resistance to antibiotics, Amazonian medicines are seen as a hopeful source for future drugs.

In 1995 the US government mounted a research programme. Administered by the National Institute of Health, this programme aims to rationalise bioprospecting, dividing areas of the rain forest among scientists while seeking to remunerate the indigenous peoples. It is too early to judge the programme as a success or failure, though many ecologists protest that the Amazonian Indians are being exploited and the forests plundered, while deforestation carries on unabated.

Plugging the hole

Antarctica is also changing rapidly as ice fields hundreds of thousands of years old melt and collapse into the sea. Mankind's attitude towards Antarctica has changed during the

EXTINCTION RATE

In the next 60 minutes six species found only in rain forests will become extinct and 9000 acres (3640 ha) of forest will be destroyed. Although deforestation is now managed in the Amazon, an area the size of Wales is still lost every year. Ecologists call for incentives to encourage industrialising nations to develop industries that make sustainable use of the tropical rain forests.

20th century. In 1900 people tended to see it as a mysterious unexplored continent, a setting for heroic feats performed by daring individuals – men such as Captain Robert Falcon Scott and Ernest Shackleton from Britain, the Norwegian Roald Amundsen and, later, the American, Admiral Richard E. Byrd. Today, experts view it as one of the most important environments on Earth. It provides an accurate measure of global climate change, while also holding the power to flood much of Earth's landmass beneath several feet of water.

In 1958, an international body of scientists, the Special Committee on Antarctic

GONE UP IN SMOKE Rain forest is often burned in Brazil to make way for short-term beef production. The land quickly becomes infertile, and the rancher then moves on to find further grazing, clearing even more forest in the process.

THREATENING THE BAHINEMOS

Logging threatens not only the world's rain forests but also the traditions of the peoples who live in them. Edie Bakker, the daughter of American missionary parents, grew up in the 1960s and 70s in a remote rain-forest region around Lake Wagu, north of Papua New Guinea's Hunstein Mountains. It is the home of the Bahinemos people. In 1993, Bakker returned:

'What brought me back to Wagu was a crisis – the Hunstein is on the verge of being logged. Some of the world's major rain forests are in Papua New Guinea. I had heard about clear-cutting in the coastal province of Madang, and the thought of such destruction in the Hunstein was intolerable . . .

'I worried that foreign logging companies would not tell the Bahinemos the truth about what logging would do to their forest, still crucial to their livelihood and culture. And did the isolated Bahinemos understand what their treasure means to the world? . . .

'I arrived in Wagu . . . but first I wanted to be reacquainted with the village and with the joy of walking the forest barefoot. This doesn't require tough feet, only an intimate knowledge of the terrain. There are dangers – nests of stinging ants and hornets, death adders, thorny vines – but once you know how to avoid them, you are free to concentrate on the unexpected patterns and colours in this world that at first glance seems only green. Plate-sized leaves of mottled orange and yellow drift from the canopy like jumbo confetti, clouds of butterflies flash iridescent purples and blues, liana vines dangle clusters of scarlet flowers 10, even 15 feet [3/4.6 m] long. The stillness is tangible – holy. To walk here is to feel the very pulse of creation. . . .

'When I first met the Bahinemos in 1964, they lived in eight villages scattered throughout their 600-square-mile [1550 km²] territory. They were recent settlements, each consisting of palm shelters . . . Traditionally, groups of three or four families had moved through the Hunstein from camp to camp, hunting wild pigs and flightless cassowaries with bows strung with bamboo fibres and gathering fruits, nuts, and the staple of their diet – starchy pulp of the sago palm . . . As I walked about Wagu, it seemed that little had changed. It was uncanny to follow the same mud path edged with hibiscus and mango trees, to touch the palm-wood walls of our old house, and to pour a cup of water from the same kerosene refrigerator. In other ways much had changed. Most people were wearing Western clothing . . . Members of my peer group looked too old to be in their early 30s . . . Logging is what I quickly began hearing about.

' "Don't be concerned about your rain forest," visiting forestry officials had told the Bahinemos. "We can always replant whatever is cut down. Our lawyers can help you write your contract so you will gain as much money as possible."

'A woman named Moyali Yalfei, about 45 years old and the widow of the head of the largest landholding clan, told me she thought she had to agree to logging. "The forestry department said they wanted it, so I'll have to give it to them, won't I?" '

Research (SCAR), was established. Then, in 1959, the United Nations brokered the Antarctic Treaty. This banned mining, military operations, the deployment of nuclear weapons and the disposal of nuclear waste on the continent. It was the first agreement of its kind, made at the height of the Cold War and involving both the Soviet Union and the United States. Nations including Argentina, Australia, New Zealand, Britain and France as well as the USA and the USSR agreed to limit work on Antarctica to scientific research. The treaty was successful, and Antarctica has remained free of industry and international territorial rivalry since then, though its seas continued to be targeted by the fishing and whaling industries.

In 1985, researchers at the British Antarctic Survey discovered an anomaly high in the atmosphere above the South Pole: a thinning in the ozone layer. This is a layer of the outer atmosphere, approximately 15 miles (25 km) above the surface of the Earth, that is rich in a type of oxygen molecule known as ozone. Ultraviolet light, part of the visible spectrum of the Sun's radiated energy, is absorbed by ozone and consequently the ozone layer prevents most ultraviolet radiation from reaching the planet's surface. Ultraviolet radiation is not dangerous in low doses – it is the radiation responsible for tanning our skins. But the Sun generates far more ultraviolet radiation than animal and vegetable life can safely absorb. The ozone layer protects us from this dangerous excess.

Using high-altitude radiosonde balloons and monitoring equipment, the scientists observed that there was a dramatic reduction in the concentration of ozone molecules every year during the Antarctic spring. The

PRECIOUS TIMBER Where logging is selective, as here in Malaysia (above), little or no long-term damage is done to the forest.

LOGGING SCARS 'Clear-cutting', as here in Papua New Guinea (below), involves the systematic destruction of vast areas of forest.

world's scientific community voiced its concern in rare harmony. Working with data provided by the Antarctic scientists, pressure groups such as Greenpeace lobbied governments to fund further research.

As early as the 1970s, scientists had warned of the dangers of ozone-destroying chemicals known as chlorofluorocarbons (CFCs). Derived from oil and other sources of hydrocarbons such as coal, CFCs were used as coolants in refrigerators and air-conditioning systems, in aerosol propellants and in plastic packaging. The USA was already starting to phase out CFCs in the 1970s. By the mid 1980s research strongly confirmed the wisdom

AHEAD OF HIS TIME

In 1896, a Swedish chemist and future Nobel prize-winner, Svante Arrhenius, predicted the effects of concentrated carbon dioxide on the temperature of the Earth. In an article published in the *Philosophical Magazine,* he explained that carbon dioxide was a ready absorber of infrared radiation and would act as a blanket, trapping heat within our atmosphere, thus heating the entire planet. It would be nearly 100 years before these ideas were taken seriously.

of this measure as it implicated the industrial manufacture of CFCs in ozone depletion.

By the 1990s Antarctic scientists found that the thinning was also happening in the summer months – ozone levels fall when subjected to temperature increases. Since then, the 'hole' has steadily increased in size and a lesser thinning of atmospheric ozone has been charted all over the Earth's surface.

A concerted effort to eradicate the use of CFCs has had positive results. In 1987 an international agreement, the Montreal Protocol, was reached which bound countries to stop the production of ozone-depleting chemicals by the year 2000. In the West, labels declaring that a product is CFC-free, or 'ozone friendly', are now frequently used to enhance its market appeal. Such measures are important, for if left unchecked the ozone hole may cause massive crop failure

ANTARCTIC PURSUITS British meteorologist Dr George Simpson demonstrating a balloon for measuring pressure and temperature in the upper atmosphere above Antarctica in 1911. An expert on thunderstorm electricity, he was a member of the team that went with Scott to the Antarctic, though he did not take part in the fateful expedition to the Pole.

COLD POSTING The Halley Bay Research Station (right) is staffed by members of the British Antarctic Survey. The base contributes to an international contingent known as SCAR which carries out continuous research into the Antarctic environment.

and millions of premature human deaths due to skin and other forms of cancer. Scientists predict that, even if the world abandoned all use of CFCs immediately, the ozone depletion will still take generations to correct.

Melting ice

Fears about a rise in average global temperature – global warming – are of particular concern in the Antarctic. According to many experts, global warming is triggered by the release of the gas carbon dioxide as a result of the industrial and domestic burning of fossil fuels. The gas acts as an insulator trapping the Sun's heat.

Research efforts – supervised by SCAR and staffed by organisations such as the British Antarctic Survey – seem to validate the theory of global warming. Yet, despite efforts to reduce carbon dioxide emissions – such as those proposed by the UN-sponsored Earth Summit at Rio de Janeiro in 1992 – global temperatures are

KILLING THE BEHEMOTH

Mechanised whaling was born in 1856 when a Norwegian, Svend Foyn, invented the rocket-propelled grenade-harpoon. This speeded up the process of killing whales, which with traditional harpoons could take several hours. The grenade-harpoon penetrated a whale's thick hide and detonated a grenade, rendering vital muscles useless and slowing the giant mammal down. At the turn of the century came the 200 ft (60 m), 600 ton, diesel-powered 'supercatcher'. For the first time whalers could speed past their prey – easily exceeding the blue whale's 12 knots (14 mph/22 km/h) – and lie in wait. In the Antarctic, onshore facilities improved after 1904 when Captain Carl Larsen constructed a whaling station on the British-owned island of South Georgia. The Antarctic ice was littered with hundreds of thousands of giant discarded skeletons and on occasion ran red with whale blood. By 1929 the whalers had added the aircraft to their armoury. Kosmos, a Norwegian firm, used Gypsy Moth planes to spot whales. By 1931, 31 000 fin and blue whales were being killed every year in Antarctic seas. Norway led the way with whaling legislation when it outlawed coastal whaling in 1904. But whaling quotas were not put in place until 1931, at the instigation of the League of Nations. It took another 63 years of highly aggressive whaling to convince the League's successor, the United Nations, to impose protective legislation on the Antarctic seas; Antarctica became a whale sanctuary in 1994.

DEATH OF A GIANT Workers on a Russian whaling ship in 1960 tackle a blue whale, the largest of all animals, caught in the Barents Sea.

still rising. What is more, they may continue to rise for hundreds of years. SCAR's findings suggest that mean temperatures over the Antarctic Peninsula have increased by 2.5°C (4.5°F) over the last 50 years. The British Antarctic Survey produced data in 1997 that revealed a southward spread of vegetation in the Antarctic islands over the last 25 years. Life is blooming on many of the islands for the first time in 100 000 years.

Six major ice shelves – large areas of ice that project from land into the sea – have collapsed this century. One recent example was a shelf twice as big as the English county of Norfolk – 4130 sq miles (10 700 km²) – which collapsed in January 1998. With temperatures around the Antarctic Peninsula rising five times faster than the global average, many experts feared the imminent collapse of one of Antarctica's largest semipermanent agglomerations of ice, the Larsen B Shelf. In April 1998 these fears seemed to be confirmed when satellite images revealed that an 80 sq mile (200 km²) chunk of the shelf had

broken off from the rest. Scientists estimated another two-thirds of the 4600 sq mile (12 000 km²) shelf would shortly break off, possibly with the arrival of the next Antarctic summer. If this happened, Antarctica would lose more ice in one go than during the whole of the last 50 years.

The threat is real, but there is also increasing evidence that the environmental changes witnessed since the 1960s could be a result of long-term environmental patterns, not man-made atmospheric fluctuations. This is difficult to confirm, however, because modern methods of observation have been systematically applied to the environment and climate across the globe only in the last 50 years. We have not yet developed a sufficiently long-term view of the Earth's biosphere – that part of its surface and atmosphere inhabited by living things – to be able to differentiate between man-made change and regular fluctuations in temperature taking place over thousands of years – these might represent a self-regulating mechanism in nature.

By the early 1980s El Niño – literally, 'the Christ child' – had been recognised as an unrivalled force for climate change. El Niño is essentially a large stream of warm water in the Western Hemisphere normally restrained by prevailing winds to the band close to the Equator. Sometimes, however – approximately every five years – wind patterns vary

GOLDEN SUNRISE Ice shelves spread out into the Weddell Sea which stretches for more than 300 000 sq miles (800 000 km²) east of the Antarctic Peninsula. In 1915 great blocks of ice like these trapped the ship *Endurance* in the Weddell Sea for ten months, stalling an expedition led by the British explorer Ernest Shackleton.

CRACK IN THE SYSTEM The Larsen B Ice Shelf is one of the largest masses of ice in the world. This vast crack appeared in the mid 1990s, indicating the danger of disintegration. Part of the shelf collapsed in 1998.

and allow the stream to break away towards the South Pacific, especially the coast of South America. The most recent occurrence of El Niño is among the largest and most destructive that has been recorded. It has changed weather patterns across the globe, bringing drought to Australia and South-east Asia, while torrential floods have swamped South America.

Similarly, conditions in the Atlantic can be changed by a phenomenon known as the North Atlantic Oscillation (NAO). This is a stream of water that during the winter months alters the movement of seas on the margins of the North Atlantic. Ground-breaking research by the National Center for Atmospheric Research in Boulder, Colorado, has linked long-term climate variations –

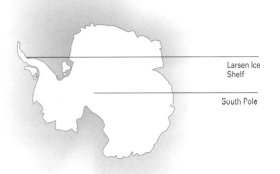

Larsen Ice Shelf

South Pole

which might be mistaken for the effects of global warming – to the NAO. Essentially, these involve a seesawing effect in temperature and pressure between different areas of the Northern Hemisphere – for example, when Denmark has a relatively warm winter, Greenland has a cold one, or when Europe has warm summers, Canada may be experiencing severe snowstorms.

By measuring changes in atmospheric pressure over Iceland and the Azores, meteorologists have been able to map the trend of the NAO over the century. They noticed that when low pressure persists over Iceland, there is a corresponding area of high pressure over the Azores. In these conditions, surface warmth from the sea is carried into Europe, producing mild winters with fierce cyclonic storms, such as the great storm which battered Britain in October 1987. The cold, harsh winters of the 1940s and 60s were probably caused by the NAO tipping in the opposite direction, with low

pressure over Europe and high pressure over the Azores starving Europe of Atlantic heat.

Who's the culprit?

The problem of separating the individual effects of the NAO, El Niño and global warming is akin to that of apportioning blame for some crimes. Evidence is muddied by the constantly changing position and activity of the suspects, while the effects of one atmospheric phenomenon may intensify the effects of another. This may be true in the case of global warming. If current spells of El Niño and NAO activity have been more damaging than before, it may be because these phenomena have been strengthened by a man-induced increase in global temperature due to carbon dioxide emissions from industry.

If the entire Antarctic ice sheet melts, the world may face its greatest catastrophe in recorded history. And some scientists believe that within the next 50 years the ice sheet may do just that – irrespective of rising global temperatures. Their theory, postulated in the late 1990s, states that Antarctica is stable and quiescent over a period of 7000 years. Snow builds up in layers, forming an ice sheet. Eventually, however, the accumulated snow begins to act like an insulator – the more snow on the surface, the greater the

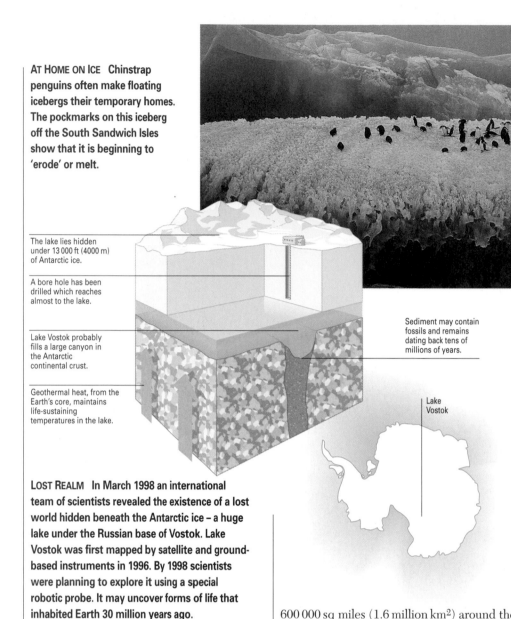

AT HOME ON ICE Chinstrap penguins often make floating icebergs their temporary homes. The pockmarks on this iceberg off the South Sandwich Isles show that it is beginning to 'erode' or melt.

The lake lies hidden under 13 000 ft (4000 m) of Antarctic ice.

A bore hole has been drilled which reaches almost to the lake.

Lake Vostok probably fills a large canyon in the Antarctic continental crust.

Geothermal heat, from the Earth's core, maintains life-sustaining temperatures in the lake.

Sediment may contain fossils and remains dating back tens of millions of years.

Lake Vostok

LOST REALM In March 1998 an international team of scientists revealed the existence of a lost world hidden beneath the Antarctic ice – a huge lake under the Russian base of Vostok. Lake Vostok was first mapped by satellite and ground-based instruments in 1996. By 1998 scientists were planning to explore it using a special robotic probe. It may uncover forms of life that inhabited Earth 30 million years ago.

insulating effect. In the end, the ice sheet reaches a critical mass and melts, flooding the oceans with water and icebergs and causing global sea levels to rise. Once the ice sheet has melted, Antarctica may then return to a 7000-year phase of quiescence, building up new layers of ice.

Whatever the true cause of the diminishing Antarctic ice cap, records of ice thickness and the frequency of ice movement have revealed a slow collapse of the ice shelves. Scientists believe that these semi-permanent shelves – which cover more than

TEARS OF THE CHILD A driver prepares to clamber to safety from his car trapped by sudden floods in February 1998. Fourteen people died after heavy rainstorms lashed northern Mexico near its border with California. The unusually violent weather was blamed on El Niño.

600 000 sq miles (1.6 million km²) around the continent's coastline – act as buttresses for the much larger ice sheet which blankets the interior. If that is true, the rapid melting of the ice shelves observed today – due perhaps to global warming – could presage the melting of the Antarctic ice sheet as a whole. In

that event, global sea levels could rise by 200 ft (60 m) with cataclysmic consequences.

If the theory of global warming as a result of carbon dioxide emissions is correct, mankind may have written its own death warrant. As the rain forests are destroyed, so their ability to replace atmospheric carbon dioxide with oxygen by photosynthesis is reduced. The contraction of the rain forests could in turn precipitate the collapse of another vital stabilising environment: Antarctica.

Alternatively, the global warming theory may be entirely wrong. In the 1970s a number of ecologists voiced concerns that pollutants in the atmosphere would reflect the Sun's energy away from the Earth and thus throw the planet into a new ice age – in effect, they were warning of global cooling. Less than 20 years later, pressure groups had forced the issue of global warming onto the international political agenda. At the Kyoto summit in 1997 some experts voiced concerns that the apparent warming experienced in the 1990s might be entirely generated by El Niño. The effects of carbon dioxide in the atmosphere may, in fact, be minimal and the fluctuations measured by meteorologists in Antarctica and elsewhere may be entirely natural. Only by continued study of the interactions of the various phenomena will scientists be able to determine the existence, or otherwise, of cyclical climate patterns which may take decades or even centuries to complete.

DAWN OF THE NEW WISDOM

THE OIL CRISES OF THE 1970S LAUNCHED A QUEST FOR NEW SOURCES OF ENERGY, AS SCIENTISTS AND ENVIRONMENTALISTS SOUGHT THE SECRETS OF SUSTAINABLE DEVELOPMENT. THE GREEN MOVEMENT BECAME A FORCE TO BE RECKONED WITH – POLITICALLY, ECONOMICALLY AND SOCIALLY. BUT IN THE POST-COLD WAR WORLD EXPERTS FACED THE PROBLEM OF ROTTING NUCLEAR FLEETS AND ECOLOGICAL DISASTER IN SOME PARTS OF THE FORMER SOVIET BLOC.

OIL CRISIS TO ECO-QUEST

OIL SHORTAGES IN THE EARLY 1970S ENCOURAGED AN ALREADY GROWING CONCERN ABOUT OUR USE OF THE EARTH'S RESOURCES

The 1970s saw a succession of oil crises. At the start of the decade, Western countries were at the height of their oil dependency. By 1973 the world as a whole was consuming 56 million barrels per day; 41 per cent of all power generated in Western Europe and the USA was derived from oil. Then came the Arab-Israeli War of October 1973. With the flow of Arabian oil interrupted, oil prices spiralled, tripling by December. The result was chaos in many parts of the developed world. Without oil, electrical heating systems failed to provide warmth, and in many places transport infrastructures ground to a halt. Transport difficulties meant that food supplies were limited. Many areas of Europe and the USA simply ran out of oil.

On January 15, 1974, the

London *Times* reported on some of the hardships experienced by Americans:

'Some schools . . . have closed temporarily and others have reduced classroom temperatures to a level where students are advised to wear sweaters. Railways have cut train speeds to conserve fuel. Scattered industries have eliminated shifts or shut down for a few days. Grain is rotting in the fields because of the lack of natural gas to feed the driers. The shortages have sucked fuel into the middle west from other parts of the country . . . Shortage of fuel at New York's three major airports has interrupted the services of United, TWA and other airlines.'

IGNOMINIOUS DEFEAT
An Israeli soldier leads blindfolded Egyptian prisoners during the Yom Kippur War of 1973.

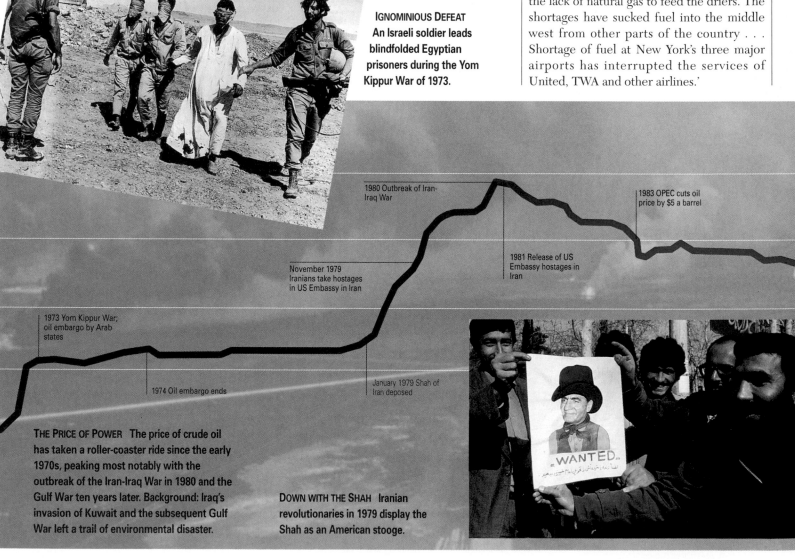

1980 Outbreak of Iran-Iraq War

1983 OPEC cuts oil price by $5 a barrel

$30

1981 Release of US Embassy hostages in Iran

November 1979 Iranians take hostages in US Embassy in Iran

$20

1973 Yom Kippur War; oil embargo by Arab states

$10 per barrel

1974 Oil embargo ends

January 1979 Shah of Iran deposed

THE PRICE OF POWER The price of crude oil has taken a roller-coaster ride since the early 1970s, peaking most notably with the outbreak of the Iran-Iraq War in 1980 and the Gulf War ten years later. Background: Iraq's invasion of Kuwait and the subsequent Gulf War left a trail of environmental disaster.

DOWN WITH THE SHAH Iranian revolutionaries in 1979 display the Shah as an American stooge.

"WANTED"

1970

1971 Greenpeace established

1973 Arab-Israeli (Yom Kippur) War; oil prices triple

1979 Shah of Iran ousted

1983 UN establishes World Commission on Environment and Development

Later in the decade, the markets recovered somewhat from the oil shock. But then came more turmoil in 1978-9, this time in Iran. It culminated in the ousting of the Shah and brought another tripling of prices. Finally, war between Iran and Iraq, which began in 1980, restricted oil production in those two countries and was another factor in keeping oil prices high.

Genesis of the eco-warrior

For the world's governments, one obvious way to tackle the crisis was to encourage alternative energies. In 1979, US President Jimmy Carter took a lead when he promoted a programme for producing synthetic fuel from shale. At the popular level, people responded by turning in increasing numbers to the various environmentalist movements, notably Greenpeace.

The history of Greenpeace goes back to 1969, when a US atomic bomb test on Amchitka Island off Alaska prompted a huge protest in the neighbouring Canadian province of British Columbia. Not only was Amchitka a haven for wildlife, it was also located in a geologically unstable zone, near a fault line in the Earth's crust; the test could have precipitated an earthquake. On the day it was due to take place thousands of protesters massed at a crossing on the US-Canadian border, holding up banners declaring: 'Don't make a wave. It's your fault if our fault goes.' The journalist Robert Hunter, an enthusiastic supporter, described the protest in the Vancouver *Sun*: 'The Monday noon demonstration against the Amchitka Island A-bomb test has begun . . . Politicians, take note. There is a power out there in suburbia, so far harnessed only to charity drives, campaigns and PTAs [Parent Teacher Associations] which, if ever properly brought to bear on the great problems of the day, will have an impact so great the result of its being detonated (like the Amchitka A-bomb test) cannot be predicted.'

The success of the event encouraged the organisers to further their efforts. Three men – Jim Bohen, a retired weapons engineer;

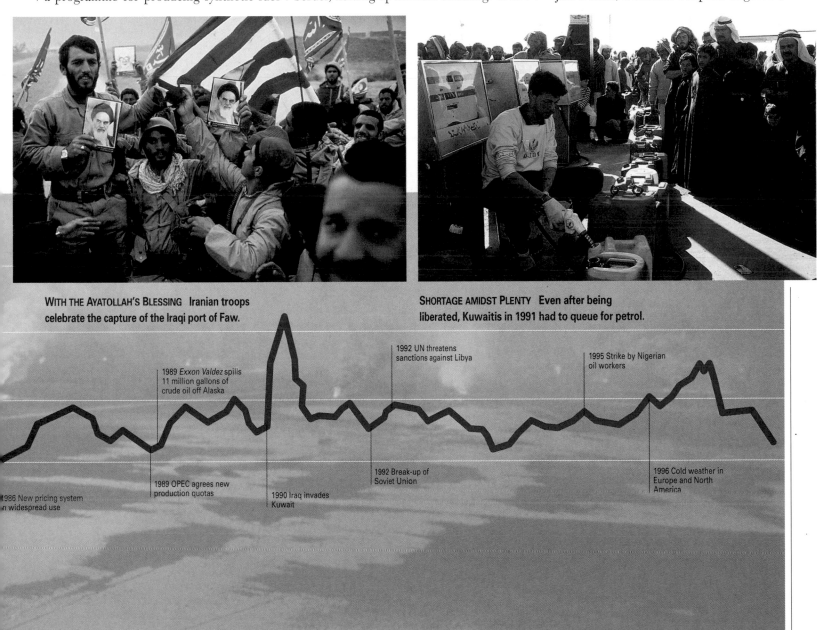

WITH THE AYATOLLAH'S BLESSING Iranian troops celebrate the capture of the Iraqi port of Faw.

SHORTAGE AMIDST PLENTY Even after being liberated, Kuwaitis in 1991 had to queue for petrol.

1989 *Exxon Valdez* spills 11 million gallons of crude oil off Alaska

1992 UN threatens sanctions against Libya

1995 Strike by Nigerian oil workers

1986 New pricing system in widespread use

1989 OPEC agrees new production quotas

1990 Iraq invades Kuwait

1992 Break-up of Soviet Union

1996 Cold weather in Europe and North America

1985 Greenpeace ship *Rainbow Warrior* sunk

1995 Shell UK halts plans to sink *Brent Spar* oil rig

Irving Stowe, a Yale-educated lawyer from New England; and Paul Cote, a law student from Columbia University – formed a 'Don't Make A Wave Committee'; this name they soon changed to the more snappy 'Green-peace'. Their first objective was to stop another atomic test on Amchitka, scheduled for 1971. They gathered the support for a further round of protests, and chartered a boat which they planned to sail into the test zone. In the event, the boat was turned back by the US Coast Guard and the test went ahead on November 6, 1971. But the protests were so successful that President Nixon cancelled any future Amchitka tests and the island became a bird sanctuary.

Then, in 1972, a UN Conference on the Human Environment was organised. Green-peace, alongside Britain's Campaign for Nuclear Disarmament (CND), established in 1958, was able to capitalise on the media attention surrounding the event. The name Greenpeace became known internationally, a rallying support for the aims of the UN

conference. CND remained at the forefront of the specifically anti-nuclear crusade, while Greenpeace had a wider remit, including issues such as protecting habitats, limiting hunting and preventing pollutants from poisoning the Earth. To ram home its point and capture headlines, it chose direct action. Greenpeace activists risked injury or even death in order to prevent fishing fleets from killing whales, and by the mid 1970s they were trying to stop the slaughter of Newfoundland seal pups, massacred with cudgels for their white fur.

RAINBOW WARRIOR The former North Sea trawler takes part in a protest against Canadian seal culling (left). By the mid 1980s Greenpeace was using it in protests against French nuclear tests in the South Pacific, and it was during this campaign that the ship met its end. In July 1985, French secret service agents blew up *Rainbow Warrior* in Auckland harbour, New Zealand, killing Greenpeace photographer Fernando Pereira. Above: In 1995 Greenpeace activists hang a banner on the North Sea oil rig *Brent Spar*, which Shell was planning to dump at sea. Below: In 1996 Greenpeace swimmers draw attention to overfishing by trawlers.

MAKING A WAVE

In 1976 Greenpeace, still a fledgling pressure group, rallied enough financial support to mount an anti-whaling campaign at sea. It chartered a former minesweeper of the Royal Canadian Navy, the *James Bay*, which set off with a crew of 36. Their target was a fleet of Soviet whaling ships hunting some 1400 miles (2250 km) southwest of the San Francisco shoreline. The 154 ft (47 m) ship was fast and could match the speeds of the whalers. She was also equipped with a mini-flotilla of highly manoeuvrable, semirigid powerboats, known as Zodiacs. The plan was for members of the crew to go out in these and form a kind of 'human shield' in front of any whale targeted by the hunters.

The *James Bay* dogged the Soviet fleet for ten days. Among the crew was the journalist Robert Hunter, who had already warned the world's media that if 'Russia and Japan decide to whale any longer, they will have to do it over our dead bodies'. Hunter's warning was nearly fulfilled as a Zodiac crew threw their powerboat onto the back of a dead whale. The vast *Daliny*

DANGEROUS PURSUITS Greenpeace's Zodiac powerboat crews dogged the giant *Daliny Vostok*, often taking great risks in the process.

Vostok, the lead ship of the Soviet fleet, was beginning the winching process, and the Zodiac's crew were almost drowned as the huge whale carcass was lifted out of the sea.

Greenpeace estimated that the *James Bay* mission saved nearly 100 whales by direct intervention, as crew members in their Zodiacs placed human shields around whales targeted by the Soviet fleet's harpoons. On top of that, as many as 1300 whales may have been protected as a result of the *James Bay*'s dogged pursuit of the *Daliny Vostok*, which in the end turned away from its normal hunting grounds and returned to its home base ahead of schedule. Robert Hunter later wrote about the confusing whirl of action during an attempt to protect a school of whales: 'Everything was in kaleidoscopic motion: twelve whales, three Zodiacs, one halibut seiner, ten harpoon boats and a looming, full-steaming factory ship like a startled rhinoceros charging to the centre of a disturbance.'

By the mid 1990s, they were taking on the might of the oil giant Shell, which was planning to dispose of a disused North Sea oil platform, the *Brent Spar*, in the deep waters of the North Atlantic. Greenpeace protested that the platform contained toxic material and posed a serious threat of pollution. Activists occupied it and orchestrated a campaign across Europe against the planned dumping. In June 1995, Shell backed down and towed the rig instead to a fiord in Norway. In the event, many experts, including those with strong environmentalist credentials, now believe that the *Brent Spar* might well have caused less pollution dumped in the North Atlantic than it is creating in its fiord where no one has yet worked out a satisfactory way of disposing of it.

By the 1980s and 90s environmentalism was 'hip'. Wearing CND logos on T-shirts

had been a fashion statement, as well as a protest, since the 1960s. Now, pop musicians such as Britain's Sting (Gordon Sumner) and the Australian group Midnight Oil embraced the environmental message. Other groups, such as The Jam, further popularised icons of the movement, including the CND symbol.

In the early 1960s, the American scientist Rachel Carson had warned of the dangers of

SAVE THE FORESTS Members of the Kayapo people of the Amazon with Belgian filmmaker Jean-Pierre Dutilleux (seated, second from right) and British musician Sting. The two Europeans brought worldwide publicity to the plight of rain-forest peoples threatened by the destruction of their homes. Inset: CND supporters at a 1983 rally in London's Hyde Park with the movement's symbol daubed on their faces.

persistent pesticide use. By the mid 1960s, James Lovelock, a British professor of biology, was putting forward a contrasting notion. He believed that the Earth would cope with the actions of mankind and compensate for our polluting ways. In 1975, Lovelock propounded this hypothesis in a book, *Gaia: a New Look at Life on Earth*. He argued that the Earth and all creatures on it should be considered as a single living entity that changes and regulates its actions in order to perpetuate the whole. According to him, this

single 'living system', named Gaia after the Greek goddess of the Earth, alters its structure to cope with change. For example, it achieves a reduction in global temperature by encouraging the growth of flowers such as the daisy. As the white daisies reflect more light than other, darker vegetation, light and heat energy coming from the Sun are radiated back into space. For its supporters, the Gaia hypothesis appears to offer a ray of hope: mankind's polluting ways will be compensated for by Gaia. However, a new

PROTEST IN BRAZIL The Australian band Midnight Oil take part in a 1997 protest against the pollution generated by São Paulo's 5 million cars.

Eden created by the compensating patterns described by the Gaia hypothesis might make Earth uninhabitable for mankind. If our activities threaten the biosphere – the

the extinction 65 million years ago of the dinosaurs happened after a giant meteorite or a cluster of comets crashed into Earth, setting off a fireball and later a protracted ice age, which destroyed much of the Earth's vegetation and animal life. The eventual emergence and dominance of mammalian life after that can be seen as an example of a Gaian response: Gaia had altered its structure to cope with change.

New wisdom

Since the modern environmental movement began, some significant changes have taken place. Government drives to increase energy efficiency have produced a shift in energy production and consumption across the Western world. In Britain, one simple measure was the introduction of improvement grants for loft insulation in older homes; this has helped to reduce domestic fuel consumption since the late 1970s. The Green

TRUSTING MOTHER NATURE James Lovelock at his home in Cornwall. A freelance inventor and scientist, Lovelock believes that the Earth's biosphere is a self-regulating system akin to a living organism.

MAKING AN EVERYDAY STATEMENT From Surfers Against Sewage to Friends of the Earth, environmental organisations are picking up increasing support, expressed on T-shirts, badges, even wet suits.

part of the Earth and its atmosphere inhabited by living things, both plants and animals – Gaia might regard humanity as unsuitable for survival and select us for extinction. Lovelock wrote:

'First and foremost, Gaia forces upon us a concern for the planet and its state of health and offers an alternative to our near-obsessive concern with the state of humanity. It is in our own interest anyway to live well with the Earth. If we do not, Gaia will live on but with a new biosphere that may not include humans. The demolition of the forests of the humid tropics and the ever-increasing burden of greenhouse gases are real threats to

Gaia and humanity alike . . . the evolution of Gaia seems to depend upon the activities of individual organisms. If these are favourable for the environment they succeed. If not they are doomed but life goes on.'

Lovelock's Gaia hypothesis has attracted some criticism from the scientific community. But his efforts to bring quantifiable scientific evidence to the hypothesis have met with a certain amount of success, and some scientists now consider that his views could be accurate. For example, it is widely believed that

Please Shut the Gate

Coombe Mill Experimental Station

WASTE CYCLE

The practice of recycling household waste first took hold in the USA during the 1970s. Denmark was one of the first European nations to encourage the recycling habit, when it started to provide separate household rubbish bins for recyclable waste in the mid 1980s.

A city the size of Paris disposes of 20 000 tons of domestic waste every day. As much as 25 per cent of that waste could be reclaimed, treated and re-used. Metals alone offer a sensible reason to recycle waste. In a year Paris produces more waste aluminium, in the form of food and drink cans, packaging and foils, than a moderately sized bauxite mine is capable of producing in the same period. Every ton of recycled aluminium is the equivalent of the aluminium found in 4 tons of bauxite ore. Waste gases produced during the process of smelting the ore, such as aluminium fluoride, would be reduced by nearly 80 lb (roughly 35 kg) per ton through recycling aluminium.

Similar results are obtained when glass and paper are recycled, and it is with these that the greatest inroads have been made in continental Europe. In the 1980s Switzerland, for example, met 60 per cent of its demand for glassware with recycled glass; by the late 1990s as much as 70 per cent of its glassware was made using recycled materials.

THE COLOURS OF WASTE More and more Western countries are establishing schemes, such as this German one, for recyling household waste.

movement, meanwhile, has succeeded in convincing governments not only to alter their energy programmes, but also that ecological matters are important – as important in many ways as health or education policy.

Europe's first Green party was the British one, founded in 1973. In the 1979 European elections it won a remarkable 15 per cent of an admittedly low vote – but no seats, thanks to Britain's first-past-the-post electoral system. The first European greens to be elected to a national parliament were members of Belgium's French-speaking Ecolo party which in a general election in 1981 won 5 per cent of the vote and five seats. Europe's most influential Green party, however, was in Germany. In 1983 *Die Grünen* made an eye-catching breakthrough when they won a solid block of 28 seats in the 497-member federal parliament. Green successes followed in other European countries, particularly after the Chernobyl nuclear disaster in 1986 and the *Exxon Valdez* oil spill in 1989 drew world attention to the ever-present risk of environmental catastrophe. In elections in 1989, 29 Green party members were returned to the European Parliament.

By then the environmental movement had been transformed almost beyond recognition. The numbers of those involved had grown from a few thousand hard-core activists in 1970, to millions of like-minded people across the globe in the early 1990s, many associated with organisations such as Friends of the Earth, Greenpeace and Earth First!

GREEN MILITANCY The German Green leader Petra Kelly. She founded Germany's Green party in 1972 and was a member of the Bundestag from 1983 to 1990.

The struggle to push environmental issues to the centre of world attention was to a large extent over. Yet the tasks facing the new generations of eco-activists remained as challenging as ever.

In Europe and the USA, for instance, car efficiency by the late 1990s had increased by 30 per cent since the early 1970s, and smaller cars had become much more the norm. Whereas an average car before the 1973 oil shock did 26 miles to a gallon of petrol (9.3 km per litre), a modern hatchback could do 35 miles or more to a gallon (12.6 km or more to a litre). This encouraging development was offset, however, by the fact that there were so many more cars than there had been 30 years before. Indeed, in many cities pollution caused by motor vehicles was now worse than ever. At the same time, worldwide carbon dioxide emissions had risen by 12 per cent between 1990 and 1995. The biggest increases came from developing countries, but even in the increasingly eco-conscious Western world emissions increased by an average of 4 per cent. The struggle to contain environmental damage was as urgent as it ever had been.

ENERGY ALTERNATIVES

THE HUNT IS ON FOR RENEWABLE WAYS OF GENERATING ENERGY: SOME OLD, LIKE USING THE WIND; OTHERS NEW, LIKE SOLAR POWER

OPEC (the Organisation of Petroleum Exporting Countries) was set up by the representatives of five nations – Iran, Iraq, Kuwait, Saudi Arabia and Venezuela – meeting in the Iraqi capital Baghdad in September 1960. Shortly joined by other countries, including Indonesia, Libya, the United Arab Emirates, Algeria and Nigeria, OPEC's aim was to ensure that its members got a fair share of the profits from their oil reserves. By standing together – above all, by

REAPING THE WINDS 'Wind farms', such as this one in Powys in mid Wales, are beginning to contribute to the world's electricity supply.

coordinating their pricing policies – they were able to face down the Western countries and companies which until then had controlled their oil industries and creamed off much of their revenues.

By the 1970s the OPEC cartel had become a powerful international body, and the oil crises of that decade prompted some major rethinking by the Western countries. From a strategic point of view, it was clear to European and US leaders that they were vulnerable to an interruption in oil supplies. From a political point of view, it was embarrassing for the world's leading nations, particularly the USA (the largest consumer of

power), to be in a position where they could be held to ransom by the OPEC nations. Two major changes resulted. Europe and the USA launched successful initiatives to locate and extract oil in their own territories – the North Sea and Alaskan oil fields were opened up in the 1970s – and a quest was launched to find alternative forms of power. This led to a re-examination of long ignored, or forgotten, technologies.

Lost techniques

Windmills were used to grind grain and pump water in both Persia and China as long ago as 1000 BC, though their use did not spread widely until the early Middle Ages and the rise of Islam. The technology was simple, and as the Muslims spread out from Arabia across much of the Mediterranean area, so did the windmill. By the 12th century the Crusaders had brought it to Western Europe. Because of their efficiency and ease of upkeep, windmills remained important until the beginning of the 20th century, especially for milling flour.

In 1888 Nikola Tesla invented alternating current, permitting the rapid expansion of electrification in Europe and the USA. This could have led to a new use for the windmill. Instead, however, electrification coincided with the discovery of oil at Spindletop in Texas and the dawn of the oil age. While the new and plentiful supply of oil helped to power one of the most astonishing periods of technological change in human history, it also, less beneficially, encouraged a wholesale rejection of tried and tested technologies, many of them renewable and sustainable.

The windmill was an example. Even as the Spindletop discovery began to change the world, one man had already proved that it was able to

1904 Larderello geothermal plant in Italy

1913 Dee Hydro tidal power plant in England

1927 Darrieus invents wind rotor

1932 First particle accelerator at Cavendish Laboratory, Cambridge
1935 US Rural Electrification Act

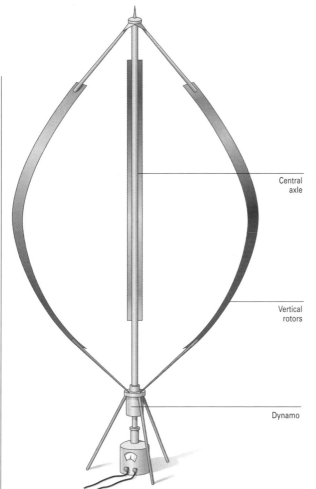

Central axle

Vertical rotors

Dynamo

ORIGINAL THINKING For his wind turbine (left) Georges Darrieus (below) was inspired by the egg whisk. It uses vertically mounted fins attached at each end to a central axle to drive a dynamo which generates the electricity.

fuel at least some of our domestic energy needs. In 1891, a Scotsman, James Blyth, professor of natural philosophy at Anderson's College in Glasgow, designed and patented a windmill electricity generator. He proclaimed its benefits at the Royal Scottish Society of Arts the following year. A Glaswegian firm, Mayor and Coulson, built his windmill generator near Montrose; it provided power for electric lights in Sunnyside Asylum. It was quite successful, producing 3 kW of power. Blyth believed that every household would one day have electric lighting, as opposed to the gas lamps which were then most common, and that it might be powered by his windmill generators. He was right about the spread of electricity, but wrong about his generators.

Nonetheless, by the 1930s great advances had been made in windmill design. In 1927 G.J.M. Darrieus, a French designer, had proposed a new design which resembled an egg whisk. Called the Darrieus rotor, this is based around a central vertical shaft, with three rotors attached to both ends of the shaft. The three rotors turn around the central shaft, irrespective of wind direction, and only require wind speeds of 12 mph (19 km/h) or more to turn the blades. Traditional wind rotors, as on a windmill, need an average wind speed of more than 15 mph (24 km/h) before they will operate effectively. The Darrieus rotor is still in use all over the world. Elsewhere, studies of aerodynamics had produced efficient, propeller-like 'sails'. Wind generators became more affordable, and potential power output from a state of the art wind turbine increased from 10 kW in 1900 to 1000 kW by 1930.

Yet windmill technology was used less and less, largely because of the USA's rapid acceptance of electrical grids – power lines running electricity from central power stations. Coal and oil-burning stations were built, and power production was centralised. In 1935 this process was hastened in the USA by the Rural Electrification Act, one of the package of measures introduced by the Roosevelt administration to try to pull the country out of the Depression. The aim was to help American farmers by making cheap electricity available to them. It fostered the building of large-scale dams, such as the Boulder (later renamed Hoover) Dam. Attempts were made to revive the wind turbine for generating electricity, including large-scale installations such as a giant 100 ft (30 m) high turbine built in 1941 by S. Morgan Smith and Company at Grandpa's Knob in the Green Mountains of Vermont. Even so, for almost 40 years wind technology was little more than a fading memory for most people.

It was a similar story in Europe. In 1915 Denmark had more than 3000 electricity-producing wind turbines, yet by the 1950s the country had followed America and rejected wind power. Throughout the continent wind power was seen as unreliable, while the cost of building capacitors (devices that store electric charge) for windless periods was seen as prohibitive. It was far better, people reckoned, to use cheap coal or oil.

WOOD OR COAL?

Which is more friendly towards the environment – wood or coal? India is planning to open its coal reserves as an alternative to wood-burning. Although coal releases more carbon dioxide and pollutants than wood, less of it needs to be burnt to get the same amount of heat energy. So, overall, it may bring pollution down.

The change came in 1979, when US President Jimmy Carter announced a programme to develop alternative energy technologies in an effort to reduce US dependency on foreign oil imports. The tensions in the Middle East resulted in a crisis which was beginning to sour Western societies' taste for oil.

Turning the blades

California was the first US state to embrace President Carter's quest. To the east of San Francisco, the Altamont Pass Wind Farm stretches across the horizon. The scheme was started in 1982 with just 100 wind turbines. Within six years 4000 turbines, generating 1000 MW of power – the same amount generated by a nuclear reactor – had been erected at the site.

The site has attracted a great deal of publicity, not all of it favourable. For example, birds crash into the fans, leading to the deaths of rare eagles and falcons. On balance, however, it is now seen as a beacon for the viability of alternative energy. It is soon to be increased to include an extra 8000 turbines – making it the world's largest wind farm. California currently produces 75 per cent of the world's total wind power, though innovation could see the Californian models being outstripped. One new design is known technically as the 'diffuser augmented turbine', and produces five times the electrical power of the older turbines. Based on research conducted

HIGH-TECH TURBINE Using research done in California, a New Zealand company, Vortec Energy, has built a prototype diffuser augmented turbine (above). Right: The cone shape funnels additional quantities of air into the turbine by creating a vortex, thus increasing the rate of spin and electrical output.

natural steam and water heated by magma from the Earth's core to temperatures of more than 250°C (480°F) emerge at the surface. Native Americans have used geothermal energy for more than 10 000 years. In modern times, it has been exploited since 1904, when a turbine was built over a pocket of geothermal steam in Larderello, Italy. Sprawling out amidst lush hills, its tall cooling towers sending out clouds of steam, the power plant is

Southampton which provides heating for its district. California's Geyserville produces 2000 MW of power, making it the most productive geothermal plant in the world. The US Geological Survey estimates that the world's geothermal areas store enough energy to produce 60 000 MW a year for 50 years. It was estimated in the 1970s that the heat stored in a 5 sq mile (13 km²) block of geothermally heated rock under the desert of New Mexico could provide the same amount of energy as was consumed by the entire world in 1973. If current trends continue, geothermal energy will be most exploited in developing nations with less dependence on traditional fossil fuels. Both the Philippines and Indonesia already have active geothermal research programmes.

Diffuser
Turbine
Main air stream
'Boundary' air stream, flowing faster than main stream

by the Northrop Grumman Company of Los Angeles in the 1970s, it has a special hood or 'shroud' attached to it which increases the amount of air channelled into the turbine; the movement of air around the blade then increases to twice its normal speeds.

Europe, meanwhile, has also begun to rediscover the advantages of wind power. The United Kingdom has a number of wind farms, including the three-bladed generators, standing 92 ft (28 m) tall, at the Carmarthen Bay power station in South Wales. Each of these can generate 300 kW. Collectively, Europe is now spending 20 times as much as the United States on wind power research.

Chasing therms
In response to President Carter's initiative, scientists embraced another alternative energy source: geothermal energy. This is extracted in volcanically active areas where

FROM THE EARTH'S CORE Geothermal energy has contributed to Italy's electricity supply since 1904, thanks to large steam turbines constructed over a natural geothermal spring at Larderello in Tuscany.

still in operation. It is capable of producing 400 MW of power and has proved the long-term viability of geothermal energy.

Although restricted to areas with the right kind of geology, the process has been used to produce electricity in a number of countries since the 1970s. Iceland, in particular, has an abundance of geothermal energy, which heats two-thirds of all its homes. Parts of the North Island of New Zealand similarly depend heavily upon it. The United Kingdom has also experimented with it; the most advanced scheme is one at Marchwood near

Wave power
Two-thirds of the Earth's surface is covered by tidal water. The movement of the tides is potentially one of the greatest sources of renewable energy available to mankind. Yet this resource, unlike hydroelectricity, has been virtually ignored in the 20th century. Where hydroelectricity depends upon the damming of rivers and the flooding of valleys – in order to create falling water to turn electricity-producing turbines – wave power depends upon the movements of the tides alone. The first time electricity was generated by exploiting the tides was in 1913. An experimental tidal power plant, the Dee Hydro in Cheshire, England, generated 635 kW of power. The scheme proved to be effective, but further development was rejected in favour of coal-fired power stations.

TIDAL POWER Brittany's La Rance power station, near St Malo, France, is the world's largest tidal power-generation plant.

Tidal power plants work by holding water from incoming and outgoing tides behind a large dam wall. The difference in the water's height on either side of the dam (akin to that in a lock on a river or canal) generates electricity as the water falls through turbines

TIDAL POWER

The world's tidal power generation potential is rated at 64 000 MW. The 20th century has seen an upsurge in interest in exploiting this potential, but it also saw the closure of the oldest of tidal power plants: a tide mill, built in 1170, in Woodbridge, England.

while the levels even out. Because these power plants depend on the strength of tides, they cannot provide a continuous stream of electricity. As with wind turbines, energy produced this way must be stored in capacitors, consisting of two or more metal plates separated by insulating layers. The charge is then drained on demand.

The world's largest tidal power plant operates on the La Rance river estuary on the coast of Brittany. Exploiting

a 44 ft (13.5 m) difference between high and low tide, the plant produces 240 MW of power. This is the first modern tidal power plant and has been running successfully since 1966. While France leads the way in large-scale tidal power projects, China has also built eight tidal plants, and the USSR built an experimental one in 1968. Still operating on the Barents Sea to the north of Murmansk, the plant produces about 400 kW of power.

Sun worship

Solar power is generated using photovoltaic cells (membranes capable of converting light into electricity). Its uses have ranged from fuelling experimental cars to powering

refrigeration units on delivery trucks. Commonly found on calculators and wristwatches, the photovoltaic cell has even fuelled orbiting satellites and manned spacecraft since the successful launch of the solar-powered satellite, *Vanguard 1*, in 1958.

Huge amounts of solar energy reach the Earth every year, and mankind has only begun to tap this virtually limitless supply. The first practical photovoltaic cell was created in 1954, the brainchild of three scientists working for communications giant AT&T – Darryl Chaplin, Gerald Pearson and

SOLAR TRUCK The British supermarket giant Sainsbury's is experimenting with refrigerated trucks that use solar power to run the cooling system.

SOLAR CELL A photovoltaic cell consists of two slices of silicon. Both are impregnated with impurities to give each an opposite charge when light penetrates them. These negative and positive charges generate an electrical current.

VILLAGE IN THE SUN Banks of solar panels, known as 'solar villages', are being built in many sun-drenched corners of the world. This 'village' provides energy for homes and businesses in Saudi Arabia.

Calvin Fuller. They treated silicon crystals and then sliced them into wafers to produce cells. These produced small amounts of electrical current when exposed to light. Although only capable of converting 4 per cent of available light into electricity, the prototype proved that solar power was a viable proposition. It took several years of further research to produce solar cells that were capable of converting up to 10 per cent of available light. By the mid 1970s, solar power was a commercial reality.

By 1988 photovoltaic cells were able to convert as much as 15 per cent of available light, thanks to new techniques devised by the Solar Research Energy Institute in the United States. The institute devised a new cell constructed of cheaper materials (copper, diselenide and indium) that resulted in

a drop in production costs. Today, office blocks in Germany and the USA are often built with solar panels as an integral part of their structure – installed in their south-facing side. Major house construction companies in Japan have designed new types of housing that incorporate solar cells instead of roofing tiles. It is hoped that these cells will make the houses self-supporting in their energy requirements. The intention is to build 100 000 of these homes with government subsidy within the next decade.

Solar power has many advantages. It is convenient and can be used in almost any environment, except the higher latitudes where the sunshine is too weak. By the early years of the 21st century, solar panels are likely to be a familiar part of street architecture. Another approach to solar power can be seen at a solar furnace built near the ski resort of Odeillo in the French Pyrenees. Here, a mammoth wall of reflecting mirrors focuses the Sun's rays onto a furnace, producing temperatures in excess of 3482°C

ORBITAL ENERGIES

In the 1970s US physicist Peter Glaser proposed a means of harnessing the power of the Sun. A space station with 25 sq miles (64 km²) of solar panels would capture 85 000 MW of solar power. Nearly 80 per cent would be lost due to inefficiencies in solar-cell technology, but the remainder would be beamed to Earth. Glaser calculated that one station would provide 10 000 MW of power: enough for New York. The USA would require 250 stations to meet its requirements – leaving little scope for other countries to use the technology.

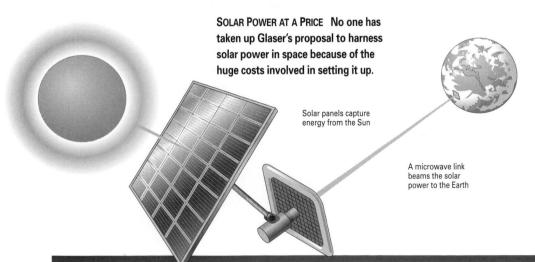

SOLAR POWER AT A PRICE No one has taken up Glaser's proposal to harness solar power in space because of the huge costs involved in setting it up.

Solar panels capture energy from the Sun

A microwave link beams the solar power to the Earth

(6300°F). The resulting heat produces steam and drives a turbine to generate electricity.

Meanwhile, scientists have been investigating a more elusive form of energy – nuclear fusion, the process that powers the Sun itself. In this, atoms join, or fuse, under intense pressure and heat, releasing enormous amounts of energy in the process.

Power from fusion

Since the 1930s, scientists have experimented with ways of accelerating atoms to make them collide and fuse. The first particle accelerator was built in 1932 by E.T.S. Walton and J.D. Cockcroft at the Cavendish Laboratories in Cambridge, and larger ones have been constructed since. Essentially, they consist of giant hollow, doughnut-like rings – with powerful magnetic fields projected into the hollow core – in which the atoms are accelerated to near the speed of light. Particularly successful in the study of atomic energy has been the European Laboratory of Particle Physics (CERN) in Geneva.

Despite decades of research, the ability to stimulate fusion without putting more energy into creating the reaction than it generates in return still eludes particle physicists. Thermonuclear weapons, an outgrowth of the atomic bomb, also use nuclear fusion, but although scientists know how to create

SOLAR SOLUTIONS
A collapsable parabolic mirror can be used in remote regions, such as Tibet here, to boil a kettle.

SUN-POWERED PLANE

In June 1997, NASA's Pathfinder broke the previous altitude record for a solar-powered aircraft. Its 100 ft (30 m) wingspan was covered with solar cells, which powered its flight to a height of more than 67 000 ft (20 500 m). It is hoped that the Pathfinder will help to further the development of hybrid passenger planes, which would combine petroleum-based fuels with energy from solar cells to power their engines.

THE ICARUS FACTOR **Solar panels on the Pathfinder's upper wing surface produce electricity, which powers the plane's six motors.**

such an explosion of energy, they have yet to harness it in the same way that we use nuclear fission to create power in nuclear power stations. If this problem were resolved, fusion could become a valuable source of power – above all, a non-polluting source, since both the materials used and the waste product are almost completely harmless. Mankind would, in effect, be able to create miniature suns to power our civilisation.

Towards a self-sufficient future

Since the oil crisis of the 1970s, Western society has begun to wean itself off some of its addiction to oil. Oil prices have fluctuated since then, but although worldwide oil consumption has continued to rise, due to our ever-growing energy demands, no inducement by producers has secured a return to the rapid growth rates of the decades before the 1970s. At the same time, the proportion of power generated using oil has dropped. In 1979, 46 per cent of the power used in the world was generated using oil; by 1985 that figure had fallen to 39 per cent. The alternative energy sector, meanwhile, has grown

steadily. Worldwide sales of solar cells grew from $340 million-worth in 1988 to over $900 million in 1997. Alternative energy provision is now a billion-dollar industry – the wind-turbine industry alone is worth US$2 billion a year – and new alternative installations could soon be going up faster than more traditional forms of power plant, such as coal and gas-fired stations.

Electricité de France, the French national power company, is committed to building 100 high-technology hydroelectric plants which will replace many of its nuclear reactors next century. A poll by Greenpeace in 1996, showed that over 51 per cent of German householders would be interested in buying solar panels for their homes. Subsequently, the regional governments of Schleswig-Holstein in northern Germany and Saarland in the west introduced subsidies for people wanting to install solar panels.

Alternative energy sources have a long way to go before they compete seriously with their conventional

FUSION INNOVATORS The father of atomic science, Lord Rutherford, stands between the men who built the first particle accelerator, John Cockcroft (on his left) and Ernest Walton. The Fusion Research Accelerator in New Mexico (left) aims to mimic the energy-producing properties of the Sun.

SOLAR ENGINEERS

The American scientist Charles Greeley Abbot began investigating the viability of 'Sun power' in the late 19th century, furthering research by the French physicist, Alexander Becquerel, who first observed the photovoltaic effect in 1839. Light is directly converted to electricity in semiconductive materials such as silicon. Abbot's research paved the way for a key discovery by Bell Laboratories in 1954: a practical method of producing a cell of semiconductive materials so as to 'tap' the Sun's power. Abbot, a firm believer in Sun power, died in 1973 less than a decade before the idea of exploiting it started to be widely embraced.

GIFT OF GENIUS Abbot's invention, the pyroheliometer (below), measured the heat of the Sun's rays.

counterparts – at present, less than 7 per cent of energy worldwide is produced using alternative sources. Nonetheless, it is clear that in the future power will be generated in a number of different ways – moving away from our dependency on a few large-scale plants. Homes with solar panels could contribute power to national grids at off-peak hours, while small hydroelectric stations, wind farms and tidal power stations will work alongside nuclear (maybe fusion) installations. This approach should help to banish the 'blackout' to history and offer a relatively painless way of replacing fossil fuels and reducing our carbon dioxide emissions.

REPAIRING THE DAMAGE

EXPERTS ARE SEEKING EFFECTIVE WAYS TO PUT RIGHT SOME OF THE POLLUTION DAMAGE DONE TO OUR AIR, LAND AND WATER

Environments are under unprecedented threat in the modern world. Since the start of the Industrial Revolution in the late 18th and early 19th centuries, mechanisation and a shift from age-old methods of farming, hunting, fishing and manufacturing have led to increased consumption of raw materials and growing production of damaging by-products and waste. At the same time, modern weapons and warfare now possess an unsurpassed capacity both to kill and to damage environments.

Across the Western world levels of industrial pollution in rivers have reached alarming levels. Mills, chemical plants and the nuclear industry all depend upon water as a coolant and as an integral part of their production processes. One of the worst river pollutants is mercury. Nearly 5000 tons of it have been lost into Europe's rivers every year since the 1920s. In the 1950s a Japanese plastics factory leaked mercury-rich waste into Minamata Bay, poisoning fish stocks and many of the people of the region.

METAL RIVER A scum of pollution floating on a tributary of the River Thame in the English Midlands. Metals such as lead and cadmium dumped in the river by local industries have poisoned it for indigenous species.

FISH KILL Shoals of dead menhaden (from the herring family) tell a sorry tale of pollution in this creek on the Maryland coast. An accident upstream can wipe out whole populations.

Years of river pollution have resulted in the development of dangerous microorganisms. One such deadly life form is the algae known as *Pfiesteria piscicida*. This thrives in waters containing large fish which it numbs as it feeds off them. The fish can become ulcerated and die. Chesapeake Bay on the eastern seaboard of the USA and the Grand

1911 International treaty to protect the northern fur seal – a conservation first

Banks have both been found to harbour the algae, provoking serious concerns that river and sea pollutants are providing an environment in which *Pfiesteria piscicida* can thrive. Research has begun into the destruction of this harmful microorganism, but it represents just one of many such problems that threaten our rivers and seas.

Some solutions to river pollution have produced good results. These include dredging, along with regular sampling and the imposition of heavy fines to prevent dumping. It is recycling, however, that offers the best practical hope of limiting river pollution and beginning the process of repairing industrial damage. Where steel, for example, is recycled, instead of being made 'from scratch' using raw iron ore, water use can be reduced by 40 per

NETTING PLANKTON
A scientist monitoring water quality with the help of a net. The presence of plankton is a good indicator of healthy biodiversity.

1950

1956 Clean Air Act enforces use of smoke-free fuels in UK cities

1972 UN conference on acid rain

1979 Three Mile Island nuclear crisis in USA

1984 Bhopal disaster
1986 Chernobyl disaster

1993 Dumping of industrial and radioactive waste banned worldwide

2000

cent, while overall pollution levels may fall by as much as 76 per cent. Similarly, it is possible to eliminate harmful aluminium pollution from rivers almost entirely – reducing it by up to 97 per cent – if recycled aluminium is used instead of processing bauxite ore.

Fish on land

The practice of restocking fish in fishing lakes has been common since the start of the 20th century. But it was not until the 1950s and 60s that the first efforts were made to find an effective way of restocking previously poisoned rivers and depleted seas.

In 1957 an experiment was initiated at the Fisheries Laboratories in Lowestoft, England. The idea was to rear 500 000 fish and then introduce them into the North Sea to help to restock it. Plaice eggs and sea water taken from the North Sea were used as test materials. The team, led by Dr H.A. Cole, made good progress over a five-year period, proving that the idea was feasible, at least on a small scale. A similar experiment was tried at Port Erin on the Isle of Man. An area of sea water was partitioned off to make a kind of tank where plaice would provide an easily harvestable supply of eggs. Initial results produced albino fish, but by adding

STEALING EGGS TO SAVE THE TURTLE A wildlife ranger in Malaysia collects turtle eggs from their beach nesting site. He and his colleagues will incubate the eggs and reintroduce the newly hatched turtles to the sea.

mineral supplements and dyes to food, and by breeding from healthier fish, this initial problem was sorted out.

International research continued, alongside the Lowestoft and Isle of Man projects. Cole had predicted that inland sea lakes could be used as fish farms, and by the late 1960s farms were, indeed, being set up in Scottish sea lochs

among other places. Today, there are more than 800 fish and shellfish farms in England and Wales alone, while 25 per cent of fish consumed in the United Kingdom as a whole originates in farms. In the United States, 5 per cent of fish sold comes from fish farms. In Europe, salmon is one of the most widely farmed fish. The salmon are usually kept in large pens until they weigh about 1 lb (0.5 kg), generally within a year of hatching. Researchers are also investigating ways of farming scallops, halibut and other fish and shellfish normally caught only at sea.

Meanwhile, as cod and plaice fisheries continue to decline and even collapse – off Canada, for example – publicly funded fish restocking programmes may be the only answer. The European Union already has a

FISH PENS Baby salmon are usually reared in circular tanks. At about 18 months, they are moved to saltwater pens, like these ones in Scotland, and 'fattened' for the table.

and France began experiments in reprocessing in the 1960s, but what was needed above all was long-term storage for this most hazardous of man-made by-products. By the 1980s the world's first nuclear power plants had developed vast quantities of nuclear waste; a typical nuclear reactor creates about 30 tons of waste in a single year.

In Britain, the government established Nirex to tackle the problem of finding suitable storage sites. Its task was to find locations that were geologically stable, free from water seepage and far enough from communities to avoid contamination in an accident. To make the job more difficult, Nirex had to find methods and locations capable of stor-

ing the waste safely for up to 40000 years. As its managing director, Tom McInerny, put it in an interview with *The Times* in March 1989: 'There is no limitation on the time-scale over which we have to consider what may happen. Effectively we have to look ahead for ever.'

In 1995 came a worrying reminder of the kinds of danger involved, when newspaper reports wrote of nuclear waste that had been dumped in the Irish Sea between Scotland and Ireland. In response, the British government admitted that low-level radioactive waste had, indeed, been dumped in Beaufort's Dyke – a 1500 ft (460 m) rift only 6 miles (10 km) off the Scottish coast. This not only lies beneath the main ferry route between Ireland and Scotland, but it is also a major fishing ground. What is more, the waste is

BURNING RAIN

Sulphur and nitrogen emissions responsible for 'acid atmospheric deposition', better known as acid rain, have been radically reduced across Europe since the late 1980s. Acid rain is caused by emissions from fossil fuel-burning industrial complexes, power plants and internal combustion engines. Since the 1970s it has been a contentious issue as one country's emissions can have a quantifiable effect on another's environment.

Norway used to receive much of the United Kingdom's sulphur and nitrogen emissions in the form of acid rain; forests and lakes were ruined as a result. In Lake Storgama in southern Norway a programme to measure acid rainfall has produced

LIME CLOUD It may look like pollution but this helicopter is dumping lime into a Swedish lake in an effort to neutralise the acid which is destroying it. Left: A protester outside Fiddler's Ferry power station in Merseyside, England.

some heartening results. Since 1980 there has been a 50 per cent drop in sulphur-rich acid rain over the lake; during that period the UK began fitting pollution-limitation devices known as 'sulphur scrubbers' to its industrial chimneys. Other schemes, encouraged by the United Nations Economic Commission for Europe (UNECE), have produced similar results across Europe, reducing acid rain by 50 per cent. However, nitrogen-rich acid rain continues to be a problem; levels have not reduced, due to the persistent use of the motor car. The greatly reduced incidence of sulphur-rich acid rain over Europe is helping the Scandinavian governments to replant forests that were decimated by acid rain before the UNECE initiative in the 1980s.

system of quotas to try to limit overfishing, but it may also have to consider a programme of restocking in the near future, as dwindling catches and contention over the quotas continue to dog the fishing industry. The USA and Norway have both attempted to restock salmon, using farmed fish.

Burying the evidence

In the 1950s, the atomic age was heralded as a period when all society's energy problems would be solved cheaply, swiftly and cleanly. Without doubt, nuclear power can contribute greatly to a nation's energy needs, as the success of France's commitment to nuclear power demonstrates. Unfortunately, the waste products are extremely hazardous to human, animal and plant tissues. The UK

DANGEROUS CARGO In 1998 the British government agreed to take uranium waste from the republic of Georgia for reprocessing at Dounreay in Scotland. The government maintained that, given Georgia's instability, it was safer to reprocess the waste than risk letting it fall into the wrong hands.

believed to lie on top of a vast cache of decomposing war munitions. The British government admitted that Beaufort's Dyke had been used by the Ministry of Defence from the 1940s to 1976 as a waste tip for millions of tons of munitions. It was almost certainly used for similar purposes in the 1920s after the First World War, though records were considered unreliable.

The combination of unstable munitions and nuclear waste so close to mainland Britain and Ireland presents a potentially serious problem. The waste is contained in metal barrels, or caskets, sealed in concrete. Should there be a leak, perhaps caused by an underwater detonation rupturing the seal of one of the nuclear caskets, parts of Ireland, Great Britain and the west coast of Europe could be irradiated, due to prevailing winds and ocean currents.

This point was brought home in October 1995, when 200 decaying incendiary devices containing toxic phosphorus were washed from the dump onto beaches in Cumbria, the Isle of Arran and Stevenson in Ayrshire. Although military bomb-disposal units successfully removed the unwanted debris, it seems very likely that many of the dumped

weapons, and possibly the nuclear caskets, missed Beaufort's Dyke during their descent from the surface and are, in fact, sitting on much shallower sections of the seabed.

Scuppered submarines

Meanwhile, the passing of the Cold War and the collapse of the Soviet Union had brought another set of problems. These events have actually increased the likelihood of environmental accidents. Poorly maintained and regulated nuclear power stations are the chief hazard, but there is also the problem of lack of control over nuclear weapons. The republics of the former USSR hold an estimated 130 tons of weapons-grade fissile material – enriched uranium and plutonium. The relatively efficient monitoring systems of the old USSR have given way to an often privatised industry prone to theft and security breaches. In 1992 nearly 4 1/2 lb (2 kg) of enriched uranium went missing from the Russian Luch Scientific Production Association (LSPA), and in 1993 10 lb (4.5 kg) of enriched uranium was stolen from a Murmansk shipyard.

There are rumours of other, similar incidents. These suggest that the infrastructure which regulated the old Soviet Union's nuclear arsenal is seriously crumbling. Since leaks and contamination are far more likely

TOXIN MONITOR
Checking chemical waste before incineration at a special plant in southern England.

SUBTERRANEAN STORAGE American construction giant Fluor Daniels bored a 5 mile (8 km) hole into the Yucca Mountain, Nevada, in order to create a dump for high-level radioactive waste.

when fissile material is being moved from one destination to another, the dangers are of grave concern to other governments. The United States, in particular, has tried to encourage the countries of the former Soviet Union to convert nuclear installations to civilian uses. It has also given a $1 billion grant to the Nunn-Lugar programmes, named after their sponsors, Senators Sam Nunn and Richard Lugar, which encourage Russia to maintain control of its nuclear arsenal and prevent weapons or technology from getting into the hands of other countries or of terrorist groups.

Damage is also being done by weapons and craft lost as casualties of the Cold War. Experts believe that a number of nuclear submarines – belonging to both NATO and the Soviet bloc – were abandoned due to technical problems. Each carried not only nuclear reactor cores, but also nuclear

MODERATING AND ANNEALING

Graphite is used as a 'moderator' in nuclear reactors. It slows the speed of neutrons travelling through the reactor, giving them more time to react with the surrounding material. Unfortunately, when the first atomic power stations were built in the 1950s, little was known about how radiation might affect graphite over time. It soon became apparent that the graphite grows in size, storing energy, and may spontaneously combust if not regularly cooled and heated: a process known as annealing. In October 1957 this led to a fire at Britain's Windscale (later renamed Sellafield) atomic power plant. The annealing process was tackled too quickly and the graphite overheated, igniting the reactor's uranium. Radioactive material was vented into the atmosphere through the cooling towers. Staff stayed at their posts – risking contamination – and took a chance that injecting water into the reactor core would douse the fire and bring the nuclear reactions under control. The core could have exploded at the moment of injection; fortunately, it stabilised. The government took the precaution of banning the consumption of milk in a 120 mile (200 km) radius of the plant. The Windscale incident is now considered to have been as serious as a partial meltdown that happened at Three Mile Island, Harrisburg, USA, in 1979.

SAFETY SUITS Workers at Three Mile Island wear sealed radiation suits in order to carry out decontamination operations.

missiles such as the Polaris. In many cases their positions are unknown. They are rotting on the seabed, and may already be leaching radioactive particles into the oceans.

Danger from unpaid bills

Similarly, many of the former Soviet fleet of 230 nuclear submarines have exceeded their life expectancies and are now moored in shipyards, such as those in Murmansk, awaiting decommissioning. Security is often lax and maintenance almost nonexistent. In 1995 the electricity supply to moored nuclear submarines was shut down because the Russian navy had defaulted on its electricity bill. Without power to their cooling plants, the nuclear reactors began to show signs of instability. The danger of a meltdown is very real in these rotting weapons of war. Many submarines still have the nuclear missiles fitted, ready for launch.

Research in the USA may offer a solution. One of the world's worst environmental disaster areas is the Hanford Nuclear Reservation in Washington state, where nuclear contractors have been dumping fissile material since the 1950s. Covering more than 560 sq miles (1460 km²), the Hanford site has 177 underground storage tanks, containing a total of 55 million gallons (250 million litres) of highly radioactive plutonium waste. Estimates suggest that 880 000 gallons (4 million litres) of the waste have leaked into the soil from 60 of the caskets, creating radiation levels that are 100 000 times greater than normal background levels.

The problem is how can the site be cleaned up without endangering lives? The US Department of Energy's Robotics Technology Development Programme is seeking an answer through the use of robots to detect leaks, analyse nuclear waste and move it to safer storage. It is estimated that the programme – which includes developing the robots and cleaning the site – will take 75 years to complete and cost billions of dollars. Despite the cost in time and money, if the technology starts to be effective within the next five years, the same robotic techniques could be applied to dismantling the former USSR's dangerously unstable nuclear arsenal.

SMOG CITY Surrounded by mountains that trap pollution and with a population of more than 15 million people, 3.5 million cars and large industrial suburbs, Mexico City is one of the world's blackspots for smog.

Atmospheric pollution has reached critical levels in the 20th century. In the Soviet Union, smog became a problem in the 1930s as the country underwent rapid industrialisation. Trees began to die and their rate of growth fell by 90 per cent. By the 1960s, after years of harsh Stalinist industrialisation programmes, nitrogen oxide and sulphur

dioxide emissions reached lethal levels in the suburbs of Moscow. Following the collapse of the USSR, the Russian Academy of Sciences stated that conditions had grown so bad that 50 million people – 16 per cent of the former Soviet Union's population – suffered from illnesses related to atmospheric pollution. They went so far as to declare the situation an environmental disaster. It has scarcely improved in the decade since the fall of the USSR; the people of the Russian Federation still suffer terrible levels of air pollution.

Anti-smog initiatives, launched across much of Europe and the USA in the mid 1960s, and enforced under various clean air acts in the 1970s, ensured a better outcome in the West. However, pollution records from the beginning of the 20th century tell a grim tale. In London, for instance, they show that in the period

TOXIC THAI COCKTAIL A Bangkok traffic policeman adjusts the mask that gives him some protection from airborne dirt and exhaust fumes.

DEADLY SMOG A visitor to London in November 1953 wears an improvised smog mask. Smogs were sometimes so thick that they prevented the normal running of buses, tubes and trains.

between 1920 and 1950 levels of sunlight in the centre of the city were 20 per cent lower than those in the suburbs. In the United States, between 1946 and 1968, the amount of poisonous lead released into the atmosphere by motor vehicles increased by 80 per cent. In Japan, smog reached its most dangerous point in 1970-2 when nearly 60 000 people suffered incapacitating headaches and bronchial conditions in Tokyo.

In 1957 Britain introduced the Clean Air Act and ensured stringent controls over emissions in city centres. Within 15 years, smog over London had fallen by 80 per cent. With more and more domestic and industrial users switching from coal to gas and electricity, city smogs became even less frequent. Today, the largest single polluter in the city is the motor vehicle, especially diesel-powered commercial vehicles which account for some 80 per cent of air pollution. Countries in Western Europe are committed to reducing car emissions by 20 per cent by 2010.

It is clear that much has yet to be done to repair the environmental damage caused by a century of development, exploitation and technological innovation. Some problems await the development of new technologies in the next century or beyond. Nuclear waste, in particular, cannot be made safe using current technology. Experts hope that one day they will find a way to break down radioactive waste at a subatomic level; this would disable its radiating properties, thus producing non-toxic by-products which could be recycled.

Similarly, stocks of fish and other sea creatures may need intervention by experts. Some marine biologists believe that many species – including the blue whale and the North Atlantic cod – have already fallen below critical survival levels. On the other hand, further protection measures, mass farming and restocking might enable these and other species to survive. For many species facing extinction in the short-term future, there may be no reprieve; in the long term, however, much of the damage done to the environment during the 20th century may turn out to be 'repairable'.

LIVING DANGEROUSLY Five-year-olds in a village outside Astrakhan in southern Russia during a gas alert drill. A gas complex in Astrakhan was so badly built that it functions at just a sixteenth of its capacity, and local people live with the possibility that a lethal leak could easily occur.

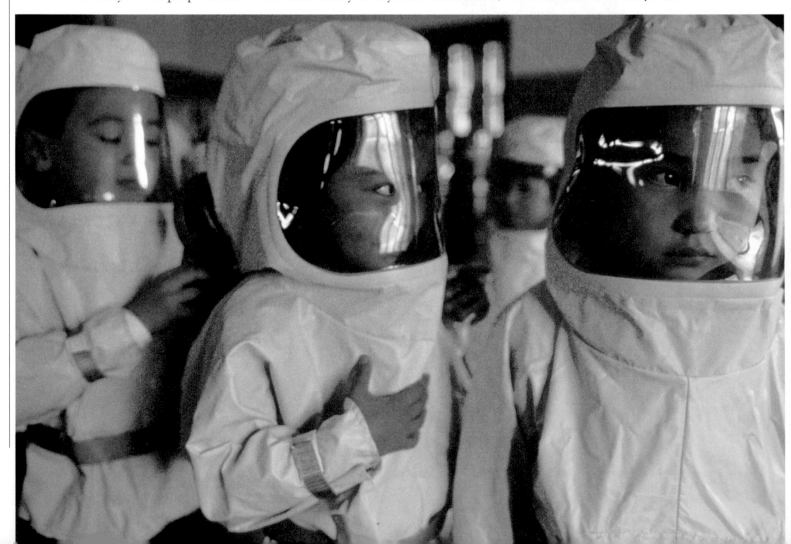

THINGS TO COME

LEARNING THE LESSONS OF YESTERDAY AND TODAY, INVENTIVE MINDS ARE CREATING THE TECHNOLOGY FOR A HEALTHIER TOMORROW

Writing in 1933, during the gloom of worldwide economic depression, the English author H.G. Wells foresaw a future of war and hardship. Mankind, he believed, would develop weapons of mass destruction; these, combined with escalating industrial activity, would pollute and damage the Earth. In the end, however, people would learn from their mistakes. In his book of political and scientific speculation, *The Shape of Things to Come*, he predicted that our grip on Earth would eventually become a nurturing one. Writing as if looking back from the distant future, he observed: 'The infinite toil of millions of tormented brains, the devotion and persistence of countless forgotten devotees, gave form and clear purpose in time to what were at first mere flounderings and clutchings towards safety. The threatened [human] race did not fall back into the abyss of extinction which has swallowed up so many of the bolder experiments of life. In pain and uncertainty it clambered past its supreme danger phase, and now it has struggled to such a level of assurance, understanding and safety as no living substance has ever attained before.'

At the start of the 20th century astonishing breakthroughs were coming thick and fast in just about every field of human activity. Many people expected the pace of change to continue – in fact, it increased. And many hazarded prophecies about how it would affect our world. Some, such as H.G. Wells in a number of his writings, were remarkably accurate. Others were spectacularly wrong, such as the men who tried to bring Lee de Forest to book. De Forest was one of the greatest of US inventors in the 20th century, responsible for more than 300 key breakthroughs in telecommunications, including the triode valve without which radar, television and computers would not have developed as they did. In 1913 he was prosecuted for attempting to sell stock to fund

MAN OF VISION H.G. Wells used a number of his books to speculate about the social and scientific future of mankind.

PAVING THE WAY US inventor Lee de Forest laid the foundations for modern telecommunications when he invented the audion tube or triode (right) to amplify weak signals.

research into what was deemed an impossible idea: international radio broadcasts. By then, international Morse transmissions (such as Marconi's first transatlantic one in 1901) had become familiar enough, but voice broadcasts were a different matter. In fact, however, the first transatlantic voice transmission had already been made, albeit unintentionally. In November 1906 two radio operators at stations in Massachusetts were communicating about the running of a dynamo. Extraordinarily, the voice of one of them was picked up by operators at a station near the Mull of Kintyre in Scotland. On October 21, 1915, a similar transatlantic feat was achieved, intentionally, when Mr B.B. Webb of American Telephone & Telegraph in Arlington, Virginia, spoke to Lt-Colonel Ferrie, representing the French government, in the Eiffel Tower in Paris.

Visionaries are so rarely understood because it is their very ability to stand apart from the established view of things that enables them to innovate. But even visionaries cannot foresee everything. H.G. Wells once commented that submarines would never amount to anything, except as a method for drowning their crews.

Measures for change

Predictions are no less hazardous at the end of the 20th century than they were in earlier decades. Nonetheless, it is almost certainly safe to say that in the 21st century change will continue at a rapid pace, affecting issues such as mankind's approach to transport, industrial production, consumption and power generation. Clues already exist to the form these changes may take. Tax disincentives, often

LEADING BY EXAMPLE The regional government of La Rochelle, France, hopes that by using electrically powered vehicles, it will encourage the general public to follow its lead and purchase similar cars.

called 'green taxes', are already beginning to bite into the pocket of motorists in some countries; governments are increasingly levying taxes on petrol and diesel. Some, the French and British governments in particular, are exploring the possibility of charging an entry fee to major cities. In the future, authorities may raise charges to the point where they effectively make the city inaccessible to the private motorist; business drivers who need their cars for work could be offered discounted rates if they have genuine services to provide in the city. Experiments conducted in the British Midlands and Parisian suburbs in 1997, indicate that such a system would be enforceable.

Some metropolitan areas are conducting experiments which take a pragmatic approach to transport. The right to own and drive a private car has been a defining factor of the 20th century, and it is a right that will not be easily surrendered. In Paris, the city is attempting to find a middle route between green public transport and the private car – the high-performance electric vehicle. Today, 120 municipal electrically powered vehicles operate in the Paris area, and in 1997 the city authorities announced that they would purchase another 50 for employees. In 1998 they guaranteed the establishment of 150

recharging points. In a poll conducted in 1997, nearly 23 000 Parisians stated that they intended to buy electrically powered cars. These have engines that can travel up to 370 000 miles (600 000 km) before they need replacing – more than twice that achievable by an internal combustion engine. They still create pollution; it just comes from the power stations supplying the electricity rather than individual engines. But this does, at least, shift some of the burden of pollution out of the cities.

This pragmatic approach may well typify policy to pollution in the next century. Another device is a form of legalised pollution or 'quota hopping', known as carbon trading. The system works by establishing an international market where the right to pollute can be bought and sold. In this market each country would be given an allocation of permitted carbon pollution. A country would

be free to trade this allocation to the highest bidder provided it was willing to forgo the industrial activity in its own economy corresponding to the amount of pollution. The USA has operated two effective emissions' trading systems since 1992. One limits ozone-damaging chlorofluorocarbons (CFCs);

ELECTRIC SEWAGE

In 1997 a British water company, Northumbrian Water, initiated a scheme to burn sewage to produce electricity. The process takes liquid sludge from the company's sewage plants, condenses it and turns it into small pellets. These pellets are burned in furnaces and the heat turns turbines which generate power for 20 000 homes in Northumberland.

the other is designed to limit sulphur emissions – the cause of acid rain. Auctions have been held where companies which no longer need their polluting allowance, because they have invested in 'green technologies', sell their pollution permits to other organisations. By January 1998, sulphur emissions had been reduced by 6 million tons from 1992 levels, with the likelihood of similar reductions by the year 2005.

The Dutch approach

The Netherlands is one of the world's most innovative developers of 'environmentally friendly' technologies. By the year 2020, it intends to produce at least 10 per cent of all

SPORTING LINES Based on the Lotus Elise, an electrically powered road-ready sports car was unveiled at an exhibition in Detroit in 1997.

1934 Ford serves soya-derived meals at Century of Progress Fair, Chicago

YESTERDAY IS TOMORROW Amsterdam's trams at the turn of the century. Faced with the problems of inner city traffic congestion, city planners around the world are beginning to recognise the value of this tried and tested technology.

model for other cities which are once again turning to the tram as a solution to the problems of metropolitan congestion and pollution. One of its beauties is that there is no need for the costly excavation and engineering works involved when building underground train lines.

The day of the teleworker
Most people take it for granted that they will travel to a place of work. It is possible, however, that new technologies – in the form of 'teleworking' and 'teleconferencing' – will do away with this need for millions of workers, greatly reducing pollution and traffic congestion in the process. The technology allows employees to work

its energy by sustainable means. One scheme is to use natural gas rather than electricity as a power source for domestic appliances – electricity is a relatively inefficient source since at least 30 per cent of energy is lost during transmission. In the southern city of Helmond, 60 houses have already been fitted with specially designed gas inlets to power washing machines and tumble driers. Experts hope that by using existing power supplies in more efficient and innovative ways, they will help to reduce the country's total carbon dioxide emissions.

Amsterdam has long boasted a sophisticated public transport system, largely based on the electric trolley-car or tram. The city's tram network consists of 17 lines, originating in the Centraal Station and radiating outwards in three spokes, to the west, the east and the south. Other lines connect these spokes, making it easy to get from one zone to another. The electric tram is an old technology used around the world since the turn of the century, but it was largely rejected by metropolitan planners from the 1930s to the 1950s when the internal combustion engine came to dominate. Amsterdam, however, like San Francisco, maintained and improved its network; today the system serves as a

COLD FUSION

On March 24, 1989, Professor Martin Fleischman of Southampton University in Britain and Professor Stanley Pons of the University of Utah, USA, announced that they had created a 'cold fusion reaction'. In normal fusion, atoms fuse together under high pressure and at high temperatures, releasing energy in the process. Fleischman and Pons believed they had achieved the reaction at room temperature by subjecting a cocktail of chemicals in a test tube to electrical charges.

Their 'discovery' could have led to unlimited power with minimal pollution and effort. For many years international research programmes have tried to create a fusion reaction – akin to the Sun's own energy source – within the confines of a large particle accelerator. But they have not made any great progress. Fusion reactions have been achieved in a number of experimental machines, including one at Germany's Max Plank Institute for Plasma Physics, near Munich. Unfortunately, the experiments demanded more energy to achieve the fusion than they produced. As a result, the suggestion that fusion could be achieved another way was met with delight by some, scepticism by others.

Initially, the physics community held its breath, wondering if a major breakthrough had been made. Sceptics, however, remembered a story from the mid 1960s, when some British physicists believed they had achieved fusion in a machine they called Zeta. The physicists later withdrew their claims as they realised that the subatomic particles produced by Zeta were not created by fusion but by other forces within the machine.

The sceptics seemed right when throughout 1989 Fleischman and Pons were unable to reproduce their experiment's results. To this day, they have never been able to substantiate their remarkable claim, other than by the data produced during their original tests. Perhaps the time will come when fusion is achievable at room temperatures, freeing humanity of its need for vast power plants and transmission grids. Cold fusion, of the kind suggested by Fleischman and Pons, would allow every home, perhaps every vehicle, to have its own fusion generator. With no pollutants and no need for costly maintenance and transmission, power would be given, in a very literal sense, to the people.

1975 Catalytic converters introduced in many US states

1983 Report states that global warming triggered by industrial activities

1989 EC agrees reduction of CFCs by 85 per cent

1995 150 nations agree targets to reduce greenhouse gases from year 2000

AMAZING MAIZE

BY CAREFULLY ISOLATING AND THEN CROSSING DIFFERENT STRAINS OF MAIZE, SCIENTISTS CREATE NEW VARIANTS OF THIS MOST VITAL OF CROPS

Maize (sweetcorn) is one of the most versatile of crops. As well as being a staple for millions in the developing world, it is the United States' most important cash crop, planted each year on 70-80 million acres (28-32 million ha). Its uses range beyond the edible. In the USA, it is used to manufacture certain kinds of biodegradable plastics, fuel and clothing.

It has also been the subject of intensive research. The Maize Genetics Cooperation programme was set up in the USA in 1932. A similar programme was established for Latin America in the 1940s – in due course, this was absorbed into CIMMYT (the International Maize and Wheat Improvement Center) in Mexico City. A key aim of both programmes is to collect samples of as many variants of the maize plant as possible, storing their genetic material in 'germplasm banks'. These include strains that have been selectively bred, perhaps over hundreds of years, in different parts of the world. They also include a few mutations induced by exposing seed samples to the atomic bomb tests at Bikini Atoll in 1946 and Eniwetok Atoll in 1948.

Using this material, researchers propagate 'inbreds' to isolate the special characteristics of a variant; they do this by making the plant pollinate itself. The inbred will usually be less vigorous than the original stock, but when one inbred is crossed with another to create a hybrid with a desired combination of traits, the hybrid's vigour will often be even higher than in the original stock. In this way, researchers develop high-yield strains that are tolerant of, say, insects and disease. One problem in South America, for example, is that four-fifths of the agricultural land has acidic soils. In the late 1970s, CIMMYT started

MAIZE IN MOZAMBIQUE From its origins in Central America, maize has spread across the globe, becoming a staple for some 200 million people.

developing a strain that tolerated such soils. Colombian researchers then used CIMMYT's results to create a variety called Sikuani. Increasing yields by more than 20 per cent, Sikuani is now widely planted in Colombia, and is being tested in neighbouring countries.

MAIZE OF MANY COLOURS Research centres have bred numerous hybrids of maize, each suitable for different climates and conditions.

from home on computers. Information is received and sent via telephone lines using a modem or along special digital lines to workplaces which may be hundreds or just tens of miles away. Some 560 000 people are already employed in this way in the United Kingdom, nearly 160 000 in Germany and 220 000 in France. The United States leads the way with almost 7 million teleworkers. Studies in the mid 1990s suggested that teleworking would be embraced in the future by 80 per cent of Europe's white-collar work force. Singapore offers a glimpse of what this may mean.

Singapore's National Computer Board (NCB) initiated plans to secure the country's place as a world leader in information technology. By mid 1998 the first phase of its scheme, 'Singapore ONE', was in place. NCB had established a fibre-optic network unparalleled across the world, linking more than 3 million people via home computer terminals to 100 services, including home shopping, movies on demand and distance learning. The aim was to link every home to this vast information network, shaping the way people work, relax and learn. Funded jointly by government and industry, the programme aimed to create fully 'intelligent homes' by 1999. High-speed links via the Singapore ONE network would give residents an extraordinary ability to monitor their homes from afar. They would be able to control central heating, security, lights and other kinds of electronic equipment, and watch it all through live video transmissions from small cameras installed in the home. They would be able to communicate with their children via video conferencing. Students were being encouraged to keep in touch with their lecturers in the same way, allowing a large number of them over a large area to work with the same lecturer. As a result, there would be less need to give up work or family time in order to travel to an educational institution.

Singapore ONE allowed firms to use smart cards – electronic cards akin to credit cards but able to carry more information – for payments. This technology, in conjunction with affordable and easy-to-use video conferencing, was expected to lead to a major change in the way business was conducted in Singapore. Instead of having person-to-person meetings, people would meet 'virtually' –

HENRY AND THE SOYA BEAN

Henry Ford, creator of the Model T Ford, believed that the soya bean held a cure for many of humanity's ills. He believed in it not only as a food source, but also as a component from which cars and other commodities could be made. Today, scientists agree with him. Materials such as carbon fibre, currently produced from polluting petrochemicals, could be made using soya beans.

In pursuit of his belief, Ford bought nearly 10 000 acres (4000 ha) of arable land in Michigan, where he cultivated nearly 60 varieties of soya bean. He had clothes made from fabrics that were spun using soya extracts, and insisted on eating soya bean products; his long-suffering family were encouraged to share his obsession at meal times. In 1934 journalists reported that Ford had served a meal at the Century of Progress Fair in Chicago that consisted entirely of soya bean foods. The menu included soya bean patties followed by soya cookies and soya coffee.

Ford used some of his Ford Motor Company's billions to fund the construction of three soya-processing plants in Michigan, where the beans were pulped to extract their oil. This oil was further processed to create paints, Bakelite-type plastic components for cars and other devices. Ford was, in fact, a true visionary, for soya products have become a standard ingredient in nearly every processed foodstuff.

In 1997 a team of American research scientists at the University of Delaware filed a patent for a new process. They had formulated a method of producing materials with the strength of metal but the weight of fabrics – from soya beans. The team proposed building a bridge using soya oil stiffened with chemicals and reinforced with fibre glass. The side panel for an agricultural baler – used to gather and bale straw – was one of the first devices to be made of the new material. It weighed only 25 lb (11 kg), whereas a panel made of metal weighs about 100 lb (45 kg). The Delaware team, led by Richard Wool, a chemical engineer, believes that their process could revolutionise engineering within the next decade, potentially sidelining metal products and replacing them with more sustainable soya products.

FLEXIBLE SOYA Henry Ford's soya bean plantation in 1942 (below). Above: Edible soya products include dried beans, soya milk and tofu or bean curd, both dried (top right) and soft (bottom).

❝ BLACKOUT

The home has become dependent upon electricity, and when electricity fails whole cities become eerily silent. In the winter of 1972 industrial strife brought regular blackouts to parts of Britain. Kenneth F. Weaver, assistant editor of *National Geographic* magazine, was in London at the time:

'Minutes ago the lights flickered, went out briefly, snapped on again. It was a warning. The electricity would last only a few moments longer, and then we would be plunged into three hours of darkness.

'Now I am writing by the light of candles that my London hotel has thoughtfully provided. Outside, no streetlights glow, no storefronts blaze, no traffic signals wink. Only the occasional flash of automobile headlights relieves the six o'clock gloom of this February evening.

'I am not the only one beset by darkness. Probably a million Londoners in scattered districts of this sprawling city share my inconvenience. For the third time today, by official edict, we are taking our turn without electricity . . . In the past three days I have covered miles of London streets, seeing what happens when modern man loses the electricity which he so takes for granted, and on which his material civilization is based . . . Along busy Oxford Street, shops and restaurants had turned off all their display lights for the duration. Inside, candles and pressure lanterns filled in during the blackouts. Impromptu corner vendors offered hard-to-get candles at inflated prices.

'Piccadilly Circus, usually a dazzling glitter of advertising signs, lay in murk except for lights over subway entrances . . . But as the three-hour blackout periods shifted from area to area and back again, people across the land fretted about whether frozen foods spoil; dairies adjusted to hours when power would be available for milking machines; factories went on part time schedules.

'Now over my battery-powered radio, I hear a newscaster announcing the end of the strike. But for three tense weeks Britain has faced an inescapable truth: Electricity has become the bloodstream of modern life . . .

'My encounter with London's blackouts was sobering. Britain's experience was a preview of things that could happen elsewhere.' ❞

they would see each other on video screens connected via the Internet. This would reduce travel and transportation costs while increasing human productivity. The technology could trigger a huge change in social and industrial activity. Road congestion and city life would change radically as the number of commuters fell away. It might even increase workers' disposable income, since they would have to spend less on travel.

But there is another approach to technology, which may in the end have a greater impact on the millions of people who live not in high-tech societies like Singapore, but

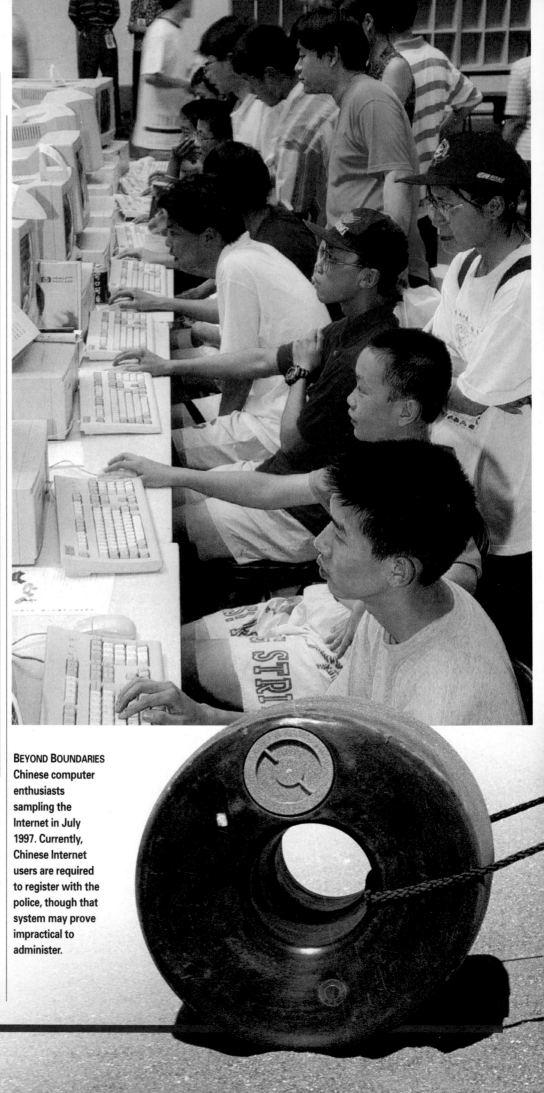

BEYOND BOUNDARIES Chinese computer enthusiasts sampling the Internet in July 1997. Currently, Chinese Internet users are required to register with the police, though that system may prove impractical to administer.

TREVOR BAYLIS AND THE CLOCKWORK RADIO

A radio that works like an alarm clock, one of the most remarkable inventions of the 1990s, was the brain-child of a British former underwater escape artist. Trevor Baylis was inspired to invent it after watching a documentary about AIDS which explained the difficulties involved in spreading information about the disease. The best way is by radio, but in Africa, where the incidence of AIDS is worst, working radios were comparatively rare because of the high cost of batteries.

The radio Baylis came up with works on much the same principle as an alarm clock: when it is wound for 20 seconds, it generates enough electricity for the radio to play for 30-40 minutes. It went on sale in the mid 1990s, and in Africa it has given many people access for the first time to information on topics ranging from AIDS prevention to adult education programmes. In Liberia, torn by civil war since 1990, clockwork radios were used to promote the message of peace and to inform voters about elections in 1996.

Baylis had already worked with disabled people, so it was decided to establish a BayGen (Baylis Generators) factory of mixed-ability employees in Cape Town. With the radios being snapped up by the Red Cross and United Nations, not to mention exports to Europe and North America, sales for the original model and a smaller, low-power model soon totalled 50 000 sets a month. In 1998 Trevor Baylis was working on a wind-up laptop computer in collaboration with General Electric of America.

those previously used. At the same time, to improve health and safety standards, the project aimed to strengthen workers' institutions and advise on workers' rights.

In this most eventful of centuries, mankind has gained power on an unprecedented scale by harnessing the atom and learned the ecological price of industrial expansion. Present trends, from electric cars to intelligent homes, give us a glimpse of what the 21st century may hold. But it is also certain that developments during the next 100 years will take many turns we cannot possibly predict. In the end, only time will reveal the true shape of things to come.

in the developing world. The prophet of this kind of technology was the German economist Fritz Schumacher whose book *Small is Beautiful* was a bestseller when it was first published in 1973. It propounded his belief that large impersonal institutions, whether government departments or business corporations, are responsible for many of the ills of society, the economy and the environment.

Earlier, in 1965, he had founded the Intermediate Technology movement, whose basic belief is that the people in poorer nations who take part in a development process should also be its architects; development is a process in which their economic power is

increased by improving their access to 'intermediate technologies', ones appropriate to their skills, incomes and environments. In the late 1990s, an example of a project sponsored by the movement was a scheme for 'artisan quarrying' in Kenya. This set out to teach methods of quarrying that were safer and less damaging to the environment than

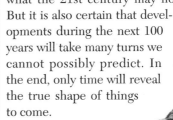

ORIGINAL THINKING   South African brothers Hans and Piet Hendrikse came up with this innovative answer to the daily chore of carrying fresh water over large distances in rural Africa. The Q-Drum can carry up to 15 gallons (70 litres) of water with a fraction of the effort involved in carrying it on the head in pitchers.

1900

The first **electric bus** runs in New York City. Called an 'Autostage', it carries 12 people along Fifth Avenue.

The Nichols Chemical Company develops the **'contact method'** for producing sulphuric acid, now used in industrial processes worldwide.

The work of Gregor Mendel, a 19th-century Austrian monk, is rediscovered by Erich von Ischermak-Seysenegg, Hugo de Vries and Carl Correns. Mendel was the first person to conceive of the hereditary nature of reproduction and to deduce the existence of information-carrying genes. The science of **hereditary genetics** is born.

1901

The Spindletop 'gusher', the first **commercial oil well**, is discovered in Texas by Captain Anthony Lucas, launching the oil age. The gusher produces 75 000 barrels of oil per day.

Guglielmo Marconi demonstrates **transatlantic radio communication** for the first time.

FIRE AT SPINDLETOP A hundred barrels of crude oil go up in smoke at Spindletop, Texas, ignited by sparks or naked flames. Fire safety was a low priority at the world's first commercial oil field.

1902

The town of Cotella is the site of the first **oil strike in Alaska**.

1903

At Kitty Hawk, the Wright brothers, Orville and Wilbur, achieve the first

successful flight of a 'heavier-than-air' machine fuelled by petroleum.

Henry Ford founds the **Ford Motor Company**.

In Britain Ebenezer Howard, author of *Garden Cities of Tomorrow* (1898), starts building the **'new town'** of Letchworth in Hertfordshire. It inspires the 'garden city' movement.

1904

Operating from City Hall to West 145th Street, the New York City Subway is the first **underground railway system** in the world that also goes under water.

1905

Arthur Macdonald's Napier is the first **motor car to break the 100 mph** (161 km/h) barrier. It reaches 105 mph (169 km/h) at Daytona Beach in north-east Florida.

Albert Einstein has his 'miracle year'. In three papers he sets out the special theory of relativity, explains the properties of light – the basis for much of quantum mechanics – and produces a paper on statistical mechanics.

1906

More than 500 people are killed in San Francisco's **'great earthquake'**.

1907

Amplification of electronic signals becomes possible with the advent of the **Audion tube, or triode**. Lee De Forest's invention makes possible live broadcasting and is an essential component of electronic systems until the invention of the transistor in 1947.

1908

Oil is struck in Persia (Iran) for the first time, at Masjed Soleyman.

The Great Road Race is won by American George Schuster, making the **petroleum motor car popular**.

The first Ford **Model T**, the motor car for the masses, is produced.

A **Declaration of Conservation** is issued by governors of the different states of the USA, outlining an intention to maintain the environment.

Swiss chemist Jacques Brandenberger develops **Cellophane**, which soon becomes much used in household packaging.

Bakelite (phenol-formaldehide) is discovered by Dr Leo Baekeland. Research begins imme-diately into possible uses for this 'wonder material'.

1909

A 16-strong fleet of US warships, **'the Great White Fleet'**, completes a trip around the world. It achieves President Teddy Roosevelt's aim of demonstrating the industrial and military might of the USA.

The multiracial team of Robert E. Peary and Matthew A. Henson complete an expedition, in which they claim to have reached the **North Pole**.

1910

Bakelite **plastic production** begins. Bakelite finds widespread use as electric insulation and in plugs, telephones, and even jewellery.

The **Haber process** is used to produce synthetic ammonia for the first time: this is a chemical much used in industry.

1911

John D. Rockefeller's **Standard Oil** is forcibly split into separate companies, following a US Supreme Court ruling that Standard was operating in a monopolistic fashion.

The New Zealand-born scientist Ernest Rutherford puts forward his theory on the nuclear structure of the **atom**. His work was further developed by the Danish physicist Niels Bohr. Bohr was awarded the Nobel prize for physics in 1922.

1912

A device for detecting **subatomic particles** is invented by Scottish physicist Charles Wilson.

1913

US chemist William Burton patents his **'cracking process'** for producing petrol from crude oil.

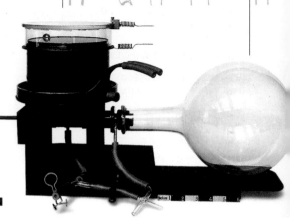

CLOUDS IN A BOTTLE This expansion chamber pioneered by physicist Charles Wilson was used to detect and examine the alpha and beta particles from radioactive elements. As the warm air in the chamber expands, it produces artificial clouds; the path of a charged ion then shows up as a track of water droplets.

The 'solar system' **model of the atom** is proposed by Niels Bohr, paving the way for the exploitation of the atom.

1914

The **Panama Canal** is completed: a direct route for the transport of oil from the east of the USA to the west.

The **American Radio Relay League** (ARRL) is founded by Hiram Percy Maxim and Clarence Tuska: a body of amateurs communicating across the USA. These 'radio hams' go on to make many breakthroughs, including singe-side band broadcasting and narrow-band voice modulation, both used by the military.

1915

The 'father' of **hydroelectricity**, Frederick Pearson, dies, along with over 1000 others when the SS *Lusitania* sinks.

The Ford Motor Company diversifies into agricultural vehicles, developing the **first Ford tractor**. Motorised farm vehicles assist the introduction of scientific methods in agriculture.

Mustard gas, developed by Nobel Prize winner Fritz Haber, is used as a 'chemical weapon' in the First World War. Some 800 000 men are estimated to have died from the gas.

Production of **Pyrex** glass by the Corning Glass Works begins.

1916

Blood for transfusions is refrigerated for the first time.

1917

Serge Voronoff begins experimenting with monkey glands to develop an **elixir of life**. In effect, his procedures were a primitive form of hormone replacement therapy.

During the **Russian Revolution**, the Tsar abdicates and the Bolsheviks

ELIXIR OF LIFE   Serge Voronoff was believed to possess the key to eternal youth. Background: Howard's plan for a garden city.

under Lenin seize power in October, establishing a communist state.

The Chemical Construction Company builds a plant for the synthesis of **nitric acid**, used in fertilisers.

1918

The first **petroleum pipeline** opens from Salt Creek to Casper in Wyoming, USA.

Sonar technology allows experts to explore the ocean floor as never before.

1919

The first **modern diamond mine** is sunk in South Africa by Consolidated Diamonds.

1920

Isopropyl alcohol is the **first commercial petrochemical**, produced by the Standard Oil Company.

Famine grips the Russian-ruled regions of Ukraine, Armenia, Crimea and the Volga river valley. An estimated 5.9 million people starve to death in the ensuing years.

1921

In Stuttgart the German scientist Friederich Berguis devises a method of **liquefying coal** to produce oil.

1922

The American Geological Survey incorrectly predicts that **US oil supplies will run dry** by 1942.

The use of Tetraethyl lead in petrol as an **anti-knocking agent** is introduced by Thomas Midgley.

A vaccine for tuberculosis, the **BCG vaccine**, is developed by Albert Calmette and Camille Guérin.

Diabetics benefit from the 'wonder drug', **insulin**. Almost inexhaustible supplies are available, extracted from pigs. Although still poorly understood, this early use of biotechnology offers a virtual cure for some diabetics.

1923

Fire destroys Tokyo city, leaving 2 million homeless. The city is rebuilt, only to be destroyed again during the Second World War.

1924

The Austrian film maker Fritz Lang visits New York. Manhattan Island's futuristic skyline and its slum dwellings inspire his film *Metropolis*.

1925

The USA proposes the **Geneva Protocol** to ban chemical warfare.

In the USA, Cleveland, Ohio, opens the world's **first municipal airport**.

Tennessee teacher John T. **Scopes** is tried for violating state law by teaching Darwinian theories of evolution. He is convicted, but the conviction is later overturned by the US Supreme Court.

1926

Echo sounders used to map the ocean floor.

1927

The Mystery Sunbeam, driven by Henry Segrave, **exceeds 200 mph** (322 km/h).

The first **weather balloon** carrying electronic instruments, the radiosonde, is released into the skies.

Charles Lindbergh makes the first nonstop **transatlantic flight** from New York to Paris.

1928

Richard Byrd becomes the first person to **fly over the South Pole**.

The action of the antibiotic **penicillin** is observed by Alexander Fleming.

1929

The Great Crash of **'Black Thursday'** (October 24) leads to bank and stock failures worldwide, and ultimately the Great Depression.

1930

The first long-distance journey by a **diesel-powered motor car**: the Packard travels the 800 miles (1287 km) from Indianapolis to New York in three days.

1931

Chemical giant Du Pont produces the first **synthetic rubber**.

Thomas Edison, creator of the electric light bulb, dies.

1932

John Douglas Cockcroft builds the first **particle accelerator**, advancing research into nuclear reactions.

English physicist James Chadwick proves the **existence of the neutron**.

1933

The chemical giant ICI discovers **polythene**. This plastic proves to be vital in the development of radar, because it offers scientists an electrical insulator that blocks electrical noise, making small radars feasible.

CHADWICK'S WAX   James Chadwick used paraffin wax in his experiments on the neutron.

Albert **Einstein flees Nazi Germany**, emigrating to the USA.

1934

Leo Szilard applies for a patent for a process of **neutron-induced chain reactions**, which might generate explosions.

1935

US chemist Wallace H. Carothers, working for Du Pont, discovers **nylon**.

1936

The Houdry process, a technique of **catalytic cracking** of petroleum, is introduced.

Jerome Namias develops the technology to make **long-range weather forecasts** possible.

1937

During her attempt to fly around the world, **Amelia Earhart** disappears, never to be seen again.

Polystyrene becomes widely available, and is used in clocks, radios, tiles and electrical equipment. It was later found to be an environmentally unfriendly product, resistant to natural degradation and producing toxic fumes when burnt.

1938

The first oil finds are made in **Saudi Arabia**.

The first therapeutic use of antiseptic chemicals, **sulphonamides**, is demonstrated. Their availability in the Second World War means that injured personnel have a much better chance of surviving than in previous conflicts.

1939

In New York, a **Geiger-Müller counter** (ordinarily used for detecting radiation levels) is used to generate a small amount of electricity by trapping 'cosmic rays', electrically charged particles which penetrate the Earth's atmosphere from space. The electricity is conducted by wire to illuminate lights at the New York World's Fair.

The Grapes Of Wrath, by John Steinbeck, depicts the 1930s **'dust bowl'** on the Great Plains of the USA.

The physicists Enrico Fermi, Otto Hahn and Otto Frisch demonstrate **nuclear fission**, heralding the start of the nuclear age.

1940

The first **wind-powered turbine** is put into service at Grandpa's Knob, Vermont, USA.

FERMI'S PILE Italian physicist Enrico Fermi played a pivotal role in the Manhattan Project, the Allied nuclear bomb effort. In 1942 he achieved the first self-sustaining nuclear reaction in a graphite-moderated reactor or 'pile'.

ICI becomes involved in the **development of the atom bomb for Britain**, via the MAUD committee. ICI makes it possible to produce weapons-grade uranium.

Catalytic reforming, developed by the Standard Oil Company, makes it possible to produce higher-octane fuel, helping the Allied air forces to outperform the Luftwaffe.

1941

Gustaffson's X-ray experiments on crops produce beneficial mutations, creating the first of the new **'super strains'** of cereal. Pest-resistant, high-yield cereals make the Green Revolution of the 1960s possible.

1942

Enrico Fermi constructs the first **US nuclear reactor** to create plutonium for the atomic bomb.

ICI **manufactures penicillin** in medically usable quantities.

1943

Joseph Mengele takes an SS position at Auschwitz concentration camp, where he continues his **racial genetics research**, using the camp's inmates as an 'experimental resource'.

Some 1.5 million people die in Bengal, India, when rice crops are devastated by the **'brown spot'** disease.

1944

The USA is first to produce the 'universal pesticide', **DDT**. Widely used in the 1950s and 1960s, DDT has since been found to persist in the environment, gradually accumulating, killing wildlife and entering the food chain.

Ukrainian-born microbiologist Selman Waksman discovers **streptomycin**, the first drug to be effective against the disease tuberculosis.

1945

In a magazine article, the writer Arthur C. Clarke describes his vision of a **communications satellite network**, which could orbit Earth by the 1980s. Clarke's article inspires the creation of such a network in the 1960s.

Hiroshima experiences the full force of the atomic bomb, dropped by US B-29 **'Enola Gay'**.

1946

The **International Atomic Energy Commission** is formed by the United Nations to supervise the proliferation of nuclear technology.

1947

Bell Laboratories of New Jersey, USA, develop the **first transistor**, revolutionising radio communication.

ATOM BOMBER On August 6, 1945, a B-29 Superfortress, the 'Enola Gay', dropped the first atomic bomb on Hiroshima.

Magnolia Petroleum Company drills for **offshore oil**, 10 miles (16 km) out to sea in the Gulf of Mexico.

The **chemical synthesis of hydrocarbons** is developed, opening up vast possibilities for completely synthetic materials.

Synthetic quartz crystals are grown by the naval research laboratories in Washington DC.

1948

The **World Health Organization** is established to provide a forum for global health issues.

1949

The USSR detonates its **first nuclear bomb**, in the Ustyurt desert – the nuclear race has started in earnest.

1950

Klaus Fuchs confesses about the **espionage of atomic secrets** from America to the Russians, and is convicted as a traitor.

Britain detonates its **first atomic bomb**, in the Monte Bello Islands.

1951

An atomic reactor is used in medical therapy at Brookhaven National Laboratories, NY. This is the first application of **nuclear technology in medical science**.

1952

The **'Bubble Chamber'**, a device for tracking the path of nuclear particles, is invented by Donald Glaser.

1953

The Union Pacific Railroad Company places the first **propane-fuelled gas turbine** locomotive in service. The locomotive hauls freight between Los Angeles and Las Vegas.

The molecular model of **DNA** is proposed by James Watson and Francis Crick in the journal *Nature*.

1954

The world's first **nuclear-powered submarine**, *Nautilus*, built by the Electric Boat Company in Connecticut, is launched for the US navy.

Capturing the energy of the Sun becomes possible with the latest invention from Bell Laboratories: the **photovoltaic silicon cell**.

1955

The **vaccine for the polio virus**, developed by Dr Jonas Salk, is proved to be safe.

Synthetic diamonds are produced by General Electric. This product is used in industrial lasers and as a coating material to strengthen machinery.

Cancer cells are removed from the cervix of a cancer sufferer, Henrietta Lacks. These cells proliferate in cell cultures and go on to be mass produced – called **HeLa cells**. They are used as the basis of cancer research around the world. Henrietta's cell line survived to the end of the century.

1956

Britain builds the world's **first industrial-scale nuclear power plant**, Calder Hall in Cumbria.

Nationalisation of the **Suez Canal** causes an international crisis and leads briefly to war. It also creates a supply problem with oil. Prices rise and governments start to look closer to home for oil resources.

1957

Sputnik, the first man-made satellite, is launched by the USSR.

British philosopher Bertrand Russell initiates the **Pugwash Conferences**, held in Pugwash, Nova Scotia, to discuss the impact of nuclear weapons on the planet as a whole.

1958

The Campaign for Nuclear Disarmament (**CND**) is established, the first anti-nuclear pressure group.

Discussions begin between the USA, USSR and Britain to agree an informal **moratorium on nuclear tests**.

CANAL CRISIS A British soldier searches Egyptian within an Suez Canal administrative zone during the Suez crisis of 1956. Background: Two British policemen forcibly remove a protester from the site of a secret US nuclear missile base in Swaffham, Norfolk, in 1958. He was a member of the Direct Action Committee Against Nuclear War.

1959

Thousands of acres of land are flooded in Northern and South Rhodesia (now Zambia and Zimbabwe) as the **Kariba Dam** is brought on line. The cost to local wildlife is incalculable.

The Air Products company builds a large-scale plant for the production of **rocket fuel**.

Texas Instruments applies for a patent for an integrated circuit, later known as the **'silicon chip'**.

A huge **gas field** is discovered off Groningen in The Netherlands, encouraging petrochemical companies in their hunt for North Sea gas and oil.

1960

A **Polaris missile** is launched from a submarine for the first time.

The Sahara Desert is the location for the first **nuclear tests by France**.

1961

Geographer **Jean Gottman** publishes his book, *Megalopolis: The Urbanised North-Eastern Seaboard of the United States*.

1962

The **Cuban missile crisis** is resolved, and nuclear war avoided.

The first **Antarctic nuclear power station** begins operating at McMurdo Sound. The power plant fuels experiments and accommodation blocks for research scientists.

Telstar 1, the first communications satellite, is launched. The satellite relays the first-ever television broadcast across the Atlantic.

John F. Kennedy initiates a programme to fit **safety devices to nuclear weapons**, so that they cannot be detonated without presidential authorisation.

In her book, **Silent Spring**, US biologist Rachel Carson sets out the need to protect health from the effects of chemical pesticides.

1963

The Americans, Russians and British – but not the French –

sign a **Test Ban Treaty**, limiting nuclear tests.

At a conference at Pugwash, the USA shares information with the USSR about **safety in nuclear devices**.

1964

The People's Republic of **China detonates** its first nuclear bomb.

1965

The first commercial communications satellite, **Intelsat-1**, is launched.

1966

The pressure group, **Los Angeles Rule 66**, makes an attempt to reduce organic solvent emissions.

1967

The Arab nations place an **oil embargo** on Britain and the USA as a 'punishment' for supporting the Israelis during the Six Day War. The embargo is rescinded as the USA and Britain are two of the world's largest importers of oil, and the producers

fear that a protracted embargo may result in a loss of market share.

The oil tanker **Torrey Canyon** runs aground off Cornwall, spilling 117 000 tons of oil and polluting 100 miles (160 km) of coastline.

1968

Paul Ehrlich's **The Population Bomb** predicts that millions will starve when world population exceeds food supply, instigating an attempt to control global population growth.

1969

After years of testing, experts find the first major **North Sea oil field**, the Ekofisk Field off Norway.

Neil Armstrong takes 'one small step for man' onto the surface of the **Moon**.

US nuclear tests on **Amchitka Island** off Alaska provoke massive demonstrations in the neighbouring Canadian province of British Columbia. In the wake of this the 'Don't Make A Wave Committee' is formed, the forerunner of Greenpeace.

British scientist James Lovelock advances the **Gaia** hypothesis. According to his theory Earth is a self-regulating living organism, which adjusts to fluctuations in climate and atmospheric conditions so as to maintain a balanced ecosystem.

1970

The **Environmental Protection Agency** (EPA) is formed in the USA, providing a forum for the discussion of environmental issues.

MOON LANDING The space race culminated in the Apollo 11 Moon landing on July 20, 1969. A stamp was produced to commemorate the event.

1971

World resistance to the use of chemical weapons in Vietnam forces the USA to **withdraw defoliants**. Defoliants destroy the jungle canopy that hides the movements of Vietcong forces.

The fledgling **Greenpeace** movement organises protests against further nuclear tests on Amchitka Island. One group charters a fishing boat which they sail into the test zone. They are arrested but not before generating worldwide publicity.

Environmentalist group **Friends of the Earth** is founded in the UK. Its first campaign involves the drinks company Schweppes. Friends of the Earth mobilise hundreds of people to dump Schweppes' 'non-returnable' bottles outside the company's London headquarters.

1972

The **Forties oil field** is discovered off Scotland.

The US Congress confronts the problem of water pollution, introducing the **'Clean Water Act'**.

1973

Leading American geneticists Stanley Cohen and Herbert Boyer prove that certain enzymes can 'cut' DNA into segments. **Gene splicing** now becomes a possibility.

Pioneer 10, a US space probe, passes within 81 000 miles (130 000 km) of Jupiter and transmits TV pictures of the planet back to Earth.

1974

The first **World Population Conference** is held in Bucharest.

1975

The first **oil pipeline** from the Forties Field to mainland Scotland is opened.

To meet new emissions standards, many automobiles in the USA are fitted with **catalytic converters**.

1976

A report states that **CFCs** (chlorofluorocarbons) deplete the ozone layer. In 1995 its authors, F. Sherwood Roland, Mario Molina and Paul Crutzen, receive the Nobel prize for chemistry.

The Cray **supercomputer** comes on line. Designed by US engineer Seymour Cray, it produces three-dimensional designs and computer animation.

1977

The **Trans-Alaskan Pipeline**, linking the port of Valdez with the Prudhoe Bay oil fields, opens.

MRI (Magnetic Resonance Imaging) is applied in medicine to produce internal images of the human body.

FRIDGE GRAVEYARD Discarded refrigerators, like these on a Swedish rubbish dump, will eventually leach CFC-rich refrigerating gases into the atmosphere. Modern refrigerators and air-conditioning devices use more environmentally friendly gases.

The World Health Organization announces that the **smallpox virus** has been eradicated worldwide. The only existing traces of it left today are held in scientific laboratories in the USA and Russia.

1978

An extraordinary baby is born in the UK. Louise Brown is the first human child to grow from an egg fertilised outside a womb, a technique that comes to be known as **in vitro fertilisation**.

The tanker **Amoco Cadiz** is wrecked off the coast of Brittany, France, spilling

223 000 tons of crude oil. It is the worst tanker oil spill to date.

1979

One-third of the nuclear reactor core at **Three Mile Island** in Harrisburg, Pennsylvania, melts. The accident could have had catastrophic consequences if radioactive gases had escaped.

Experiments succeed in producing human insulin, synthesised by genetic engineering. **Synthesised insulin** is recognised as 'human' by the body, and so works without causing an antibody response.

The search for **alternative energy** resources gets a boost when President Carter announces a drive to reduce US dependency on foreign oil.

1980

General Electric patents a **microorganism for cleaning up oil spills**. This has serious implications for the future of biology – implying that industry has the right to own particular forms of living organisms.

Natural Bridges Monument, Utah, is the site for the first **solar-cell electric power plant**. The plant heralds a new era of experimenting with solar power in the USA.

1981

NASA's first re-usable spacecraft completes its first full mission. **Space Shuttle** Columbia carries John Young and Robert Crippen on a two-day journey orbiting the Earth, successfully returning to land at Edwards Air Force Base on April 14.

1982

The Acquired Immune Deficiency Syndrome (**AIDS**) is first described. The syndrome is suspected to have

affected humans since at least the 1930s, but no general theory had yet been formed to account for the mysterious deaths now attributed to the AIDS virus.

1983

US astronomer Carl Sagan publishes his theory of climactic devastation – the **'nuclear winter'** – after nuclear war. Campaigning with other scientists, Sagan lobbies the US government to reduce nuclear arms.

OPEC agrees to **reduce its oil prices** for the first time. Twenty three years after its creation OPEC has acknowledged that oil is becoming less attractive to many consumers.

1984

Famine in Ethiopia gains global media coverage. Bob Geldof establishes the charity **Band Aid**, which raises £8 million for famine relief with the Do They Know It's Christmas? record.

Some 2000 people are killed in **Bhopal** by an accidental release of toxic gases from the chemical plant owned by Union Carbide.

1985

French agents bomb and sink the Greenpeace ship **Rainbow Warrior** in Auckland harbour, New Zealand. The ship was on its way to monitor French nuclear tests on Moruroa atoll. Photographer Fernando Pereira is killed in the bombing.

The **Live Aid** pop concert raises a further £48 million for famine relief in war-torn Ethiopia.

FOOD RELIEF Ethiopian famine victims in the 1980s depended on food aid provided by the international community and distributed at relief centres, such as the one at Tigré.

The British Antarctic Survey discovers a large **ozone hole** over the Antarctic.

1986

The worst nuclear accident on record takes place at the **Chernobyl** nuclear power plant, near Kiev in the USSR. Radioactive dust spreads, affecting many European countries.

The launch of **Space Shuttle Challenger** goes horribly wrong, exploding during takeoff. All seven astronauts on board are killed.

1987

Construction begins on the Superconducting Super Collider (**SSC**) in the USA. The SSC is to be

LIVE AID Rock and pop stars of the 1980s gave freely of their talent at the Live Aid Concert, organised by Bob Geldof, to raise money for famine relief in Ethiopia. Background: A worker at the Chernobyl plant monitors radiation levels following the explosion on April 26, 1986.

the world's largest particle accelerator, built inside an oval tunnel 52 miles (84 km) in length.

The **Montreal Protocol** lays down international commitment to the replacement of CFCs.

Genetic fingerprinting is introduced by the British police force. It becomes one of the key methods of crime detection in the 1990s.

1988

One of the most ambitious scientific studies ever undertaken is instigated when the **Human Genome Organization** is set up in Washington

DC. The project aims to map and record every element of human DNA.

1989

The **Exxon Valdez** oil tanker runs aground off the coast of Alaska, spilling approximately 440 000 gallons (2 million litres) of crude oil into the sea. The disaster becomes one of the worst oil spills in history, damaging areas of natural beauty and poisoning fish stocks.

1992

The **Rio de Janeiro Earth Summit** is the first major international attempt to set limits on pollution.

HAARP, the High Frequency Active Auroral Research Program, begins in Alaska. The project is designed to monitor weather patterns and to find ways of limiting the effects of the aurora borealis on satellites.

1993

The **Canadian Cod Fishery closes**. Fish species which once populated the Grand Banks have been hunted to virtual extinction.

1994

More computers are sold this year than televisions, demonstrating the immense impact of the **computer age**, not only on business but on leisure time as well.

1995

The first accurate **map of the ocean floor** is produced, providing a wealth of information on structures yet to be seen by man.

The European Laboratory for Particle Physics (**CERN**) in Geneva produces the first antiprotons with a particle accelerator, proving the existence of antimatter. The nine antiprotons exist for only 30 billionths of a second before being annihilated on contact with matter.

In September, France breaks a three-year moratorium on nuclear testing when its explodes a nuclear device beneath **Mururoa Atoll** in the

South Pacific. It is the first of a series of tests that cause an international outcry. In January 1996, President Chirac calls off the tests.

1996

Some 72 000 tons of oil are spilled when the tanker **Sea Empress** runs aground near Milford Haven, Pembrokeshire, Wales. Thousands of birds, fish and other wildlife along the Pembrokeshire coast are affected by the spill.

1997

Dolly the sheep, the first mammal cloned from an adult cell, is born. The potential misuse of this technology prompts many nations to question the ethics of such research.

The **World Food Summit**, held in Rome, highlights the environmental cost of the scientific approach to agriculture. Reducing the variety of crops and cattle worldwide, it has left agriculture open to potentially devastating effects from disease.

Man-caused **forest fires** rage in indonesia, covering nearby Malaysia in thick smog. The health effect on the inhabitants of Malaysia will not be fully known for many years.

The **Kyoto Summit** is staged as a successor to the Rio de Janeiro Earth Summit. World governments attempt to decide on future environmental policy. Disagreements over the need for a reduction in carbon dioxide emissions dominate the talks, with the USA refusing to conform to the requests of the other states.

1998

India carries out underground **nuclear weapons tests**, provoking a worldwide outcry. In retaliation, India's regional foe Pakistan carries out its own underground nuclear tests. Record **floods** devastate Bangladesh and, later in the year, parts of Central America.

INDONESIA ABLAZE Malaysian firemen join their neighbours in Indonesia to combat the forest fires raging in Bayung Lincir, central Sumatra, in October 1997.

INDEX

ACKNOWLEDGMENTS

Abbreviations:
T=top; M=middle; B=bottom; L=left; R=right

CBUK = Corbis/Bettmann
MEPL = The Mary Evans Picture Library

3 SPL/Brian Brake, L; Science & Society Picture Library, LM; Popperfoto, RM; Tom Stack & Associates/Inga Spence, R. 6 Panos Pictures/Heidi Bradner, BL. 6-7 Hulton-Getty. 8 Brown Brothers, BL. 8-9 Popperfoto. 9 MEPL, TR, MR, BR. 10 Panos Pictures/Alberto Arzoz, T; Magnum Photos/Elliott Erwitt, BL; Poster: *Stop de Neutronenbom, stop de kerwapenwedloop*, N. Schonfen, bureau: Walr.v. Hallweg 17, 1063 TB, Amsterdam, MR. 11 Magnum Photos/Thomas Hoepker, T; Katz Pictures/George Steinmetz, MR, B. 12-13 Magnum Photos/Franklin Stuart. 14 Magnum Photos/Paul Lowe, TR; Bradbury & Williams, BL. 15 SPL/David Parker, background; SPL/Sheila Terry, L; The British Petroleum Company plc, M; CBUK, R. 16 Brown Brothers, BL, R; Jean-Loup Charmet, MM. 17 The British Petroleum Company plc, TM, TR. 18 Brown Brothers, TL; Culver Pictures, BR. 19 Bilderdienst Süddeutscher Verlag, ML; The British Petroleum Company plc, BR. 20 Graham White, TL, BL, BR; The British Petroleum Company plc, MR. 21 Popperfoto, TL; Brown Brothers, MM, MR. 22 Gamma/Frank Spooner Pictures, TL; The British Petroleum Company plc, TR. 22-23 The British Petroleum Company plc, B; Magnum Photos/Paul Fusco, TM. 24-25 AKG. 25 Popperfoto, TL, MR. 26 Michael Freeman, TL; AKG, MM; Science & Society Picture Library, BR. 27 CBUK, BL; BAL, TR; Christie's Images, BR. 28 SPL/Manfred Kage, TL; CBUK, BL, BR. 29 SPL/Sheila Terry, TR; Bilderdienst Süddeustcher Verlag, BL; Bradbury & Williams, BR. 30 SPL/David Parker, ML. 30-31 Katz Pictures/George Steinmetz. 32 CBUK. 33 Hulton-Getty, TL; Planet Earth Pictures, BR. 35 Greenpeace/Beltra, TL; Popperfoto, BM.Bradbury & Williams/Artwork based on: General Bathymetric Chart Of The Oceans (GEBCO); Mercator Projection – Scale: 10 000 000 at the Equator: Published by The Canadian Hydrographic Service, Ottawa, Canada/IHO and the IOC (UNESCO), 5th edition, 1979; reprinted, 1993. © Minister of Fisheries and Oceans Canada, 1993, TR; Still Pictures/Gil Noti, ML; Planet Earth Pictures/Robert Hessler, BL; Graham White, BR. 36 Courtesy David T. Sandwell and Walter H.F. Smith, TL; © CSIRO/R.A. Binns, from JAMSTEC's 'Shinkai-6500' Submersible, BL 36-37 ELF/M. Davalan. 37 Planet Earth Pictures/Robert Hessler, MM; CBUK, TR. 38 Dr William Fenical, Center For Marine Biotechnology & Biomedicine/Scripps Institute of Oceanography, UCSD/Photo by H. Schleyer, TR; Planet

Earth Pictures/William M. Smithey, BM. 39 Environmental Images/Pierre Gleizes, TR; Environmental Images/Martin Bond, BM. 40 Roger-Viollet/Harlingue, BL; Roger-Viollet/Boyer, background, B; Popperfoto, BR. 41 Ullstein Bilderdienst, TL; CBUK, BR. 42 Martin Woodward, TL, MR; Brown Brothers, BM. 43 Martin Woodward, ML; CBUK, TR, BR. 44 CBUK, TR; SPL/Brian Brake, MR; Martin Woodward, B. 45 Popperfoto, TR; CBUK, M; Popperfoto, BL. 46 Brown Brothers, BL; CBUK, TR. 46-47 CBUK. 48 AKG, TR; Hulton-Getty, MR; CBUK, BL. 49 Brown Brothers, TL; Popperfoto, BR. 50 TBA, TL; SPL/Michael Martin, BL; Hulton-Getty, BR. 51 Popperfoto, T; AKG, B. 52 SPL/Sandia National Laboratories. 53 SPL/Carlos Muñoz-Yargue/C.E.T.P./EUREL IOS, background; Roger-Viollet, L; MEPL, LM; Popperfoto, RM; Still Pictures/Mark Edwards, R. 54 The Kobal Collection, MR. 54-55 AKG. 55 Lewis W. Hine, TL; Brown Brothers, TR. 56 Cadbury Limited, TR. 56-57 Hulton-Getty. 57 MPEL, MM. 58 Roger-Viollet, BL. 58-59, 60 Still Pictures/Mark Edwards. 61 Popperfoto, TL; Tony Stone/Chad Ehlers, R. 62 Roger-Viollet/Boyer. 63 Environmental Images/Martin Bond, TR; Tony Stone/Martin Mouchy, BL. 64 Popperfoto, B. 64-65 CBUK/Richard Hamilton Smith. 65 Science & Society Picture Library, BR. 66 Magnum Photos/Bruno Barbey, TL; Still Pictures/Mark Edwards, BR. 67 CBUK/Underwood & Underwood, TR; Hamish Hamilton, from *Silent Spring*, by Rachel Carson, 1963. 68 Panos/Sean Sprague, TL. 68-69 Still Pictures/Nick Cobbing, BR. 69 CBUK, TR. 70 SPL/Sinclair Stammers, T; Express Newspapers, B. 71 CBUK/David Reed, TL; Hulton-Getty, BR. 72 Bilderdienst Süddeutscher Verlag, BL; Roger-Viollet, BR. 73 Brown Brothers, TL; From: *The Theory of the Gene*, by Thomas Hunt Morgan, Yale University Press, background, TL; Ray Grinaway/From *The Theory of the Gene*, Thomas Hunt Morgan, Yale University Press, BR. 74 AKG, TL; SPL/Michael Davidson, background, TL; 'PA' News, BR. 75 Wiener Library, TL, B; Bilderdienst Süddeutscher Verlag, ML. 76 Popperfoto, TL; SPL, MM. 77 SPL/Richardson/Custom Medical Stock Photo. 78 Popperfoto. 79 CBUK, TR; SPL/Russell D. Curtis, MM; Martin Woodward, BL. 80-81 SPL/E.R. Degginger, BL; SPL/Nelson Medina. 82 SPL/Carlos Muñoz-Yague, TL; SPL/David Parker, TR; Roger-Viollet, BL. 83 CBUK. 84 Popperfoto, TL; Brown Brothers, BM; SPL/NASA, background, BM. 85 HAARP, TL; SPL/Sanford & Angliolo, B. 86 Tony Stone/Rich Iwasaki. 87 SPL/Rosenfeld Images Ltd, background; David King Collection, L; The Wildlife Collection/Martin Harvey, LM; Oxford Scientific Films/Doug Allen, RM; Bradbury & Williams, R. 88-89 David King Collection. 90 Magnum Photos/Marc Riboud. 91 Bradbury & Williams. 92 Aspect Picture Library/Mike Wells, T; Still

Pictures/Mark Edwards, BR. 93 Popperfoto, TM; Still Pictures/Mark Edwards, BR. 94 Magnum Photos/Steve McCurry, TL; Popperfoto, BR. 95 SPL/Rosenfeld Images Ltd, MR; Woodfall Wild Images/D. Woodfall, BM. 96-97 Tom Stack & Associates/John Shaw, BL; Tom Stack & Associates, T; Tom Stack & Associates/David M. Dennis, BR. 98 DRK/Larry Ulrich, BL; CBUK, TR. 98-99 Ray Grinaway. 99 Auscape/Anne & Jacques Six, TR. 100 Auscape/D. Parer & E. Parer-Cook, BL; DRK, Stephen J. Krasemann. 101 Auscape/Jean-Paul Ferrero. 102 FOE/Andrew Testa, TR. 102-3 The Wildlife Collection/Martin Harvey. 103 Popperfoto, TR; The Wildlife Collection/Martin Harvey, BR. 104 Oxford Scientific Films/Doug Allan, TM; Still Pictures/Mark Edwards, BM. 104-5 Oxford Scientific Films/Richard Kirby, T; Still Pictures/Thomas Raupach, BR. 106 Tom Stack & Associates/Inga Spence, BL. 106-7 AKG. 107 Environmental Images/Irene Lengui, TR. 108-9 Still Pictures/Herbert Giradet. 110-1 Environmental Images/Alexis Smailes. 111 Gerald Cubitt, T. 112 Popperfoto, BR. 112-13 Ecoscene/Robert Weight. 113 Popperfoto, BR. 114-15 DRK/Kim Heacox. 115 Popperfoto, TR; Martin Woodward, MM. 116 Auscape/Jean-Paul Ferrero, TM; Martin Woodward, ML; Popperfoto, BR. 117 Environmental Picture Library, background; MPEL, L; Tom Stack & Associates/David M. Dennis, LM; Vortec Energy Limited, RM; Friends of the Earth, R. 118 Hulton-Getty, ML; Magnum Photos/Abbas, BR. 118-19 Magnum Photos/Steve McCurry, background; Colin Woodman. 119 Magnum Photos/Jean Gaumy, ML; Magnum Photos/Abbas, MR. 120-1 Greenpeace/Gleizes. 121 Greenpeace/Gleizes, TR; Greenpeace/Newman, B. 122 Greenpeace/Weyler, TM. 122-3 Environmental Picture Library. 123 Popperfoto, TR; Hulton-Getty, BR. 124 Environmental Images/Charlotte Macpherson, TL; Friends of the Earth, TR; OOA, Copenhagen, ML; SPL/Anthony Howarth, BR. 125 Still Pictures/Thomas Raupach, TR; Magnum Photos/Thomas Hoepker, BM. 126 Environmental Images/Martin Bond. 127 Martin Woodward, TL; Jean-Loup Charmet, B. 128 Vortec Energy Limited,TL; Martin Woodward, MM; Environmental Images/Alex Olah, BR. 129 Environmental Images/John Novis, TL; Courtesy of Sainsbury's, BL; Martin Woodward, BR. 130 Martin Woodward, BL 130-1 Topham Picturepoint. 131 Roger-Viollet, BL; NASA/Dryden, MR. 132-3 Katz Pictures/George Steinmetz. 133 Brown Brothers, MR; Topham Picturepoint, BL. 134 Environmental Images/Robert Brook, BL. 134-5 Oxford Scientific Films/Survival Anglia/Mike Price. 135 Tom Stack Associates/David M. Dennis, BR. 136 Tom Stack & Associates/Inga Spence, BL. 136-7 NHPA/Laurie Campbell. 137 Still Pictures/Mark Edwards, MR; NHPA/David Woodfall, BM.

138-9 Murdo Macleod. 139 Environmental Images/David Hoffman, BL; AP Photo/Lennox McLendon, TR. 140 SPL/Alexander Tsiaras, TL. 140-1 Colorific/Fred Carol. 141 Popperfoto, BR. 142 Popperfoto, TL; Magnum Photos/Fred Mayer, B. 143 Hulton-Getty, ML; MEPL, MM; Brown Brothers, BR. 144 Environmental Images/Stan Gamester, TL; Popperfoto, BR. 145 AKG, TL. 146 Popperfoto, ML; SPL/Peter Menzel, B. 147 SPL/Françoise Sauze, T; Brown Brothers, B. 148 Popperfoto, TR. 148-9 © P.J. Hendrikse – Q-Drum 1994. PO Box 4099, Pietersburg, 0700, S. Africa. 150 Popperfoto, ML; Science & Society Picture Library, TR. 150-1 MEPL, background. 151 CBUK, ML; Science & Society Picture Library, TR. 152 Science & Society Picture Library, TR; Hulton-Getty, MM. 152-3 Popperfoto, background. 153 Hulton-Getty, BL; NASA, MR. 154 Still Pictures/André Naslennikov, ML; Panos/Neil Cooper, BR. 154-5 AKG, background. 155 Bradbury & Williams, ML; Popperfoto, BR.

Front Cover: Courtesy David T. Sandwell and Walter H.F. Smith, T; Tony Stone/Chad Ehlers, B; NHPA/David Woodfall, L; Roger-Viollet, LM; Woodfall Wild Images/D. Woodfall, RM; SPL/Richardson/Custom Medical Stock Photo, R.

Back Cover: Courtesey David T. Sandwell and Walter H.F. Smith, T; Tony Stone/Chad Ehlers, B; Auscape/D. Parer & E. Parer-Cook, TL; Still Pictures/Herbert Giradet, TR; CBUK, BL; Environmental Images/Irene Lengui, BR.

Endpapers: John Frost Historical News Archives.

The editors are grateful to the following individuals and publishers for their kind permission to quote passages from the publications listed below:

Petroleum Exploration Society of Great Britain from *Tales from Early UK Oil Exploration, 1960-1979* by Richard Moreton, 1994
National Geographic magazine from 'Rebirth of a Deep Sea Vent' by Richard A. Lutz and Rachel M. Haymon, November 1994; from 'Gorillas and Humans: an Uneasy Truce' by Paul F. Salopek, October 1995; from 'Return to the Hustein Forest' by Edie Bakker, February 1994; from 'The Search for Tomorrow's Power' by Kenneth F. Weaver, November 1972
The Times, Christopher Walker, April 30, 1986
Houghton Mifflin from *Silent Spring* by Rachel Carson, 1962

DAY, OCTOBER 23, 1962 ... 3d.
© 1962, by the Daily Sketch

BLOCKADE

Ultimatum to Krusc

Summit sets up security partnership

Russia and Nato bury the Cold War

By MICHAEL EVANS, BEN MACINTYRE AND OUR FOREIGN STAFF

have the right to veto Nato
Russia blew away

Expert

TB

World pledge global

Toxic tide Europe's

dela Gooch in Madrid reports
the battle to save a wildlife
ven from a flood of acid waste

TEAM of experts
was battling yester
day to stop a tide of
toxic mud pollut
ng one of Europe's
ant bird reserves
te reservoir
rup

which is used to channel the
waste into the sea.
However, the river
the reserve and
certain

eny link between antibiotics given to animal

Supermarkets move
growth-drug meat fr

The Guardian Thursday March 19

ealth Organisation of failing to check spread of killer diseas

the rampage again

Soviets
Nuclea

Automatic choke: after years of severe traffic congestion. California is set to lead the world in anti-car, pro-public transport legislation. A series of measures to be introduced include car-sharing schemes and fines for driver-only commuting

Save the world — forget the car

NEXT to the dog, many people
think it is man's best

By the end of the next century there will be seven billion of them. For the Rio conference the

DAILY

Lighting-up: 9.39 pm to 4.33 am

TUESDAY AUGUST

Smoke hides city 16 hours after greatest secret weapon strike

HE BOMB THAT HA
HANGED THE WORI

told 'Now quit'   20,000 tons in g   3